# Marrying Wealth, Marrying Poverty

*Gender and Bridewealth Power in a Changing African Society:*

*The Igbo of Nigeria*

Patrick E. IROEGBU

© Copyright 2007 Dr. Patrick Iroegbu.
All rights reserved. No part of this publication may be reproduced, stored in a retrieval system, or transmitted, in any form or by any means, electronic, mechanical, photocopying, recording, or otherwise, without the written prior permission of the author.

Note for Librarians: A cataloguing record for this book is available from
Library and Archives Canada at www.collectionscanada.ca/amicus/index-e.html
ISBN 1-4120-8100-9

*Printed in Victoria, BC, Canada. Printed on paper with minimum 30% recycled fibre.*
*Trafford's print shop runs on "green energy" from solar, wind and other environmentally-friendly power sources.*

*Offices in Canada, USA, Ireland and UK*

**Book sales for North America and international:**
Trafford Publishing, 6E–2333 Government St.,
Victoria, BC V8T 4P4 CANADA
phone 250 383 6864 (toll-free 1 888 232 4444)
fax 250 383 6804; email to orders@trafford.com

**Book sales in Europe:**
Trafford Publishing (UK) Limited, 9 Park End Street, 2nd Floor
Oxford, UK OX1 1HH UNITED KINGDOM
phone 44 (0)1865 722 113 (local rate 0845 230 9601)
facsimile 44 (0)1865 722 868; info.uk@trafford.com

**Order online at:**
trafford.com/05-3097

10 9 8 7 6 5

# CONTENTS

|  | Preface……………………………………….............5 |
|---|---|
|  | Acknowledgments… .……………………............16 |
|  | Dedication…………………………………….....19 |
| Chapter 1 | Introduction……………………………………....20 |
|  | The Central Issue...……………….…..…………....20 |
|  | Action Research, Questions, and Significance……..…….23 |
|  | Kola nuts, Oji and Bridewaelth……..……………….30 |
| Chapter 2 | Ideology and Bridewealth……..…………………....31 |
|  | Making Sense of the Ideology of Bridewealth…….............31 |
| Chapter 3 | Igbo Society…………………………………….....36 |
|  | Sociocultural Perspective… ..……..……………….37 |
|  | Igbo Culture Areas……………………………….39 |
| Chapter 4 | Igbo Sensitivity to Marrying …………………….....46 |
| Chapter 5 | Stages of Traditional Marriage: *Ije di, ije nwanyi*……………62 |
|  | Stages of Marriage: *Usoro alulu* ……………………....63 |
|  | Meaning of *Di* and *Nwunye*.………………………..64 |
|  | Inheriting a Wife: *Ikuchi nwanyi*…………………….........65 |
|  | Search for a Partner: *Icho nwanyi na icho di*……………..67 |
|  | Exchanging Marriage Visits: *Ije nleta*…………………….69 |
|  | Bridewealth Ceremonies: *Emume ikwu ugwo alulu*….…............73 |
|  | Paying Bride Price and Taking a Bride Home: *Ikwu ugwo isi nwanyi na ikporo nwanyi*……………………………….......74 |
|  | Staying on the Road: *Ino n'uzo alulu*………………….......77 |
|  | Fertility Cock and Vagina Yam: *Okuku elu ikpu na ji ikpu*….77 |
|  | Shedding Tears and Going to Marital home: *Ibe akwa ila ebe di*……………………...………………….............83 |

|            |                                                                      |
|------------|----------------------------------------------------------------------|
|            | Symbolism and Marriage: *Omuma na alulu*..........85                 |
|            | Change and Diversity in Partner Selection..........89                |
|            | Chapter Wrap-up..........94                                          |
| Chapter 6  | Sensitivity to Poverty and the Poor..........95                      |
|            | Defining and Explaining Poverty..........95                          |
|            | Etiology of Poverty and Targeting the Poor..........102              |
|            | Oscar Lewis and Culture of Poverty..........108                      |
|            | Gender and Poverty Reduction Programs..........112                   |
|            | World G.8 Spotlight on Poverty and Development Reforms....118        |
|            | Marrying Poverty and Online Chatting..........126                    |
| Chapter 7  | Theory of Gift Swap-over of Bridewealth..........130                 |
|            | Power of Giving and Receiving..........130                           |
|            | Before and After Colonialism..........131                            |
| Chapter 8  | Diaspora, Trendy Cash Economy, and the Impact..........136           |
|            | After the War..........136                                           |
|            | Tensions and References to bridewealth..........144                  |
| Chapter 9  | A Changing World..........152                                        |
|            | Changing in the Cutting and Trailing Edges of Change....152          |
|            | Eaters and Keepers, Producers and Bringers..........157              |
|            | Matrilineal and Patrilineal Faces..........160                       |
| Chapter 10 | Gender, Sexual Power, and Igbo Healers..........165                  |
|            | Why Consult Healers..........166                                     |
|            | Exiging the Patriarchal Dominance..........169                       |
|            | Social Independence and Empowerment..........175                     |
| Chapter 11 | Gender and Development in Decades to Come..........178               |
|            | Critical Development Debates and Women..........178                  |
|            | Gender, Health, and HIV/AIDS..........192                            |
|            | Social Power and Safe Sex..........194                               |

|  |  |
|---|---|
|  | Sexual Behavior Practices and Implications……………..…..197 |
|  | HIV/AID Prevalence and Fear………………………..…198 |
|  | Transmission, Gender, and Combative Methods………....201 |
| **Chapter 12** | Male Feminists, Gender, and Feminist senses…………..…..205 |
| **Chapter 13** | Summary and Conclusion……………………………….....220 |
|  | References……..…………………………………….....226 |
|  | Endnotes…..…..………………………………………....236 |
|  | Index……………………………………………………251 |

# Preface

Bridewealth is a striking customary practice and exchange device. Bridewealth after marriage is a complex issue that is little studied and lopsidedly and poorly understood; yet, it remains a part of every marriage considered culturally tenable in Igbo society. There is a need to explore the senses and representations, presently unaccounted for in scholarly discourse, of bridewealth power after marriage. This present work is essentially devoted to understanding gender and bridewealth power in a society facing change.

This book is based on the premise that, although research on gender from a cross-cultural perspective is ethnographically well documented, the reality of gender and bridewealth power after marriage has been established neither in a culture specific way, nor in the context of a changing society. Since gender and marriage in intercultural relations and positions intertwine within native and diaspora realities, the experience of Igbo society provides an important context. Not only does it offer a key milieu from which to examine new realities of gender relations and positioning between women and men, it also reveals the dynamics of gender and bridewealth before, during, and after marriage.

This book, therefore, seeks to explore several issues: how bridewealth power in a patriarchal structure is constitutive of the degree of relationship and power women and men share; how the denigration of women in Igbo society is embedded in the power of bridewealth, which is often not understood by the women themselves; how the ideology of bridewealth is explained and its impact on gender practices; what gender relationship means for the Igbo and how the factor of bridewealth conveys the power and pattern of relationships after marriage; how bridewealth accentuates psychodramatic experiences previously fully recognized in gender issues, and how these experiences influence the reality of everyday life, particularly in terms of development. It also aims to show how the theory of bridewealth gift exchange is both constitutive and constructual of kinship alliance and marriage in Igbo life and culture, as well as to highlight what feminist senses (that is, the collective representation of feminist theories, concepts, and ideas, and their application) attempt to portray in ongoing feminist movements, including, but not restricted to, how they are used, and how non-feminists should view, and respond to, those senses in a changing gender world.

In large part, the work will explore the feelings and psycho-sentiments expressed amongst the Igbo when marriage economic-rites of passage[1] occur, and how this, in turn, affects gender power. Literature shows that marriage issues have been much debated. Even so, marriage rites and ideologies continue to evoke even more discussions about gender relations in a changing African society. This indicates that African societies consider marrying wealth, or marrying poverty, very crucial because of its potential to be the turning point in advocating for the level of both gender status positioning and identity keeping. At the occasion of every marriage, family and extended relatives are fully involved; much of this kin membership involvement existed before, during, and after colonialism, and kinship participation continues to play an important role in marriage-related social payments. This is in contrast to western society where 'falling in love' is the foremost factor in mate selection, even to the exclusion of kin group members.

Given the culture of marriage involving social payments, this book will explore the gender relations involved, and provide insight into the strong tradition of bridewealth power. The term 'bridewealth' embodies meanings and ambivalences connected with beliefs about the assumed paternal and maternal roles of fathers and mothers. The book emerged not only out of fieldwork and personal and intercultural experiences but also as a corollary of conference papers submitted to the 'First Annual Women's History Month Conference of the African American Studies' of the Temple University, Philadelphia (March, 2004) and, prior to that, the University of Leuven gender school discourses (1999-2001), which provided the inspiration for examining the systemic connotations of gender and bridewealth. In addition, fruitful discussions with students in *Gender, Age, and Culture Courses* at the Grant MacEwan College-University Studies contributed significantly to this work. Ultimately, this book endeavours to show that gender is a constructed difference between women and men, and can be increasingly grasped, more constructively, as a relational and positional concept.[2]

The concept of bridewealth, as a whole, reflects the fact that every culture, in some manner, operates a marriage-exchange system. In some cultures, this system maps people into networks of kinship interactions and in others it links people through some other form of social identity or political alliance. Crucial to this argument is demonstrating that when relationships involve wealth exchange as a device for attaining social status they are often attached to sensibilities that commonly render women and men visible or invisible, empowered or disempowered, noticed or ignored, or elevated or reduced in their capacity to exercise control. This draws out not only a vivid ideological picture of the challenges women and men face in their lives but also demonstrates critical transformations in the repositioning of women and men in a changing world.

The lives of Igbo and African women and men in diaspora have increased gender sensibilities, thus impacting the usual meaning and power of bridewealth social codes. Invariably, both women and men are culturally marked by power and gender issues, both in and out of perceptual ideological spaces of gender distinction and dominance (Brettell & Sargent 2001, 2005; Lancaster & Leonardo 1997). The gender question has come to refer to many things, drawing out different approaches that both women and men impose on their relationships.

Given the hypothesis that bridewealth is a social code of denigration after marriage, this book is calculated not only to demonstrate that fact but also to show multilayered meanings and applications beyond that fact. Women have failed to recognize the ideological implications of asking for bridewealth and the wisdom behind the asking is ambivalent and often elusive, thus trapping both genders in the underlying cultural forces bridewealth inscribes. That notwithstanding, ethnography often depicts the gender question as a matter of ideological war, which is sometimes, and sometimes not, understood. As a device for negotiating power, bridewealth inevitably becomes a challenge at some point in the gender struggle.

It is essential to consider both home- and diaspora-sought bridewealth dynamics together, and seek actions and devices for achieving new gender roles in the complex mechanism of culture and gender negotiations. This must be accomplished with input from both female and male circles, and this work proposes the theorizing of this intercultural thinking. It illustrates and represents this view with cases drawn from fieldwork conducted among the Igbo of Nigeria over a twenty-month span. It also attempts to suggest ways in which women and men can better critically face the changing gender challenges in decades to come.

As far as 'gender' is concerned, the term is generally used here to refer to the ideas, behaviours, and social cosmology associated with maleness and femaleness within cultural and social constructions and reinforcements.[3] That is, gender involves culturally patterned and socially learned behaviour that embodies psychological and emotional expressions and attitudes. These same psycho-behavioural expressions distinguish married males from married females within the context of the power of bridewealth.

In terms of the power of bridewealth, it is important to keep in mind that when dealing with the interface between male and female horizons each society shows specific historic, political, social, and economic developments. Methods of gendering people and their society are products of not one but two parallel sex positions sensitized within, and exclusive to, those same positions. Such gendered positions rehabilitate culturally defined and culturally bound systems of sexism and classism. Igbo women and men, in particular, are defined not only by their sex and age but also by their increasingly powerful gender clauses, social origins, stereotypes, occupations, kinship roles, and other important distinctions in society. Bridewealth is a device and process of the politics of identity and status in a patriarchal foundation, particularly in kinship and descent rules as they pertain to being male or female. I show that bridewealth not only symbolically represents how men and women enter into the transaction of embodied kinship relationships but also illustrates the way men and women are tied together in a web of generatively stratified power and status. The analysis offered is essentially for the purpose of gaining a better understanding of the fact that local systems of knowledge exist on the same level as scientific ones, and each can speak productively to the other in constructing gender and personhood (cf. Rosaldo 1989). That the Igbo have a unique gender system was first commented on by Leith-Ross (1939), one of two colonial anthropologists who studied Igbo women in a colonial setting in the 1930s and 1940s, and who revealed Igbo women's feminism and ambition for power in both the public and private spaces of gender relations. Gender constructions were mediated by the flexibility of culture toward self-distinction, and influenced the community in such a way that men and women competed, in varying degrees, for achievements and social positions.

It should be emphasized that the concept of gender is both a social institution and one of the major ways human beings organize their lives. In *Structuring Gender Conversation,* Judith Lorber simplifies the idea of constructing gender when she says, "everyone does gender"[4] even without thinking about it. Thus, my contention is that the bridewealth power, as a whole, is a broad based *mis-en-practice* as it is captured within the Igbo group's social and cultural activities and discourses. In particular, the Igbo patriarchal construction of women and bridewealth is played out in 'doing gender.' There is no doubt that gendered people are identified not just by biological features and notions, but also by the exigencies of the ideological order and social conditions of which bridewealth is a huge part.

Considering the above, this book was written with the primary objective of understanding specifically what bridewealth in Igboland constitutes after marriage. It explores cases related to how bridewealth power is expressed, and how both male and female genders feel about it. It sheds light on the argument about whether men and women actually understand the implications of overstated bridewealth celebrations. The reader is guided through the central purpose of the discussion by focusing mainly on the theme of bridewealth at home and in diaspora as it is seen in today's changing Igbo society.

Bridewealth is analyzed in detail, showing specifically how it sheds light on tensions between men and women. I focus on what people say about bridewealth and then offer suggested strategies for resolving gender issues. Viewing bridewealth as symbolic and relational reveals a circulatory exchange process that accumulates power. Understanding how it is constructed and deconstructed, based on reality rather than just speculation, leads to an emphasis on it as a mechanism for weaving authority. Marcel Mauss and Pierre Bourdieu's notion of exchange and reciprocity of cultural capital, therefore, underlines the field of "origin" and the field of "destination"[5] in bridewealth transactions. Frequently unnoticed, the power of giving speaks to how the bridewealth device locates and relocates or, rather, uproots women from their fathers or mothers' homes and reconfigures them in unequal gender relations in marriage. I argue that bridewealth portrays a field of rights and obligations, as well as underlining authoritative meanings and powers that produce the social organization of gender.

In analyzing bridewealth, I consider it necessary to acknowledge the divergent uses and definitions of 'culture,' in the explanatory context of gender, gift exchange, and power relations, as a group phenomenon, as a learned and symbolic concept, and as a reference to the integrative forces of biological and hereditary realities. In other words, people learn their culture—on the one hand by growing up with it, and, on the other hand, through a 'systemic enculturation' passed on or borrowed from one generation or society to another. People are not born into a society in possession of all the attributes necessary to 'fit in.' Rather, they learn the social, economic and political skills that are fundamental to their acceptance by other members of the cultural group. One is not born with the cultural sagacity of bridewealth, but develops and cultivates the kinship logic and patterns tied to bridewealth. In that light, bridewealth can be considered an acculturative force. In this regard, anthropologists would here view 'culture' as consisting of the shared ideals, values, beliefs, and practices of a people. Feder, (2004:20) of course, has viewed culture from archaeological perspective and shows that it is the extra-somatic means of adaption. Using the terms "extra" and "somatic" he refers to "the beyond the body strategy of survival." In other words, those elements of human existence, beyond what our body offers, that enable us to live meaningfully. Culture respents the things humans think, invent, produce and reproduce, share, distribute, transmit as knowledge and symbolize in varied ways.

As will be demonstrated, this view allows for the examination of not only one aspect of a society but of all aspects as interelated parts of the whole, resulting in the ability to consider the importance of old, new, and discordant realities. Culture, being used in that context in this enthographic pursuit, will basically serve as a tool that will lead us to the concrete reality of bridewealth rather than the imagined or partial truths and fictions.

Primarily, then, bridewealth is customary and is used to interpret experiences and regenerate behaviours that reflect its place in society. Culture, therefore, generally refers to bridewealth values, beliefs, and practices specific to the society. Expansively, however, culture also refers to the production of art, rituals, and penetrative transactions that represent the beliefs and practices of a people. As such, this analysis includes the cultural mode of discerning bridewealth in that I question how the culture of bridewealth is commodified and consumed. In other words, how it is viewed in terms of its exchange value and power within the contestive ideological foundations and positioning of genders. Bourdieu's concept of "habitus"—the structuring of structures of gender—in the disposition of bridewealth helps us examine the principles that generate and organize bridewealth practices and representations as they pertain to attaining kinship and social ends. I attempt to understand bridewealth as the agency of, and pretext to, the actual moment in which a particular social position between genders is established. Subsequently, I am concerned primarily with how bridewealth is formed, powered, entered into, and perpetuated after marriage in gender relations specific to the Igbo. In exploring the stages of indigenous marriage celebration and marriage types, the focus is on the psychocultural and psychoanalytic logjam of the code of bridewealth.

It is hoped that engaging in such a work will offer sensible insight and initiate change that, in one way or another, will reveal the 'gendered human worlds.' Not only do researchers offer systematic accounts that relate to gender ideology, identity, and sex roles, they also show how gender orientations are produced and reproduced in concrete cultural ways. The dangers of not speaking out when one should are illustrated in the power of the 'unsaid.' This is especially true in a world that challenges, in many ways and on a daily basis, simplistic and grand theorized movements of gender realities. Unraveled beliefs about how people are, and how they should be, significantly influence gender arrangements in and after marriage. This becomes even truer based on how researchers see and describe the world.

I have tried to reflect the specific issues outlined above in the organization of the book, which appears in thirteen chapters with themes cross-cutting through content according to relevance. Chapter one presents the main issue of the text by focusing on bridewealth at home in Igboland, Nigeria, and the changing pattern caused by the influence of migration. It also highlights the adopted fieldwork approach and outlines questions relating to the objective of the book. Chapter two, besides further focusing on the study, also draws out the sense of the ideology of bridewealth and establishes its importance in Igbo society.

Chapter three offers a look at the sociocultural state of Igbo society, pointing briefly to the debate about Igbo origins and their socially, culturally, and economically conditioned migrant way of life. Readers are also introduced to the underlying dynamics of Igbo life and culture in the context of gender relations and social organization in both pre-colonial and modern times. Chapter four focuses on the Igbo sensitivity to marrying and brings out the Igbo cultural notion of the 'prize' of marriage. General expectations and social positions of both men and women in relation to marriage rites, gender ideology, roles, and identities are further highlighted.

Chapter five addresses the stages and rites of traditional marriage, and provides insight into the symbolism of the traditions and stages involved, ranging from seeking out a bride to taking a bride home. Sensitivity to poverty and the position of the poor are discussed in chapter six, highlighting the etiology of poverty, and reaching an understanding of how the poor view poverty in respect to traditional and modern marriage. While chapter seven explores the theory of gift swap-over and bridewealth power, chapter eight exclusively examines diaspora, the trendy cash economy, and the impact of these on negotiating genders. Chapter nine deals with and emphasizes the important fluctuating edges of change, and demonstrates how women initiate specific efforts and coping strategies to either accept, or reject, the obligations of bridewealth. This is expanded in chapter ten by drawing examples from Igbo medicine and ritual forces, which women look to in order to negotiate better opportunities and more power. Obviously, negotiating sexual power is crucial to gender dynamics in society.

An outline of implications for development in gender relations in decades to come is put forth in chapter eleven, and advice for women and men is provided. As chapter eleven expatiates on gender and health issues, including sexual behaviour practices and implications on the issue of HIV/AIDS, chapter twelve discusses male feminists, gender, and feminist senses from the angle of identity creation, and power and gender categories. Finally, chapter thirteen lays out the summary and conclusions of the book, and claims that change is necessary. However, for change to be successful, both genders—women and men—need to understand the basics and mechanisms of bridewealth in the first place, and then respond by becoming more pro-active.

Overall, efforts have been made to deal with trendy gender politics and bridewealth in a straightforward way. The various chapters are short and guided by the motive and central objective of clearly conveying the forces influencing gender and bridewealth power in Igboland. It is my view, and hope, that this book will be useful to researchers, teachers, students, and the general public. The gender feminist movement has been central to anthropological theory for the past two decades, and focusing on bridewealth after marriage provides an in-depth contribution to gender, sex, age, and cultural perspectives in a changing world.

Taking feminism seriously in this light suggests that men and women should become more aware of their gender privilege, question it, and act as defectors to that privilege and circumscription with a view toward shaping a new-world gender order largely provoked by critical feminism and masculinism in a global society. The book's encompassing use of case studies, moreover, provides a useful perspective that further illustrates bridewealth as an important field of cultural theory. It also shows a way in which significant gender ideas and forms of ideological power fit into challenging notions of gender and basis of feminist senses in a changing world.

**September 2006**

# Acknowledgments

Many people were involved in the researching, writing, and producing of this work. To all of you I give special thanks for the various supports you provided. In particular, my thanks to Professor René Devisch, who provided me with intellectual mentoring and also shared genuine experiences with me in the field in Igboland of Southeastern Nigeria. To all my informants – the various people I worked with in the field, I am truly thankful. I also thank Prof. Dr. B. Saunders and Prof. Dr. M. C. Foblets for their encouragement and, more particularly, for initiating the forum where the gender problem and its changing dynamics were brainstormed. Prof. Saunders also inspired me to take this bridewealth discourse further in the international knowledge-paths.

I wish to express specific appreciation to Nick Igbokwe (Houston, USA) and Nigerian Igbo Women in Leuven and Edmonton, with whom I shared some inspiring discussions and developed my views. Thank you also to Dr. Adenike Yesufu, Terry Aihoshi, Lisa Mutch, Leslie Dawson, and other colleagues at Grant MacEwan University Studies Programs for their various supports. I thank Dr. Cynthia Zutter (Chair of Anthropology, Economics and Political Science), who found time to read parts of the initial draft, provided useful comments, and encouraged me to publish this book. Special appreciation is expressed to the Grant MacEwan Research Council for the "Faculty Research and Scholarly Activity Fund" extended to me to finish the preparation of the book (Project N#: 05-109 and Account#: IG-RHZZBI). Without this very important assistance, this work would not have come out when it did.

Norma Jean Linfoot, I want to thank you especially for bringing to bear on this effort your meticulousness in transcribing the text, which greatly improved the work. Your queries and the answers they initiated, as well as general discussions on the text, contributed significantly to the work. Moreover, the additional hours you volunteered in order to ensure a consistent quality of work demonstrate your commitment to professionalism. I would be remiss should I forget to mention my gratitude to Chief Christian Chukwumezie and Lolo Engr. Sonya, who provided related photos and support that helped to deepen my grasp of gender issues, insights, and analysis in the field.

My immense gratitude also goes to Prof. Dr. Pantaleon Iroegbu for his multiple inspirations and support. I extend my gratefulness also to Dr. Phil Okeke-

Ihejirika of the Women's Studies of the University of Alberta who took time out of her schedule to read the initial draft and offered constructive suggestions.

If Igbo gender ethnography is to continue to evolve and become suitably expressed, invented, experienced, and shared, it must essentially rest on the senses we produce and reproduce about the political and gender experiences in today's intercultural Igbo-Nigeria and the world beyond. If I have not made the most of, or have not fully reflected, the useful suggestions recieved in the course of writing and reviewing this manuscript, I take sole responsiblity for any resulting shortcomings in the work.

# Dedication

This book is dedicated to:

1. Women in Igboland and in Diaspora

2. Nneoma Lolo Mary, and Umuada Iroegbu

3. Chizoba, Kingchilee, Annette Ezinma

4. Memory of Nze, Ogaranya Titus Ononiwu, and Dr. Stefan Bekaert.

# Chapter 1

# Introduction

In this chapter, I will present the main issue of bridewealth and gender and develop my argument within the framework of the impact of migration, gender, ideological pragmatism, the power of social payment, and life after marriage. The chapter, by looking at what hopes prevail in accepting a suitor either from home or in diaspora, will show that females and males are inclined to negotiate gender constructively and socially. This also entails exploring the dynamics and implications central to marriage and bridewealth considerations and choices, both within and outside of extended ethnic neighbourhoods.

**The Central Issue**

In the Igbo of Southeast Nigeria, when gifts celebrating a child's success are brought into the family as expected wealth, they are received warmly. The Igbo at that moment are gaily thrown into a bodily moving song: *a gari ma nwa, ewezuga nwa, onye ga enye m,* literally translated as 'without a child, who will give me?' This type of enthusiastic show of pride is echoed in some famous Igbo songs of *egwu omumu* (childbirth, initiation rites, and status transformation ceremonies.) Such songs are so ennobling that they are regularly expressed at ceremonies involving gifts and children. In the example above, the phrase *"onye ga enye m"* is an idiom that, taken alone, means 'who would have given me gifts' (*onyiye*)? The obvious implication is that the 'child gift' (*onyinye si n'nwa*) is a happy, expected benefit of motherhood and fatherhood (*ibu nne na ibu nna*). I was privileged to witness several traditional marriage ceremonies in Igboland, and participated in several of them directly when I immersed myself into the Igbo daily and seasonal cultural affairs.

Not only is the Igbo traditional marriage ceremony a high point of public marriage celebrations, it also marks many things for the couple, the families, and the entire community involved. Friends and relatives of the young couple are involved in the marriage and I observed that, indeed, all are obligated to reciprocate participation as part of the pattern of kinship and gender arrangement. The whole arena shows that young couples setting out to enact the bond of marriage prepare for it well in advance. Marriage is a social celebration viewed and practiced as a rite of transition, and the day of the ceremony is eagerly anticipated. The level of preparation for the marriage social gathering depends on the social standing of the young man and woman and the two families involved. The families of the bride and groom work hard to provide a feast for communities or lineages, friends, and relatives, who gather to celebrate their wards' rite of transition into marriage. In Igbo, a kinsperson does not need to be officially invited to the celebration with a written, or otherwise formal, invitation. Simply hearing about the date of the marriage is considered sufficient notice, and it is expected that everyone will participate and contribute.

In many cases, the question of whether a prospective suitor will actually pay out wealth causes tension. If he does, the ceremony will be a highly jubilant affair that automatically situates the young girl into a position of favoured appreciation with her kinspeople. Young girls often pray they will be lucky enough to marry a wealthy husband, and into a wealthy family. Poverty is dreaded—no one prays to marry poverty. These were my preliminary impressions when I began my research on Igbo bridewealth and what bridewealth versus poverty translates into after marriage.

In deciphering the cultural environment and subjects of my research, I formulated the hypothesis that bridewealth is as a condition of social payment without which the marriage is not considered worthy of an atmosphere of public display. I was also concerned with showing that bridewealth is a matter of nuances tied to the trust of relationship. Equally, I wanted to know if the bridewealth process is aimed at receiving payback for the expenses incurred in raising a girl—and, if it is, how families and kin-group members calculate what they deserve to receive from a suitor in return for a young woman. I also needed to evaluate whether bridewealth is a symbolic expression of alliance through gift exchange or the expectation of an economic transaction expressed in the idiom 'in-law must pay' (*ogo ikwu ugwo*). I wanted to know how bridewealth works for the people, since much of it is aimed at expressing a maturity of gender in regard to purpose and status, which entails the formation of new household units and the realization of self-concept in addition to the development and assimilation of the mainstream social aspects of senior adulthood and cultural responsibility. I found, in the process of exploring these issues, that delayed age of marriage and age initiations before marriage are, for males, also important phases linked to marrying wealth or marrying poverty.

In my analysis of bridewealth power and gender, I pondered these questions: Why do the Igbo celebrate bridewealth and cherish it so much? Who desires bridewealth more between the male and female genders? What are the implications and gender ideologies surrounding bridewealth? Is trendy marriage exchange and bridewealth power changing, and if it is, how? And if it isn't, why? And, finally, how is Igbo migration to various parts of the world influencing gender and bridewealth power in the face of intercultural competency and globalization?

With these questions in mind, I decided to take an action-based approach to my research. That is, I became involved with the main players in the process of bridewealth activities in order to understand and relate how bridewealth is experienced and expressed in everyday lives. Igbo tradition is such that if a child is not well behaved, or is unable to understand local proverbs and idioms, he or she is ridiculed using references to bridewealth (*aku ejiri luo nne*). For instance, it is said that the child's mother was acquired at a loss of wealth (*asi onye atura ilu kowara ya, ego ejiri luo nne ya furu ohia*). All of these concepts, as a whole, are very meaningful to the Igbo and need to be thoroughly understood from their unique perspective. What the ideology behind all of this is, and how it can be fleshed out, becomes the most urgent question for critical anthropological analysis.

## Action Research Questions and Significance

Central to anthropological and related social-science discourses is the fact that knowledge is produced by a combination of experience and fieldwork. Using fieldwork to produce knowledge, Edward Said reminds us, means being present in order to see things that the 'other'— that is the subject or object—cannot see in an expert way. In other words, both the researcher and researched must invest extended quality time into discourse that results in understanding, bridge building, and the transmitting of knowledge. This affords us the opportunity to discover and connect underlying local or urban experiences that are not yet well accounted for or reported, thus providing a more thorough understanding through firsthand observation. Moreover, this produces rich comparative perspectives, and informed and experienced analytical attention. The goal is to construct reality without violence and hostility toward the identity of difference, and without posing a threat or displaying vicious ignorance. Fieldwork results in the researcher and researched assuming new levels of awareness, different from those present during the theatrical excitement of their first meeting.

*Igbo quest for wealth versus poverty and gender positioning*

Given the main issues of bridewealth, gender, and marriage, I applied these principles during my fieldwork⁶ among the Igbo and adopted a cultural valuation of

*A Daily Life Scene at Aba-Branch in Ehime Mbano and Area*

the chauvinistic ideology of bridewealth rooted in men's power over women. Bridewealth acts as an example of men's symbolic social-control ideologically, rooted in the power of giving and taking. I focused on deconstructing and reconstructing the foundation of the gender relationships that bridewealth embodies. With this in mind, I posed this question to a group of people involved in a nursing training session: "Who would like to marry a rich person for a rich bridewealth at home or in diaspora?" Almost every hand in the class, comprised of 95% females, went up.

Exploring the gender element further, I asked the females, "Who would like to marry a rich man for a rich marriage wealth?" and I asked the males, "Who would like to marry a rich woman?" I was surprised to observe clear differences and preferences underlined by the ideological ethos of male and female genders. The differential responses that emerged quickly signaled that females desire to marry rich men for rich bridewealth. The data showed a correlation of 100% between desire and wealth for females, and only a 60% correlation for males. This observation points to the female gender's overwhelming desire to marry rich partners. Finding the opportunity to do so is a passion for most women, who tend to hunt for mates in diaspora at the expense of males at home. Expressing concern in an example related to this trend, Sunny Igboanugo describes a case in which the focus of women's appreciation ranged "from their (celebrants') attires to the drinks guests took." He stated that there was no doubt that the bride, 30-year-old Ifeoma, who had graduated from one of Nigeria's Polytechnics and worked in an accounting firm, had finally "hit it big." Prior to this, Ifeoma's worries had caused her increasing anxiety. Ifeoma's beauty, good morals, and social standing, however, met the approval of her suitor's sister-in-law, who brokered Ifeoma's marriage to a successful sweetheart based in the USA. This event turned Ifeoma's world around. Overcoming the difficulty of joining her husband in the USA after marriage is, however, another story altogether (*nigeriaworld.com*, May 12, 2004).

The case of Ifunanya Munonye is another useful one. Ifunanya graduated from nursing at the University of Nigeria Teaching Hospital and married USA-based Chinedu Emezue. This was considered by her relations and friends to be a lucky match—a dream come true. But now, in attempting to join her husband after gaining the perceived social benefits of marrying someone in diaspora, Ifunanya has hit the immigration wall. Stories of these preferred, and supposedly profitable, relationships with mates living abroad are increasingly common, and invariably include difficulties that often cut short life-long dreams of living in diaspora. Aramide Oikelome emphasized how highly this trend is valued by females when he said, "I am happy for you Vicky! This is a dream come true," after realizing that Vicky's fiancé was based in America and would soon be coming home to celebrate a traditional wedding and pay and celebrate the bridewealth, soon after which the church and registry ceremonies in the USA would take place. Vicky's friends were amazed and envious, "Vicky must be so lucky," they all thought (see Daily Independent Online, April 27, 2004). Literature and mass media reports show several examples of trends in the marriage market, and the preferences females have for suitors living in diaspora. But there is a problem here. As Murtala Habu noted, Nigerian women in America and other foreign countries must consider that African society was not built on how much individuals own, but on agreement in terms of their sincere attitudes toward relationships. He cautions, "I strongly believe that materializations and flamboyance are denying Nigerian women from existing properly, and that Nigerian women cannot continue to hang around for Mr. 'Bridewealth' Right in the diaspora at 30s, 40s, 50s and even 60s" (*www.gamji.com*, April 4, 2004).

It is understood that aligning into a rich marriage will result in the dispensing of a generous bridewealth. The implication here is that, while both females and males appreciate having wealthy partners, females have a greater desire to marry into riches than do males.

Male pride causes anxiety at the thought of the possibility of being socially de-gendered. That is, males feel they must avoid domination by a female because, as folklore has it, 'he who pays the piper dictates the tune.' Many view it as culturally acceptable if a man dispenses the wealth, but a man whose wealth is gained through his wife is often ridiculed by his peers and members of the community, who will allude to it often. Cited cases, in which informants quickly noted the influence of Western education on male pride, exemplify this. At the same time, discussions in local and urban communities regarding pride are quite common. For example, relationships are issues people like to talk about, as the following box (showing

Chioma Anyagafu's capturing of the impact on male pride if his partner/s earn more than he does, therefore reinforcing the very fear men try to hide) indicates.

| *Vanguard Online* | *Chioma Anyagafu* |
|---|---|
| Questioning who earns more and who feels fine with it in regard to equality and inequality of gender relationship? | ***Saturday, February 18, 2006***<br>Do men care if their partner earns more money than they do? Short answer, yes. Even if they try to hide it and say that it's okay, the truth is that when a woman out-earns her man, it's a blow to his ego. That said, not all of men are comfortable being the breadwinners, either. Being responsible for someone else's financial stability is a huge amount of pressure. It's a catch of 22 thing. |

Research continued to corroborate these results through a visit to a collective of 80 people, consisting of 58 females and 32 males, in a village community of 1,870 inhabitants. I wanted to discover whether the social consciousness for marrying wealth is associated with home and diaspora connotations. And, if it is, what strategies are being adopted in the diaspora playing fields that influence the desire to marry wealth? Do female and male genders in urban areas share a common mindset with the local community in terms of the conspicuous culture of bridewealth?

I found that there is a tendency to more often seek marriage with mates in diaspora—for both males and females. But, at the same time, the desire for the riches and social status this affords is more pronounced among females, as the majority of suitors coming from abroad are male—it is rare for a woman to return home to look for a husband.[7] What does all this amount to? Initially, it appears to demonstrate some powerful psychological wishes for a life with family and wealth.

I have been increasingly intrigued by these observations, and realize now there is more to this research than initial impressions suggested. I have come to wonder whether Igbo gender behaviour is due to ideological kinship reinforcement or the result of Westernization and the cash economy. I am drawn to understanding the underlying cultural basis of this differential gender behaviour through the minds of adults in post-secondary education, professional institutions, and communities. One may view what is going on not only from the resource-grabbing theory of bridewealth displayed on the screen of globalization, but also as a challenge of the application of feminist emancipation from poverty. This ultimately questions the implications of the Igbo inscriptions of bridewealth on the male mind and the female body.

In analyzing what bridewealth means after marriage, I set out to understand the position that men and women take in negotiating gender practices in the context of bridewealth devices and dominance. What is the underlying power of bridewealth after marriage in Igbo gender ideology, roles, and identity negotiation and positioning? Answering this question demands that bridewealth be unraveled and placed in the context of wealth, women, poverty, power, and the impact of migration.

I also set out to use my experiences to increase awareness and debate regarding changing bridewealth age, kinship, and gender and economic power relations (cf. Salins 1974). Marshall Salins and his followers once observed that wealth distribution in the context of reciprocity occurs in three basic strategic forms: generalized, balanced, and negative. It is interesting to explore how these concepts occur in bridewealth discourse, and whether they also hold true to the gender-development environment. Is it obvious that the poverty of women was an invention of civilization (Salins 1974:36-7)[8] and, by extension, so is gender bridewealth negotiation? How cultural beliefs are recognized, reconfigured, disseminated, appropriated, hegemonized, domesticated, refused, reproduced, and practiced are issues that border on, and challenge, the cultural frame of gender negotiations of power and bridewealth that manifest after marriage.

In addition, questions and findings arising from fieldwork summarize the fact that the desire to be rich is culturally aligned to sources of ideology behind the exchange of bridewealth devices. The way in which bridewealth is culturally played out also suggests that it is deeply related to ideological reinforcements of the gender question, and the power of control that is perceived to work best for the society.

The overall point here is that the desire to own wealth through marriage is shared by the female and male genders, and this holds true irrespective of the large disparity between the male and female drives for achieving this. I focused on finding answers to the following questions: Where is the power of bridewealth positioned after marriage? Have women suffered or benefited because of the implications of bridewealth? Why is the pursuit and celebration of bridewealth events considered so prestigious? What forms of transition are made socio-culturally meaningful by it? The answers to these questions demonstrate how modern Igbo women are struggling to become liberated from or maintain feminine mystique and clichés, masculinist jealousies, and the virility of bridewealth.

The central issue is that, despite important bridewealth studies,[9] deeper issues that shape gender roles and positions after marriage remain unclear. In structural-functional discourse, it is agreed that the ways in which men 'exchange' women in many societies vary, and these variations affect kin allegiance and the reproduction of community. Yet, how bridewealth manifests itself—if it does—after marriage in modern terms remains obscure. Recent studies of gender and power tend to focus on factors that render women powerless and disadvantaged, or create conditions for their collusion in that (Stamp 1990). As a consequence, Western critics have continually supported the image of African women as socially and economically oppressed. Increasingly, women in Nigeria, exposed to this discourse, express the same opinion.[10] However, there are other issues, unrecognized by feminists, that are also emerging and complicate the issue. I will refer to those issues[11] as they apply to understanding the ideology and power of bridewealth.

## Kola Nuts, Oji and Bridewealth

In great part bridewealth is a bondable belief and practice marked symbolically with kola nuts. It is therefore an event that organizes the celebration of kola nuts to positively conjure up and smooth out the body and mind. Given its high potentials including the fertility and peace power it embodies, events for community development and rite-giving such as gathering together and celebrating bridewealth usually begin with the presentation, blessing, sharing and eating of kola nuts in Igbo life and culture. Kola nuts in varying types and shapes as will be further mentioned in the course of the text are so important in ceremonies for the Igbo when marriage and other human related social exchange matters are to take place.

In their worldview centered beliefs and practices, the Igbo see the rite of kola nuts as a fact of bringing the body and heart together. It is a way to first open the mouth and heart through blessed prayers placed upon the timeless forces of good health and life. It entails sharing and eating the kola nuts equally followed by some general social talks to help pass information about current affairs, as well as settle down the participants' psychological mindsets before any event, ceremony and negotiation at hand. Kola nuts play out the symbolism of social commensality and discourse. Several steps are involved in the ceremony of sharing kolanuts and the whole scenario means a lot for the community. Commonality and valorization of the significance of kola nuts is captured in an Igbo proverb which says that *onye wetara oji wetara ndu*, and this literarily means "he who brings kola nut brings life" (Achebe 1958). Obviously, it anchors the entry point that making a guest/s to feel at ease and experience warm reception is all very important for dignity, respect and honour. Let us begin and continue this work by saying *oji nmuta abiala*, kola nut for knowledge has come out, as the plate here offers.

Here, Mr. Richard Chukwu and others present kolanuts to guests in 2005.

# Chapter 2

# Ideology and Bridewealth

In this chapter, I will define 'ideology' as it is intended to be used here. I will also relate early discourses on ideology, explain how the Igbo express what their ideology entails in terms of understanding gender and bridewealth power, and suggest that bridewealth ideology is a systematic Igbo gender construct that guides the way men and women behave, and view themselves, within it.

**Making Sense of the Ideology of Bridewealth**

In order to make sense of the ideology of bridewealth we must first clarify what ideology means and refers to, and how it ties in with the forming of gender relations. The term 'ideology' has a long history, and was first used by French scholar Claude Destutt de Tracy (1754-1836) in his series *Elements d'Ideologie I-IV*, written between 1801 and 1815. Destutt used the term to refer to a "science of ideas" in a sensorialist sense. That is, in the sense of interpreting ideas and calling for action. In other words, ideology deals with a system of interpreting a push for action based on a related belief informing that action. Put yet another way, for Destutt it means a scientific approach to the interpretation of ideas and, in addition, a calculated system for initiating action in society with the goal of consequential change (Iroegbu & Izibili 2004:167).[1] In effect, this suggests that the roots of the ideology of bridewealth stem from lived experiences of individuals or groups—in this case, married males and females locked in the beliefs and practices of bridewealth. Destutt and his followers in France were concerned at that time with reformatory ideas in socio-political life in the National Institute in France. For Wiredu (1980)[2] however, in terms of African philosophy and culture, ideology refers to a set of dogmas imposed on society, even by the use of necessary force.

Ideology evolves over time, taking into consideration the feelings, sentiments, reactions, and views that the people in a society put forward as they shape their survival strategies and positions within that society. Thus, ideology initiates individuals and groups into certain opportunistic beliefs, skills, and competencies that dominate their life profiles and development as they follow and live out their ideas in any given time, place, and circumstance. In this regard, Destutt's use of the word 'ideology' was not congruent with this philosophy of the mind, which, indeed, has little to do with empirically verifiable premises of rationalistic emphasis or ideas.

Of interest here is to show that ideology functions, in part, as an evolved, systematic consciousness that may help people understand themselves and their societies. In this way, the reality of a society may be understood, or not, and consciousness as a whole may be elusive or fixed in the changing context of society and culture. I use the term 'ideology' to refer to the body of ideas and expectations woven around bridewealth and gender power, and to denote the set of Igbo beliefs and expressions that form the basis of political, economic, and social systems of gender construction. Men and women in Igbo commonly expect their gendered roles and positions to follow the expected behaviours that society attributes to each gender. The increasing biases that genders face make apparent the complexity of the answer to why bridewealth after marriage often assumes power that goes beyond the ordinary terms of daily life.

As I quickly discovered, the debate on bridewealth transactions is well documented (e.g., Goody and Tambiah 1973; Stone and James 2001).[3] But, despite this rich ethnographic information, some important fundamental relationship issues between women and men still need to be illuminated. Ongoing debates on women's issues make this not only relevant to academic discourse but also in the deciphering of masculinists' perceptions and experiences of relations that are culturally and inventively adopted as pet-topics. Bridewealth is entwined between Igbo women and men in such a way that it generates constant gender politics of considerable impact. The metaphors, and practices, of bridewealth subtly explain gender anxiety, power distinction, and dominance. As a whole, bridewealth stems from the indigenous concept of constructing, acquiring, and possessing wealth by sustaining marriage and community kinship based alliances.

Bridewealth (*aku nwanyi*)[4], which is as old as Igbo society itself, once served the pragmatic processes of forming kinship and network ties. However, when sex/gender was introduced by missionization and colonialism the practice calcified (Amadiume 1997; 1987).[5] In the name of 'traditionalism,' emphasis on bridewealth was heightened in order to encourage male control of such things as bridewealth, child-marriage, polygyny, widowhood, property inheritance, fertility/puberty rites, female circumcision, etc. (Ranger 1983; Dolphyne 1991).

Across cultures, the solution to the puzzle of society in relation to women also exists in this traditionalism (Brettell & Sargent 2001, 2005). Previously, these institutions and practices were not as demeaning to women as they are presently, even though the ideology behind them was clearly patriarchal. Daughters were once valued as much as sons and the birth of a daughter was celebrated as a source of bridewealth. Parents and close kin showed pride in girls by giving them names that reflected their importance as symbols of wealth. Igbo names such as *adaku* (daughter of wealth), *ihuaku* (face of wealth), *nwaku* (child of wealth), *mmmaku* (beauty of wealth), *eziaku* (real wealth), and *Jideaku* (hold or beget wealth) were common and meaningful. Often an exchange of daughters united lineages, with both patriline and matriline of the bride(s) receiving and giving bridewealth as wife-givers and wife-takers.

This book, however, rather than focusing on history, is more concerned with exploring what bridewealth amounts to in Igbo society today in terms of the making and unmaking of genders, and it is through the prism of gender that we will examine it. I suggest that, more than anything else, new configurations (building on Christianity, colonial structures, and a cash economy) have created conditions in which bridewealth has come to denigrate women on one hand, and create anxiety for men on the other. These new configurations are played out through a psychodrama of distinction and dominance by Igbo men as a gendered 'tool bar' for 'editing' Igbo women out of society.

Among the Igbo, bridewealth remains absolutely crucial, even against the clamour of urbanization and modernism. It focuses on, and is translated through, a variety of tensions (neglected in scholarly literature) that are not only concerned with distinction and dominance but also with change—though this change is rarely for the better. Remarkably, women themselves support the system, and that support is essential to its maintenance and—as paradoxical as it may seem—to the accentuation of gender roles. Not only are women tied to this system, and compliant with it of their own will, they help constitute it as the central mechanism through which Igbo society objectifies gender relations.

Next, I describe the significance of bridewealth from an Igbo gendering perspective before examining how it affects relations after marriage, in particular in regard to women's status. Without downplaying the historical primacy and imperativeness of Igbo bridewealth, I want to emphasize that, in the context of a cash economy, it has become the means *par excellence* of negotiation and control.

Consequently, I focus on traditional stages of marriage in order to extract the underlying symbolism of bridewealth. Marriage types, and their transformations from a traditional to modern state, will not be given exclusive and detailed analysis; rather, the focus is on the significance of the 'power-that-belittles' (*ndi alualu,* as the married folk say). The most important point to note is that everything that occurs in Igbo life is played out against the backdrop of occluded layers of social 'payment.' Despite this backstage power play at home and, by extension, in diaspora, which in one sense locks women into absolute subjection, there are nevertheless signs that bridewealth is ideologically and practically the site of social bonding and resistance on the part of individual and collective subjects.[6]

# Chapter 3

# Igbo Society

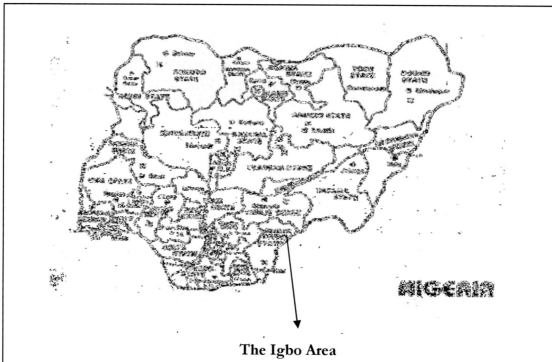

The Igbo Area

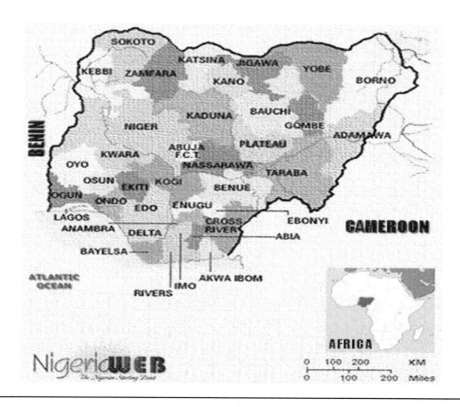

# Purpose

In chapter three, I explore the sociocultural context of Igbo society, and its system of beliefs and practices. The focus will be on bridewealth and gender dynamics as constitutive of cosmological fields of gender stratification, ascribed gender roles, politics of identity, and the framing of power between men and women.

## Sociocultural Perspective

Igboland is in Southeast Nigeria, covers about 45,000 square kilometers, and is home to some 30 million inhabitants, constituting some 23.5% of the total Nigerian population. There are two major climatic seasons: the wet period (*udu mmiri*) and the dry period (*okochi*, with harmattan, *uguru* included), the latter being when

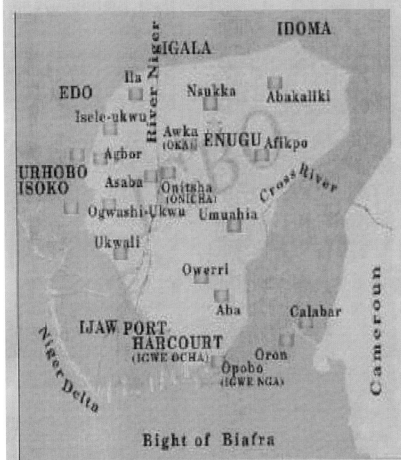

most ritual festivals and marriages take place. Between the two main seasons, the Igbo indulge in leisure time. They engage in craft work, tend their houses, travel, and participate in folkloric dances, music, and rituals. People are surrounded by relatives, and are constantly appreciated, nurtured, encouraged, and cared for in a spirit of mutual obligation. For example, if someone becomes ill, relatives invariably visit and stay to offer help and support until the illness passes. In the same way, relatives are brought together for the duration of ceremonies and funerals. The people take great pride in maintaining the convivial homes, farms, kinship relations, and marriages in which bridewealth is shared (Iroegbu 2002, Nnoromele 1998, Isichei 1976). Uchendu (1965, 1995) argued that individuals in Igbo society are entirely aware of their dependence on the kin group and community. Each individual—female or male, adult or child—is aware of his or her own contribution to the group to which so much is owed. Productivity, hard work, achievement, and success are still highly esteemed.

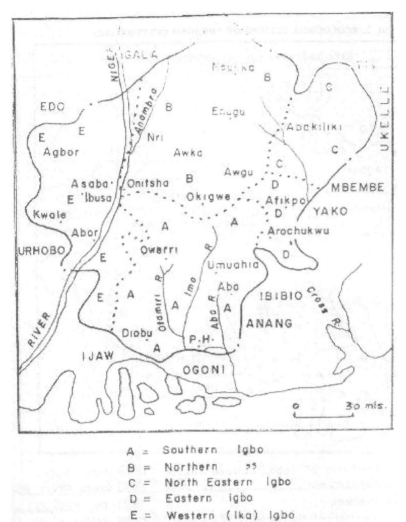

A = Southern Igbo
B = Northern ”
C = North Eastern Igbo
D = Eastern Igbo
E = Western (Ika) Igbo

In addition, the Igbo are a fluid community with an extremely migratory culture. This is attributable to the imbalanced political and economic hostility they experience in the midst of other ethnicities in Nigeria because of, it is claimed, their boundlessly industrious nature. Other migratory factors include compact settlements, land hunger, natural disasters, the open nature of society, and a passion for achievement and status.

**Igbo Culture Areas**

Igboland shares borders with other groups, such as the Ibibio, Idoma, Edo, and Urhobo (Onwuejeogwu 1987, Emeka 1991, Ohadike 1994). Since the 1970s, political regroupings of ethnic peoples in Nigeria have carved out five political Igbo states, known as Anambra, Imo, Enugu, Abia and Ebonyi. Because of this, the Igbo culture areas are currently surrounded by the Cross-River, Benue, Kogi, Edo, Delta, Akwa Ibom, and Rivers States. Each sub-Igbo community is known by its kinship settlement's "call name."[7] Igbo is the common language spoken, and the name 'Igbo,' by itself, is associated with the Igbo's earliest neighbours' perception of them as 'forestland' people.

Today the word 'Igbo' is polysemous: it can refer to the Igbo homeland, to native speakers of Igbo, the Igbo language itself, and/or the social and political ethos, or 'feel', of the entire Igbo world, including gender constructions and relationships between men and women, both at home and in diaspora. The word 'Igbo' encompasses all things Igbo, notwithstanding time and place. It is where they settle and live out their lives, and it is their values and social identities. It is no wonder that anywhere the Igbo settle they are easily identified as they participate actively in life among other ethnic nationalities.

Igbo origins are fraught with controversy. Some oral accounts claim that the Igbo are a primordial people (Isichei 1976:3, Afigbo 1981). Others suggest that their ancestral forebears settled in Igboland (Onwuejeogwu 1987). A number of theorists have attempted to link Igbo origins to Egypt, North Africa, and Israel (Ezeabasili 1982; Afigbo 1987; Ohadike 1994).

Whereas Shaw (1972) recounted how the migration of the Jews into Igboland—Igbo-Ukwu being an important intercultural global center for North Africa and Arab-Indian trade at that time—resulted in the Jewish ethos having distinct influences on the Igbo, Vansina (Vansina *et al* 1982:9-11) asserted that the Igbo are the cultural survivors of the lost sons of Judah, who joined the southward migration of Jews, Arabs, and Berbers through the Sahara Desert to Igboland (circa 2500 B.C.). Suggestive of these origins was the tendency to view the Igbo as purely emigrational, thus placing them in the geopolitical axis of the Niger Benue confluence. It has, hence, been argued that the settlers moved southward to their present location because of population pressure (Orji 1990:14-15). Amadiume (1987: 21) claims that, where ever the Igbo came from, "the colonial invasion was the milestone in their history, when hitherto autonomous groups came to be grouped together as Igbo."

The explanation for their dispersal is also contested; some claim the ever-widening frontier came about through trade and business relations, others maintain that it was the result of the Igbo's desire to found independent villages, and yet others allege that expansion was provoked by a combination of population pressures and natural disasters (Uchendu 1965:3). Given the ethnic politics in Nigeria today, the Igbo currently see themselves as the primary aboriginals. Their claim of ancestral origin in Igboland places them within the obvious territorial autochthony in the southeast. The contention is that there is no strong historical link that can show that they migrated from another place. Furthermore, to our knowledge, most Igbo cultural symbols of autochthony, such as the ritual symbols—namely *ofo*, *ogu* and related taboos—bear no resemblance, either directly or indirectly, to those of other societies elsewhere.

The Igbo have become known for their "high achievement skills" (Ohadike 1994). In the pre-colonial period, the Igbo demonstrated an exceptional capacity for political and economic adaptation, social coherence, and ideological self-assurance (Davidson 1965). They practiced agriculture, trade, and medicine. Life revolved around subsistence activities (farming

***Ofo:*** *Symbol of Igbo Authotchtony*

and trade) and the practice of medical therapeutics, or 'healing rituals.' Igbo character was described as assertive, cohesive, and community spirited. Their 'ethos' was characterized by a strong commercial orientation and a practical, unromantic approach to life. It was an open society in many respects, in which every person was encouraged to regard themselves as equal to everyone else—a belief which encourages competition (Chuku 1993).

The post-colonial period is characterized by an "intensive cultural renaissance" (Amadiume 1987: 22), even though Nigeria as a whole has, until recently, been controlled by military kleptocracies.[8] Since 1999, and for years before that, the Igbo claim was apparently that of being marginalized, a tendency promoted by their outward mobility across Nigerian borders. Currently, in the new democratic dispensation, the Igbo tend to work harder to recapture their erstwhile national position, which was lost due to the civil war of 1967-1970. Ottenberg (1968)[9] introduced the dual-descent system of the Igbo, with particular reference to the Afikpo village-group. In much the same way, Nsugbe (1974)[10] emphasized the Ohafia matrilineal organization, which shares neighbourhood with Afikpo and Biase in the Cross River State, where matrilineality is a pronounced form of kinship social arrangement.

In pre-colonial times, Igbo social organization began with the matricentric unit—the *mkpuke* (Amadiume 1997: 147). This was a mother-focused social category occupying distinct space in the compound comprised of mother and children. In 1956, R.T. Smith coined the term "matrifocal" to refer to households constructed around a key female decision maker. In such households women held authoritative roles and controlled incomes and decisions. While some scholars, such as Mohammed and others (1988) in the study of Caribbean families, have sometimes viewed such maternally conceived families as 'deviant structures', they are cherished amongst the Igbo, as wives give social loyalty to males even though the females control incomes and decisions as a part of the stabilization of households. Matrifocal households were economically self-sustaining, and their ideological base was bound in the spirit of common motherhood and the ideology and ritual of *umunne*—children of one mother. This ideology is a synthesis on forging a "uterine family" (Wolf 1972, Devisch 1993)—a family based on powerful relationships between mothers and sons such that they serve primarily as a safety valve for women. Uterine families allow women to act as kin-keepers, while also fostering and perpetuating channels of communication. They can, as need dictates, plan, stage, and participate in elaborate family rituals. The place of women in men's lives was consistently viewed as that of nurturers, caretakers, and helpmates. Moreover, these important roles necessitated women's ability to weave together the networks of kin relationships that they, in turn, take comfort in, exemplify, and rely on in order to function with social respectability.

A woman's role in rituals focused on worship and spirituality, as the *okwu*—the altar or shrine to the successive line of mothers—was built in the woman's kitchen or bedroom. The *obi* stood above the *mkpuke*, was the ideological seat of a male-focused ancestral house, and involved the social category of fatherhood—although that role could be equally fulfilled by a woman in the practice of woman-to-woman marriages (*nwanyiilu nwanyi buru di*).

A daughter could also become a male and a son (male daughters—*nwanyi-nwoke*, or *nwoke nwanyi*), and replace her father in an *obi*. "Woman marriage" (I shall discuss this further in Chapter 4) was termed by Nnoromele (1998:51) as a counterpart to polygamy. In Igbo, however, it is held that women do not practice polyandry for reasons that remain far from being established, but, rather, that it was accepted that women could marry other women in order to establish their own households. Amadiume also refers to "female husbands" (Amadiume 1987, Iroegbu 2002). Rather than being fashioned as homosexuality, the reasons why women married, and still marry, other women range from a desire to cover up barrenness and family dearth to the wish to exhibit a show of bridewealth the same way men do.

At the wider organizational level was the patrilineage, or *umunna*, which encompassed formal duties and powers symbolized in particular practices. Wealthy women could buy their way into some of the societies formed by the patriline in order to protect their interests. In the socio-cultural gender construction, daughters of the patriline were classified, along with their brothers and other males, as superior in authority to wives. There were always exceptions however, and women sometimes organized into councils, or bought their way into male interest groups or the *Nze na Ozo*—a socially prestigious cult. Women always constituted a viable autonomous system in their own right, which complemented the patriarchal system (Amadiume 1987: 149).

It must be stressed that women's cultural subordination was fostered by the inversion of the old gender order that the patriarchy faced when British colonial structures penetrated the system. Within these new structures, men were favoured over women in the organization and implementation of social issues, thereby creating an unbalanced gender notion.[11] With this, the pre-colonial cultural subordination manifested itself in male-child over female-child preferences, and in rigid gender-specific roles based on biological features and social make-ups. This supports the argument that gender relationships often incorporate power disparities that are shaped by biological sex and age, as well as women's limited power to control or change things that happen to them sexually and economically. In addition to the manifestations already mentioned, certain customs developed, including some harmful widow practices and the exclusion of women from certain privileges, such as inheritance entitlements and participation in rituals. An example of this is that of the kola-nut (*oji*) blessing, where women are culturally excluded from active participation when men and women gather together for the blessing and breaking of the kola-nut. While the culture does allow for the kola-nut to be shown to women, they are not allowed to touch it when it is offered at gatherings.[12] The patriarchal culture reflected in the kola-nut blessing is reinforced by the myth that men are 'holier' than women.[13] Adding to this reinforcement is the myth of the sacredness of the kola-nut itself. Other gender structuring can be traced to the Nri myth of Igbo origin, which includes a variety of crops, such as the male yam and female cocoyam.[14] Also, the gender position of women in the society is emphasized as being either married or an exchangeable daughter awaiting marriage.

In addition to womens' social organizations and practices, the elders (*ndi ichie*), who were the pillar of collective memory, and thus powerful, constituted their own social formations. In participating in all forms of community gatherings and debates until a collective agreement was reached, women achieved status through giving birth to and rearing a preferred sex, age, ability, oracular dexterity, and moral discipline. It could, therefore, be argued that Igbo social organization was once composed of multiple groups rather than being a simple patriarchy (cf. Anyanwu 1993: 119).

*Women and Men Engaging in Roadside Fast-food Services to Enhance Life*

# Chapter 4

# Igbo Sensitivity to Marrying

In pre-colonial Igbo times, *alulu* (marriage) was considered essential. Ideally, marriage was an alliance between two families and their extended, or stem, families.[15] Indeed, marriage would have been less meaningful if it had not been anchored in the politics of enhancing lineage. Crucial to the integrity of the system was its all-inclusive nature. Generally, at least in principle and practice, premarital pregnancies are highly stigmatized, and penalties are often called for when they occur. Punishments serve the purpose of declaring premarital pregnancy completely unacceptable; it is considered to be an abuse of the cultural value of true spinsterhood before marriage, and an offense against the kin groups, and youth and religious societies that one is connected to. Avoiding having children out of wedlock, as well as maintaining virginity, is a highly prized virtue in women. Before the mid-1970s, when universal primary education reached every household and girls became more educated, virginity was used primarily as a means for women to win favoured grooms, families, and lineage connections. Although virginity in unmarried women is still largely honoured, and even more so across the Islamic cultures (Delaney 1991),[16] the penalty for the offence of premarital sex resulting to pregnancy is mostly measured in symbolic fines charged and collected from the erring girl and calculated to serve as a deterrent to others. Nothing, to my knowledge, happens to the male involved, other than having the pregnant girl forced on him (marriage by force) if she is marriageable. If she is not marriageable, it is hoped that support from the male will be negotiated until such time as she delivers—this, however, happens only rarely today. Ridicucling and cajoling the offending parties, including gesturing toward the offending genitalia of the male, is within the cultural strategy to contain such behaviours. Another deterrent is the limitless gossip that accompanies the discovery of such a development. Considering that the people generally deem the act of premarital pregnancy to be a devaluation of bridewealth income, these measures appear logical. It is always hoped that marriage will be marked by elaborate ceremonies of bridewealth, and parenthood is reasoned to be legitimate only in marriage (Uchendu 1965, Iroegbu 2002, Amadiume 1987, Okehie-Offoha 1996). The case of Nkeiru illustrates this reality:

> Nkeiru, a 19 year old student, was unlucky when she became pregnant. She was ill-equipped for it, and her condition prevented her from finishing her high school education.[17] She was banished from school—her school, it was said, had no place for expectant mothers. When the news broke publicly, the gossip was endless. The episode also offered the chance for general discussions about high school students and unwanted pregnancies. Increasing complaints and protests against the loose life of young girls and boys in the community were launched by parents, and concerned parents advised the school authorities to tighten up sexual discipline among the youth. Madam Joyce Ofoire, Nkeiru's mother, was confronted with the issue of premarital pregnancy, and, more particularly, the implications of her own daughter's premarital pregnancy. When asked how she felt upon hearing that her daughter was pregnant out of wedlock, she lamented her loss—that loss being her pregnant daughter. In her plight, Nkeiru's mother declared that

Nkeiru had brought shame upon her and the entire kin-group. She was adamant that Nkeiru had messed up her life, and therefore faced a dark future. She wondered if any man at all would marry a 'second-hand girl.' In addition, Nkeiru had denied her mother the chance to receive the bridewealth due her, and which every parent anticipates rejoicing over. Mrs. Ofoire blamed her *chi* (personal god) for not doing enough to prevent her from having to face the shame and indignity brought to her by her pregnant daughter. She also could not imagine how she would live without receiving a good son-in-law and suitable bridewealth, all because of the misfortune of her daughter's premarital pregnancy.

This case narrative is clear; it describes the agony of a mother hoping to receive and share bridewealth and finding herself denied. Parents take bridewealth seriously, and any behaviour by their wards that would deny them the opportunity to receive it is met with deep anguish and severe disappointment. A daughter is expected to earn wealth in compensation for her up-bringing; her parents and relatives expect this and hope that their daughter will, in turn, foster that same value. Daughters meet that expectation by adhering to the community's moral rules regarding sexuality, thus bringing their families the required bridewealth. Failure to observe the rules and values results in consequences that impact not only the female involved but also other relatives and members of the community. The pride and honour of the girl is diminished, and the bridewealth income is affected to the disadvantage of all involved. It is argued that the dignity of a daughter who experiences a premarital pregnancy, even if she does marry, will never be comparable to the dignity of one who does not. A variation on this view occurs in cases where an intended husband is responsible for the pregnancy; the church authorities involved are sure to frown on such pre-wedding pregnancies. Female sexuality is always a serious concern in terms of kinship solidarity; it is considered honourable to bring a daughter, in her best culturally expected form, to a marriage, which in turn attracts the greatest bridewealth and honour.

Because premarital pregnancy is so serious, one can point to numerous reasons why unmarried women would do whatever it takes to avoid it. Informants' references to, and discussions about, high abortion rates demonstrate that ensuring that a woman is properly married prior to having children is vital if she wishes to avoid the entwined stigma and gossip that arise in manifold ways. Of course, there are contributing factors that lead to couples engaging in sexual behaviour before marriage that often results in premarital pregnancy, as it did in many studied cases. Such factors include poverty, and inadequate information about, little knowledge of, and limited access to, contraception. Another factor is the economic, gender, and general inequalities that characterize women's positions in marital and non-marital relationships. In Igbo, social security and honour are linked to having a good marriage. Failure to marry is failure to 'be Igbo.' Marriage rites—gift exchange, feasting, parental blessing—legitimize and empower the new couple and, by extension, their lineages.

The compatibility of the two lineages was also important in ensuring a good marriage.[18] There are several significant categories that families fell into: poor family *(ezi ogbenye)*, rich family *(ezi bara uba)*, slave family *(osu + ume)*, freeborn family *(ezi diala)*, or polygamous family *(ezi ogaranya)*. Family traits to avoid, or seek protection against, when looking for a marriage match were such things as the presence of stigmatizing illnesses *(ara)*, a history of quick death *(onwuike)*, a tendency to criminality *(oshi na ama)*, a reputation for infertility *(enweghi omumu, atughi ime)*, and known pacts with the spirit world *(ihe nzuzo nke ndi mmuo)*. Traits to be sought after included the possession of a hardworking attitude, a proven propensity toward success in life, and exemplary behaviour *(nwa eji amatu)*. The stability of a marriage was often the result of good consultation between the families and the assurances that are extracted in that.

Through marriage exchange, daughters stepped into wifehood and motherhood, and control passed from the natal to marital lineage (originally, however, this occurred without degradation or a loss of power.) Passionate or sexual love, emphasized by modernism, had no significance in local morality. Instead, a woman was expected to be virtuous (virginity increasing her 'value')—anything approaching passion might develop later. When a woman was positioned to marry, she was bound both by notions of co-operation and by a debt of loyalty. Under traditional marriage norms, a woman, irrespective of her background, was exchanged and, upon customary settlement and establishment into the family circle and kindred division of chores, she became the all-inclusive default mother of her family's household unit. 'Default' mother, or parent, refers to the hands-on parent, who has a greater intimacy with the children and to whom the children turn first for their needs. Parenting is, in no way, optional for the default parent—he or she knows the children's needs and schedules and attends to them (see Walzer 1988 cited by Townsend 2005:105). A default mother is, by and large, a gatekeeper and mediator in the social process of gender attachment and development.

Since the beginning of colonial times, there has been a saying in Igbo: *uwa nwoke na nwanyi abughi otu* (the worlds of man and woman are not comparable). This belief connects with the notion that men and women are conditioned differently, and function equally in separate, but related, spheres. According to Ekejiuba (1995) a woman was often regarded as the "hearth-hold," and the abundant resonances of domesticity allude to a woman's body as the space a man should fill. In the absence of marriage, women were considered fundamentally 'empty' (*idi oghe*). For a woman, an unmarried life was a complete disaster, and her inability to marry was considered a curse (*uwa ojo*) patterned much like an illness - *azi di igba nwanyi* (cf. Uchendu 1965).[19] Men, on the other hand, were never left in an unmarried state—irrespective of how unattractive or poor, in terms of material wellness or standing, they were.

A woman's position was secured by appropriate motherhood (with children of the 'right' sex), by being 'loyal,' and by adhering to 'good' behaviour (*ezigbo omume, ibu ezigbo nwanyi*)—without this, she was powerless. Her default position and role became shaky and nerve-racking if she was stressed by the burden (*iku eze, madu iri onwe ya, ahu akwaghi ukwa*) to produce and reproduce. High fertility, therefore, was a woman's ultimate virtue (*ugo, aku*), while infertility was a curse (*azi, abu*). Blessed with motherhood, a woman would be protected, but without it she was nothing (*afo oghe*). Adoption was not acceptable—only with one's own biological children, conceived with a legitimate husband, was it possible for a woman's honour to shine forth. The status and respect a woman commanded was thus entirely dependent on the husband, and was expressed by the saying: *ugwu nwanyi bu di* (a woman's honour is her husband), and *mma nwanyi bu di* (the beauty of a woman is her husband). Men differed in this respect—with much less of a man's status connected to his wife, the beauty of a man was his wealth (*mma nwoke bu ego*).

Modern marriage, introduced by missionaries and the British colonial administration in the 18th and 19th centuries, now co-exists with traditional marriage forms. In general, the form of Christian marriage has superceded traditional norms in Igbo life, although many echoes of traditional marriage remain. Foremost amongst these traditional echoes is bridewealth. Although overlain by a Christian framework, Igbo society remains basically polygynous. Normally, depending on his economic condition and the constraints of bridewealth, a man can only afford one wife; in theory however, and in practice for the wealthy, a man having multiple wives is an acceptable and legitimate practice. A man's status has always been measured in terms of his age, his productivity, and his contributions to the welfare of society. In pre-colonial times, polygynies were encouraged, as women were not only partners to men in the regeneration of life but were also their associates in economic production (Nwankwo 1993: 6). Polygyny, an important feature of Igbo ancestry (cf. Uchendu 1965, 1995) and the legacy of traditional society, legitimized the organization of social status in two ways:

i. it furthered the ideal of a woman's honour being attached to her being married.
ii. it furthered the ideal of *ogaranya*—wealth and success symbolized by many wives and children, comprising a large homestead.

Women never had a problem sharing a husband—only in the modern Christian marriage does a woman's self-esteem rely so heavily on her husband's whims. Co-wives were, and are, the sources of solidarity, child rearing, labour sharing, and affection, and loving sentiments are often found between co-wives. Powerful wives could, and can, take their own wives. In situations where a woman was *di bi ulo,* the 'family head', she could also practice polygyny with many wives (with children fathered by male lovers). Barren women could find a surrogate mother for her husband's children, which would then become her own. In these circumstances, the need for adoption never arose—although social maternity was, and still is, practiced (Etienne 2001:32). Because Christian marriage requires serial wifedom, which so often generates tensions, forms of traditional polygyny flourish alongside it, with no signs of disappearing.

The ideology behind polygyny serves many pragmatic purposes and remains a powerful force. Polygynist marriages tend to be more stable than both Christian and civil marriages.[20] The fertility of polygamous women is, in essence, 'shared,' so the fertility of any one specific woman is not as large of an issue. (see also Ukaegbu 1970).[21] Women are able to participate in meaningful activities in the public realm, and emancipation is encouraged. The downside is that the husband may actually be neglected—a notion that is enshrined in folklore: 'a man with many wives may die of hunger' (*nwoke otutu nwanyi aguru na-egbu*). As far as the women are concerned, however, their solidarity and pragmatic imaginations are enhanced by the collaboration needed to maintain a polygynist household. In addition, the problems of social status, belongingness, and security in the kinship system are solved by creating room for women to conduct their own independent affairs, whatever those may be. There seems little incentive to oppose this mode of gender relation and organization. On the contrary, there seems every reason to imbue it with recognition for the new possibilities and opportunities that it provides.

A number of theories have sought to explain the different forms of polygyny, how it started, and why it persists. In truth, the majority of societies known to anthropology have shown us that marriage is often not comprised of the one man/one woman model. Rather, many societies allow a man to be married to more than one woman at the same time—a system known as polygamy. There are two forms of polygamy—polygyny and polyandry. Polygynous alignment, as explained above, permits one man to marry and live with more than one woman and it has been revealed, through the societies that practice it, that it is a mark of a man's attainment of great wealth and status. Only wealthy members of the society can, or are expected to, be involved in it because of the complexity of managing a large family unit. Polygyny involves being able to support more than one wife as well as being able to effectively handle the difficulties and jealousies associated with multiple co-wives. To reduce tensions among co-wives in a society, men may engage in 'sororal polygyny'—that is, the marrying of women who are sisters or come from the same village.

'Non-sororal' polygyny—the marrying of women who are unrelated by kinship and/or villagization—is also common and, in such cases, the co-wives have defined rights in matters of sex, economics, and personal possessions. The most senior wife in such a situation is conferred the prestige of *isi nwanyi* (head wife), and is consulted and respected as such in family-related matters. As previously noted, polygyny has economic and political advantages; apart from providing enough agricultural and market labour, women also tend to be influential in their communities. For the Igbo, as it has also been observed as true for South Africa (Anderson 2000), women stated that they married a man with other wives because the husband could afford it. In addition to that, other wives could help with child care and household chores, provide companionship, and free one another up to come and go at their will. It also answers the problem of the shortage of single, successful, and wealthy marriageable gentlemen.

'Polyandry,' in its simplest form, refers to a system of marriage in which a woman is married to more than one man at a time. I did not witness any form of polyandry in the studied culture area, but ethnographic accounts show that in some societies, such as the *Toda* of India, the *Sinhalese* of Sri Lanka, and some Tibetans, the practice of 'fraternal polyandry' is decidedly evident. In these cases, brothers are not concerned about biological paternity; no attempts are made to establish a biological link between children and a particular brother and all children are treated alike (*Ember et al* 2005:365). One explanation for the practicing of polyandry is a shortage of women in the society. In societies where female infanticide is practiced, such as with the *Toda* of India (Stephens 1963:45), the excess of men, though rare cross-culturally, is certainly plausible. Another explanation is that polyandry is an adaptive response to severely limited resources, such as in the case of the Tibetans occupying the northwestern corner of Nepal. With an elevation of over 12,000 feet, it is difficult for the inhabitants to find cultivatable land. Here, fraternal polyandry is the rule in that it prevents the partitioning of a family's already limited land and animal resources. Thus, brothers adapt to these limitations, and preserve the family assets when they share one wife.

Overall, the persistence of polygyny has been theorized to be the result of it being permitted in societies that observe a long *postpartum sex taboo*.[22] According to this child-rearing belief and practice, a couple is to abstain from intercourse until their child is one- to three-years old. Because of health issues linked to the breast milk children receive when nursed by their mothers, couples are required to abstain from sexual relations for a long time; it is considered that any interruption in nursing (such as may occur as the result of a subsequent pregnancy) will affect the child's wellness.

In these terms, a man having more than one wife is a cultural adjustment to the taboo. Women prefer their husbands to bring other women home as co-wives,

*Women in Daily Market Struggle*

which allows for the women to have some control of the situation, and also contains, within the family, resources that may otherwise be spent by the man in seeking outside relations.

Other theories consider the imbalanced sex-ratio as a primary issue. In societies where women greatly outnumber men this problem is addressed by allowing multiple marriages, thus providing spouses for the surplus of women, which in turn ensures moral and social stability. The delayed age of marriage for men is yet another condition that promotes the polygamous lifestyle, as it invariably creates an increase in the number of marriageable women. It is assumed that these two factors—the excess of women and delayed age of marriage for men—are predictors of polygyny.

It must be stressed, even further, that polygamy is a strong virtue in the gender organization of the society. This, however, is contrary to the position of some social commentators, who view it as a "cancerous issue in Nigeria." Some Nigerian based internet websites—*www.gamji.com* (Oct. 1, 2004) for example—post articles on polygamy, and argue that it is a cancerous cultural behaviour that must be abandoned by those seeking top political offices in Nigeria in the new age. This contention is erroneous; the issues of male and female relations and gender struggles constitute everyday activities that define both genders on a continuing basis as they advance toward genuine gender relationships. In his book, *The Case for Polygamy*, MacFarlane argues that "whether the question of polygamy is considered socially or religiously, it can be demonstrated that it is not contrary to the highest standards of civilization." I believe we must add that Africans, particularly those who practice polygyny, behave in a way that is congruent with civilized gender accommodation. Significantly, gender accommodation offers a healthy, practical remedy for the Western problem of destitute and unwanted females—the alternative is a continued increase in prostitution, concubinage, and distressing spinsterhood (which the Igbo pejoratively, and justifiably, call *oto n'aka nne,* literally meaning 'leftover in one's mother's hands'). The shortage of men in comparison with the excess of women seeking relief and respectability is a recognized issue in almost every society.

While some societies have addressed the issue of the unbalanced sex-ratio through such things as plural marriages, others allow for the practice of same-sex marriage or single parenthood. The cultural processes that construct same-sex sexual preferences have been shown, in a number of societies, to be both a resistance to fixed marriage and a way to resolve the threat that unmarried women pose to men's control of their wives (Blackwood 2005:268). This can be seen in female-focused households in the Caribbean, in the practice of multiple-sexuality by Afro-Surinamese *mati* (women), and in the same-sex relations of the sisterhoods among the Chinese. The issue of unbalanced sex-ratios has become more critical than ever, and it appears to this writer that it engenders a social worth in society for the Igbo and related cultures. That is to say, one possible solution against the excess of women and the challenges they carry along remains the practice of multiple marriages, which create healthier families and a more stable society.

Monogamy, as a universal marriage system, is only one form of marriage lifestyle existing across cultures, and it has not sufficiently resolved the dilemma of excess women in any society. Polygamy, as Prof. C. von Ehrenfels of Prague powerfully declares, "is the general order which is much superior to monogamy." On the basis of scientific grounds, he asserts that "polygamic marriage order has become necessary, and will succeed monogamy because it is morally superior."[23] One may be tempted to fall in agreement with von Ehrenfels in that this would be a positive change. At the same time, this is not to suggest that a polygamic culture would be appropriate for those whose laws and social relevance run contrary to it. Besides, given that culture is not static, it further suggests that the tendency for humans to recreate gender relations in challenging circumstances can obviously serve critical purposes.

Only recently, beginning in the 1960s, did the feminist movement start advocating for equal rights and the opportunity to exercise the fundamental human rights granted to others in their societies. Women's rights including all forms of informed choices and relationships have become human rights and vice versa. Since that time, gender issues have intensified, resulting in same-sex marriages and homosexual rights and accommodations for 'marginalized' groups in workplaces and institutions.

With the current trend of focusing on human rights issues, one may envisage that polygamy will, sooner or later, be viewed seriously from both the biological and cultural sides of gender relationships. Though it has worked, to some limited extent, as a religious definition of gender praxiology, it will, in time, return to the natural-gendered society as a resolution to the gender conflicts and biases that arise in forming relationships. Commentators, such as French sexologist, Dr. Le Bon, predict that European legislation in the future will recognize polygamy, and contend that polygamy is the natural relationship between the sexes, which will remedy many evils: prostitution, venereal infections, abortion, and 'unmarried-life-ness.' Disproportions between the sexes, adultery, and forms of gender jealousy will be mitigated. The single lifestyle is a consequence of the obligatory monogamy required, under normal circumstances, of young people between the ages of twenty and thirty-five in Western civilization. We must recognize the cultural imperatives and wisdoms behind marriage practices that have effectively served gender relational needs.

It is also worth pointing out that history has a lot to teach us about polygamy as a natural social condition for solving gender-related problems such as an excess number of women, and for ensuring the stability of female virtues and the quality of society. Irresponsible sexual behaviour, social immorality, unprecedented promiscuity, and armed robbery are alarming conditions that disrupt public safety and moral expectations. In addition to dealing with these things, polygamous leaders should not also have to be concerned with deflecting complaints about the way they manage their homes and worship God. It is subjective to compel men and women to respond to one another only within the constraints of monogamy. Why do we do this? What compelling reason and condition exists that dictates that only the model of one man and one wife can serve society? In Igbo culture, polygamy is an accepted part of life, and gender organization harbours the fact that it is not meant for all persons but only for those who can maintain the ancestral order of the *Ogaranya* status. Cultures that do not accommodate polygamy have strong socio-cultural reasons for patterning their relationships in that way. In like manner, societies that appropriate polygamy tell us what it entails and how it makes sense for them. The belief and practice of polygamy is like comparing cultural differences in technology for adpation to the environment. Said otherwise, as one informant has clearly put it; "it is a 'social care technique' and politics" which enables women and men to be accommodated in relationships. It also offers them a measure of security of some gender balance for everyone." It is, because, a society that expects everyone to be married in order to be considered responsible must equally device means of ensuring that the opportunity to get married is there for everyone – age and status notwithstanding.

It was common in Biblical history for eminent prophets and temporal citizens with large households, abundant blessings, considerable leadership skills, and a firm faith in God to be considered exemplary citizens. For example, many of the ancient Israelites were polygamous, some having hundreds of wives. King Solomon, David, and Jacob had multiple marriages and concubines. Both Solomon and David portrayed God's will and blessings in the Christian faith. Having several wives, rather than weakening their service to God, fortified them for the responsibilities and challenges they faced in helping and leading others. Christianity, for a host of reasons, challenged cross-cultural gender lifestyles and imposed the monogamous lifestyle. The implications of this, in regard to women being denied access to marriage because of an insufficient availability of men, have not been analytically addressed. Celibacy as a life option for the clergy serves its purposes but, again, blinds the ordinary person in society to the true causes of the one man-one wife doctrine being regarded as necessary to the practice of effective Christianity.

Monogamy, as opposed to polygamy, became an integral part of Western culture when it was accepted by Christianity as one of the cardinal principles for organizing gender relationships in religious circles. Initially, it was intended to prevent men from acquiring an excess of women, thus depriving many of them of their needs. Secondly, it was viewed as a way to reduce the conflict and struggle incurred in the accumulation of women by the powerful. The side effect of this is that this gender organization in society became problematic as it resulted in an excess of women. As it stands today, monogamy promotes more evils in society than it helps resolve.

As recent as the 17th century, polygamy was practiced and accepted by the Christian Church.[24] Monogamy was introduced into Christianity at the time of the Apostle Paul, when Christianity underwent many revisions in order for the Church to conform to the Greco-Roman culture, where men were monogamous. Those same men, however, owned many slaves and were free to use them sexually. In that sense, unrestricted polygamy was available to the Greco-Romans of the time. Today, in Western society, with divorce being commonplace, serial polygamy has become the order of the day. A critical cultural eye will see the increasing celebration of divorce rather than make people feel ashamed of it; they have come to argue that it is change for the better and deserves to be accorded celebration to mark the end of the union as it was marked at the beginning *per se*. No longer is marriage seen as a permant cultural outfit but a mere relational contract that can face change any time.

I recall an argument in a Belgian (Glabeek) apple farm in 1997, where a male Belgian derived pleasure from joking about Africans and their plural taste for women. When asked if that taste for women was a bad idea or, rather, a natural thing in society regarding gender relations as they are specifically practiced by a given society, he seemed to search for reasons to support his position. When he was reminded that the Europeans express that same taste for women through high rates of divorce and serial polygamy, he was at a loss to defend himself. Apparently, there are contradictions between what the essences of monogamy and polygamy offer, and owe, to society in gender observable facts.

In the Igbo world, as previously noted, polygamy is considered both natural and socially valid. The practice legitimizes the ancestral institution of *Ogaranya* (status standing whereby marrying more than one wife and having a large household is the expression of gender accommodation normativity). Polygamy summarizes both the nature of man and nature itself as it is associated with women. A more honest understanding of gender must recognize the genuine place of polygamy in gender beliefs, identity, and roles in terms of the problems unmarried women and even men face. Left without husbands and support, women urgently attempt to advance their own social independence through illicit relationships in society, which, more often than not, result in illegitimate children. Free-sex between two or more consenting adults, particularly in Western society, is not helping developing nations sustain their own cultural morality, which finds happiness in cohesive marriage relationships within their societies. An abundance of irresponsible sexual relationships results in numerous fatherless children and unmarried teenage mothers—all of whom become a burden on the country's welfare system. The West is undeniably at a crossroads regarding bloated budget deficits and other burdens faced by powerful nations such as the USA, Canada, and Britain. Saleh Yamusa, among others, has argued this in a similar way (*www.gamji.com* Oct., 1, 2004).

At this juncture, I will turn to the consideration of how the Igbo enact the stages of marriage, and highlight the symbolism of these stages in 'doing gender.'

# Chapter 5

# Stages of Traditional Marriage

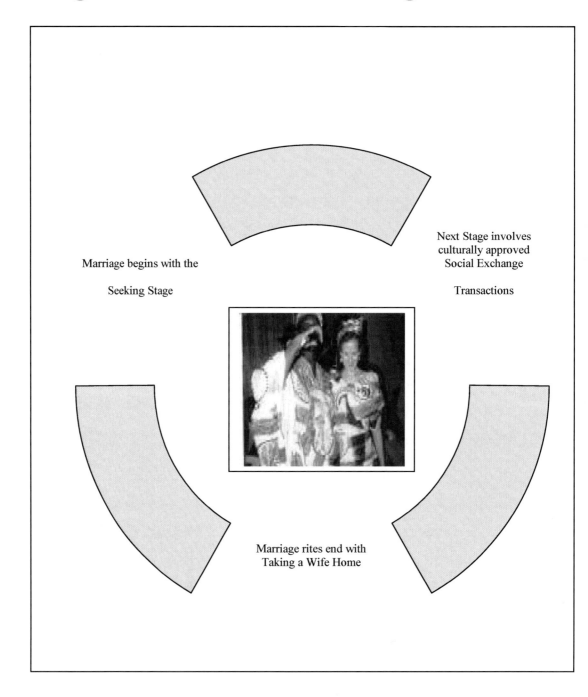

Marriage finds its foundation in the predominant folk theory of kinship, which brings culturally designed exchange symbols, beliefs, and gender aspects greatly into play. Unlike mating, which is biological, marriage is chiefly cultural and symbolic in that the social honour that traditional marriage and its symbolism can create is well acknowledged. The goal here is to draw from research, experience, and discussions to gain insight into the sequences of marrying, as well as bring to the fore the symbolism of this tradition. My overall approach, therefore, will be experiential, descriptive, semantic, and interpretive. The changes to, and continuity of, marriage traditions intertwine with modern symbols of traditional marriage to disclose, rather than cover up, the reality of life and cosmology, both functionally and meaningfully. And it is to these adaptive and transformative significances that attention will be paid.

## Stages of Marriage, *Usoro alulu*

The tradition of marriage affects family, kinship, unwanted pregnancy, modernism, and the inclusion of polygamous virtues (cf. Uchendu 1994).[25] In central Igbo in particular, negotiating bridewealth is an important feature of marriage. In her book, *The Igbo Village Affairs*, Green (1964)[26] noted that several traditional forms of marriage were observed before the arrival of 18th century external influences. Today those forms still exist, with useful adaptations to modernism.

Up to the late 1970s, marriage was not based primarily on 'falling in love.' A wife needed to be discovered, recommended, investigated, and formally approached. The sociocultural background did not necessitate a system that would permit engaging in a love relationship before marriage. Such behaviour would, in fact, be considered provocative, ethically inappropriate, and unacceptable. If friendship existed between young men and women, it was under the strict supervision and control of their families. Traditional marriage was, rather, focused on family- and kin-relationship involvement from beginning to end. This allowed for an exuberant celebration of marriage through traditional ceremonies. These ceremonies, I contend, established a sense of involvement, acceptance, comfort, and protection for the Igbo.

## Meaning of *Di* and *Nwunye*

Before I delve further into the stages of marriage, I must first explain the terms *di* and *nwunye* or *nwanyi* in conjunction with 'going to marry' (*ije alulu*). These terms, although briefly covered earlier, must be explained in more detail here, as they provide some linguistic details about the gender relationship between men and women. From an ideological stance, males and females are distanced from one another in terms of power and assigned lineage roots. In the case of marriage, this is demonstrated by the fact that the terms *di* and *nwunye* connote relations of gender and lineage authority. The term *di* is, in itself, both a word and a prefix to a word, sentence, or phrase. By the rule of binary linguistic opposition, there are words that are quickly associated with, and stand opposed to, one another—in Igbo, for instance, *di na nwuye* (husband and wife), *oke na nne* (male and female), *nwoke na nwanyi* (man and woman), and *dimkpa na nwata* (adult and child).

In addition, the word *di* refers to an achieved status and specifically means a husband, a master, a specialist, and a leader. A *di* is a master to someone, namely a wife, or, in terms of a master/patron relationship, a boss to his or her followers. Examples of words and phrases formed with *di* include *di mmadu* (someone's husband), *di nwanyi* (a woman's husband), *di nta* (master or lead hunter), *di mgba* (master wrestler), *di oshimiri* (master swimmer), *di ochi* (palm wine tapper), *di ala* (core person of a land, place, and earth), and *dibia* (healer). Applied to gender relations, we can therefore see that a husband, to the Igbo, is the master (*oga*) or director of a wife, family, and household (*di-ulo, di-bi-ulo*).[27] Technically, *di* means a strong pillar that holds in place, and supports, a household.

Whereas *di* refers to a carrier or base pillar, *nwunye* means 'the soft layer of sand.' That is, the soft soil that the *di* penetrates so that he can stand up. In this sense, the wife is the supporter. Husband and wife complement one another in the household setting and in marriage; hence, is recognized as a relationship between *di* and *nwunye* (man and woman, or male and female) realized within kinship solidarity and observance of gender norms and practices (Iroegbu 2002).[28] Nowhere, I argue, is the semantic relationship of *di* and *nwunye* made more meaningful than in the senses of bridewealth, and the implications and responses ascribed to it by the communities involved. Evidence of the power and uses of bridewealth is further tendered in, and by, the type of marriage relationship endorsed by the society, as the following themes will illustrate.

**Inheriting a Wife: *Ikuchi Nwanyi***

One type of marriage that may occur is a traditional adherence to levirate, termed as 'augmenting' (*inochi*). Both symbolic and practical, this form is displayed through widow-inherited marriage—that is, marriage of a brother or other close kinsman of a deceased man to his widow. 'Taking over' (*ikuchi nwunye*), as it is called, means that a man, upon the death of his brother, will acquire his brother's wife. Folklore surrounding this form of marriage is drawn from a widow's tears and lamentations over her loss. One informant stated that a widow laments before the kinsmen to draw their attention not only to the consideration of how best to bury her husband but also to the matter of who will 'take her over' (*ikuchi ya*). As the kinsmen discuss these matters, it becomes clear who the widow will approach for all of her needs. This practice is aimed at protecting a deceased man's household, ensuring that his off-spring and name will not be threatened by outside male intruders (*iko*) into the family blood and solidarity. This wife (widow) automatically exercises rights and privileges as the male inheritor's adjunct wife. If the young man was not yet married before inheriting his dead brother's wife, he is expected to marry his own wife (*ilu nke ya, ilu n'aha ya*). Polygamy that is widely spoken about has become generatively sustained in this way. Inheriting a wife is a clear indication that, once married, a wife remains the property of the husband's family. The following case illustrates and reflects changes that have occurred due to religious, particularly Christian, diversity.

> Umunnakwe was 38 when he died suddenly in 1998, leaving behind a young wife, 30- year-old Chikeremma. Two children had been born to the marriage. The deceased was the third child out of seven brothers, whose aged parents were still alive. During discussions about the burial arrangements, the fate of the widow—whether she should go back to her parents, be inherited, remarry, or have her own male friend/s (*iko*)—became a crucial point. The elders involved in the discussion advised that tradition holds that responsibility for the widow fell on two of the brothers (immediate senior or junior) of the deceased. Either of these two would inherit the widow and ensure that her needs were met. Further negotiation resolved that the immediate senior brother, 42-year-old Kelechukwu, would take that responsibility. Accepting this duty, Kelechukwu suggested that he would not share a bed with the widow, but that she could have a male friend—with the condition that no further children would be born to the family as a result of any sexual affairs she might have in order to maintain her physical and mental health. With Christianity and Catholicism quite dominant in the community, the brother sleeping with her would have amounted to polygamy. Thus his position was accepted by the group, and the conditions were clearly laid before Chikeremma, who accepted them and promised to work hard to train her children and represent her dead husband's family line to the best of her ability (*nga ike na ngbali ya ha*).

This is an exceptional case in that the inheritor, Kelechukwu, was quite apprehensive of contravening the Catholic doctrine of monogamy. This case also demonstrates that sexual relations are not necessarily a part of the equation when a male member of the family inherits his dead brother's wife. Rather, instances vary, and informants referred to numerous examples that showed flexibility in the sort of sexual relationship that might follow after an inheritance of this kind.

## Search for a Partner: *Icho nwanyi na icho di; Ije di na Ije nwanyi*

When a man is ready to marry, his family initiates the search for a bride. This

*New bride and groom*

search often follows a circle of relations beginning with ego and proceeding from inside to outside or asking close relations (*iju ikwu na ibe*). That is, the search begins with close kin and valued friends, and then moves to other kin, neighbours, and villages or towns. A bride is only searched for outside when the close kin circle fails to provide or endorse a bride. Upstanding and successful women in the village are approached first, and asked to introduce sisters and close relations as candidates for marriage. Of course, a less than 'upstanding' woman would not be approached in the same way. The search for a wife begins when a young man is considered mature; that is, he has been initiated into the masculine skills considered necessary for survival. Girls, on the other hand, are considered mature when they have mastered hygienic, househould, and socially related feminine chores. Males, with the help of their families and relatives, make known to their friends their intention of finding a 'good' girl to marry. Markets and ceremonies are visited with the purpose of observing and inquiring about marriageable girls (*icho nwanyi*). Usually, several girls will be selected for closer observation until the suitor settles on one through a process of *iju ajuju* (inquiries surrounding the selection of a bride and determining marriage suitability). The girl's family will also make similar inquiries so that they can refuse a suitor if they are not satisfied that their daughter would be comfortable in the groom's family. This refusal may occur even after the formal approach with palm wine and kola nuts has taken place and the intention to marry has been declared. This refusal is referred to as *ekweghi n'ije olulu a*, literally meaning, 'we do not accept this proposal.' Metaphorically, it also means 'the road did not go' for the suitor (*uzo ekweghi oguga*). Emphasis is placed on the compatibility of families as a major issue when considering the suitability of marriage partners. In the event the girl has received important gifts such as unused wears, jewels, money, and pictures, it is expected that she will arrange to have them returned—keeping them would weigh heavily on her conscience to such a degree that it might affect her psychological balance, possibly even leading to anxiety disorder or what is referred to as 'violent crisis' and 'forms of difficult misfortune' (*ihu ojoo, azi igba*), or 'bad world' (*uwa ike, uwa akpu*).

If it is the man who decides that he is no longer interested in marrying a family's daughter, the process for withdrawing is different; any subsequent traditional market days of 'wine carrying' (*ibu mmai ogo*) cease, and no excuses are made for withdrawing. No apology is made, no efforts are made to reschedule the event, and the indication of the man's intention to discontinue the courtship is clearly understood by the girl's family.

Marriage inquiries are directed toward different issues of individual and collective importance and also serve to officially inform the parents and the girl of the suitor's intentions so that they can accept or reject his advances (*igwa nne na nna* and *iju nwata nwanyi ma okwere ekwe*). Soliciting acceptance, both privately and publicly, from both the man and the woman is a task performed by kinspeople prior to the commencement of payments of the significant expenses constituted in the bridewealth. On the one hand, the groom's family concentrates on looking for a morally, physically sound, and appealing *agboghobia* (bride). On the other hand, the bride's family focuses on securing a financially capable *okorobia* (groom) or suitor who will be able to pay out a rich bridewealth (cf. Okehie-Offoha 1996:66, Nnoromele 1998:44). The families' divergent hopes and expectations are played out depending on the number and category of suitors who approach the girl's family with the intent to propose marriage.

## Exchanging Marriage Visits: *Ije Nleta*

After the investigative process (*ohia ajuju*—bush of inquiry), the next phase of traditional marrying consists of the young woman paying a visit to the groom's home. This phase, however, is not rushed. Proper care is taken to ensure that all efforts are made by the families to familiarize themselves with, and assess, the important features of both the young man and young woman involved. This phase occurs only after the engagement is already enacted and witnessed by representatives of the wife-giving and wife-taking lineages. A market day (*orie, afo, eke,* and *nkwo* being the traditional days) is selected as the day when the visit will take place. On the appointed day, the girl chooses two or three girls and a woman from her maternal home to accompany her. Sometimes the girl's baptismal sponsor (*nne-ukwu aha mmiri nso*) will escort her to the groom's home. This first visit is called *iga nleta ije di* (going to view a husband's home). The obligation to provide listed gift items and money is

*Bride and groom through to palm wine sipping rite*

fulfilled on this day, and each person escorting the bride shares in whatever is realized from this celebrated visit. The groom invites his friends and relatives to exuberantly welcome his proposed wife and bestow on her the highest appreciation.

This serves as a means for the bride to evaluate the strength of the solidarity the groom enjoys. In addition, she is offered clues through jokes and discussions that arise from the payment negotiations that occur during the 'washing of hands,' which the bride and her companions engage in before eating. Courtesy requires that the bride have her hands washed, appreciated, and 'paid' for by the groom before she eats the food that is provided (*ego isa aka* or *ikwo aka*). Symbolically, this common rite emphasizes cleansing and purity, and also serves as a declaration of cheerful hearts and bodies at the commensality provided in the groom's home. Invited friends and kinspeople contribute various amounts of money as a show of appreciation and support for the visit, and to signify their solidarity in welcoming and accepting the bride into their fold. The combination of all these practices aid the bride and her entourage in assessing the 'team spirit' of the groom's kingroup, and help her to decide whether events will continue to progress toward a marriage celebration or be brought to a close.

Following this 'one day road knowing visit' (*imata uzo*) is a four-day trial visit in which the bride lives with the groom's family (*ije di abali ano*). And, following that, if she wishes she may remain with them for another eight days (*ije di abali asato*). In some cases, there may be another visit that lasts for sixteen days (*izu ano*—four Igbo market days). Each of these visits affords the bride the opportunity to be addressed as the wife of her husband, and the groom to be addressed as the husband of his wife. It also gives the bride the opportunity to become acquainted with her in-laws. In addition, 'viewing visits' (*iga nleta*) provide an opportunity for the girl to become acquainted with other members of the family. She is told stories and taken to visit farm lands, local streams and markets, and churches and festivals as a demonstration that she is welcome.

The bride's visits to the groom's home, besides allowing her to view and evaluate his situation, also provides an opportunity for her indoctrination into the local gender and marriage beliefs and practices of the lineage. Elder women and the most recently married wives of the lineage take it upon themselves to expose and impart the implications of accepting bridewealth gifts and blessings in order to impress upon the bride the fact that marriage is a serious issue and any bride who loves her life and her family would not play games or act irresponsibly. In this way, the bride is instructed in the gender rules of showing respect, displaying loyalty, and working hard. The women who do the instructing often point to themselves as good examples of these virtues. Also of significance is the instruction the bride receives on invoking the local deities and oracles as a part of the daily life of the lineage.

*Mother (centre) and her Married Daughters: Umuada*

The terms of relationship that a new bride must adhere to within the lineage in order to be blessed in her marriage will also be emphasized. Equally, the dangers that await a bride should she refuse the marriage or attempt to run away after the bridewealth processes are fulfilled are accentuated. Educating the bride on issues of proper living and cooperation is the privilege of elderly men and women, the most recently married women, and the groom's father and mother. Daughters of the lineage also play a role in the orientation of the new bride. Over all, the orientation of the bride is a gradual process that is effective in assisting the bride in the process of adjusting to married life in the patrilineage.

Invariably, the need to please and 'play nice' to everyone will prevail on the bride to create spaces of acceptance that validate of her as a wife worthy of being cherished—at least at the beginning of insuring her personhood. One Igbo proverb reinforces this when it states that a new bride sweeps family compounds or yards beyond boundries and is appreciated for that, even by the enemies of the groom's homestead (*asi na nwanyi ohuru amaghi mgbe o na-azafe ezi tinyere eze ndi iro umu di ya*). In other words, a new bride does not draw lines of enmity while negotiating acceptance and favours from the groom's kin-group. An English proverb literally summarizes this as 'a new broom sweeps clean' – at least until the conditions of the environment change the shape of the broom.

**Bridewealth Ceremonies: *Emume ikwu ugwo alulu***

In the Mbano area specifically, once the traditional familiarity and assessment visits are finished the next thing to occur is the carrying out, stage by stage, of the bridewealth payments. These include, but are not restricted to, 'knocking on the door' (*iku aka n'uzo*) and the involvement of marriage arbitrators (*ndi ebe*, witnesses) in the negotiations. Recognition of the woman's mother (*ihe nne*) and father (*ihe nna*), male youth (*umuokorobia*), female youth or lineage daughters (*umu agboghobia*), the collective lineage community (*ihe obodo, ama ala, umunna*), and the village head (*ihe onye isiala*) is undertaken. All these phases involve elaborate feasting, the giving of listed gifts, snuff sharing, singing, dancing, commensality, talking, chatting, negotiating, and much more. During this time, the home of the bride is visited regularly by the groom and his friends and relatives. Cooking for, and entertaining, visitors from the groom's side in a fitting manner are common efforts that require considerable resources. It is, however, expected that visitors will, from time to time, give money and other types of gifts to the bride and her parents as a matter of reciprocal social courtesy and genuine affiliation.

**Paying Bride Price and Taking a Bride Home:** *Ikwu ugwo isi na ikporo nwanyi*

Usually, a separate day is selected for negotiating the bride price and, when

**Cow: *Obu aku, ehi***

this is settled, the marriage is concluded with a traditional wedding or blessing known as *ihe nkporo* or *ihe atu,* which is parallel to the modern Christian wedding. The amount of the bride price is paid in money or goods,[29] depending on the social standing of the bride's family and of the bride herself; educated or skilled and highly-resourceful girls tend to attract a higher bride price. Bride price may take the form of material goods such as cows (*ehi, obu aku*). A cow is symbolic in its equation with a bride's worth in that cows are the most valuable domesticated animal in the area, and the traditional use of a cow in paying bride price exemplifies the extreme value of the bride.

The pattern of negotiating the bride price differs from one locality to another, and is also influenced by the ability of the marriage witnesses or 'go-betweens' (*ndi ebe*). Negotiations are prolonged deep into the night, or day, and the bride may be asked to present herself so that she may be praised (*ija ya mma, itu ogo*) by the wife-givers and appreciated (*ina-bata ya, iri ya mma*) by the wife-takers, thereby motivating the wife-takers to make a higher offer. While some groups negotiate orally, others use counting sticks called a bundle (*ukwu nkpa*—burden). A bundle is used in such a way that the wife-givers will pass a bundle of, for example, 100 short sticks to the wife-takers. The sticks may be cut broom-sticks, or chewing sticks. For that reason, an informant stated, the bundle is called *ihe atu* (chewing stick, or measuring stick). The bundle signifies a measurement of the bride's value. Regardless of the material used, the sticks convey both metaphoric and symbolic nuances.

The wife-takers receive the tied bundle, count it, remove a certain number of sticks from the bundle, and return it to the wife-givers. The returned quantity signifies how much they have agreed to pay. With the wife-takers and wife-givers taking turns adding and removing sticks, the negotiations continue in that fashion until an agreeable sum is reached and endorsed. The wife-takers are generally cautious about not offering too little, which would be considered belittling and that would result in them being ridiculed by the wife-givers. So it is that the wife-takers do make an honest effort to pay out a sum that will be

*Some Bridewealth Items*

pleasing to the wife-givers. In like manner, the wife-givers are careful to avoid asking for too much, which might cause the wife-takers to consider them relentless, money-grabbing, in-laws. Achieved in all of this is a negotiation that ends with both sides having entered into a mutually beneficial in-lawship that will tie them together through the expressions of social payments and other related gender and kinship alliances.

The pattern is sometimes so dramatic and so symbolic that the Igbo believe strongly that marrying *is* the negotiation. The use of expressive, powerful proverbs and speeches make the transaction one that serves to strengthen their ties and reveal the potentials of the parties involved. With the intensification of the Christian religion, *ihe nkporo* may be conducted on the night preceding the wedding day. Receptive forces of change from within and outside of the culture have incorporated this into the 'bachelors' eve,' during which the groom's age grade members and social peers facilitate and participate in the dedication and blessing rite.

## Staying on the Road: *Ino n'uzo alulu*

During the whole period of marriage negotiations and visitations, the bride and the groom regard each other as being 'on the road' (*ino n'uzo alulu*). The bride, in particular, terms her movement between her natal home to her future (husband's) home as *ino n'ije di* (staying on the husband's road). During this period, she travels from one home to the other on a regular basis. In like manner, the groom regards his travels to his wife's home as *ino n'ije nwanyi* (staying on the wife's road). For him, this period is characterized by his preoccupation with paying bridewealth. All of these references and metaphorizations come to an end when the bride is finally escorted, with gifts and blessings, to the dwelling of her husband, where (assuming all goes according to plan) she will live in the patrilineal home for the rest of her life. For the fortunate, living in wealth is part of the experience of married life. Others, however, are not so lucky and, for them, marriage is characterized by poverty and the hope that that poverty will one day be overcome when a child of the family comes into a fortune.

## Fertility Cock and Vagina Yam: *Okuko Elu Ikpu na Ji Ikpu*

'Age grades' are one of the important social institutions of the Igbo. Men particularly, and sometimes women, belong to age grades in their communities. The functions of an age grade are social, cultural, political, and economic. Age grades bring into union and action a category of an age set of men and women. It is, therefore, a club of social empowerment recognized by the members' age category. Communities use the age grading of members to create levels of hierarchy and entry into manhood and womanhood. In an age grade, each member is equal in all respects to any other member in terms of rights and privileges. Age grades help discipline their members, foster respect for one another, and support one another's welfare.

In terms of the stages of marriage, for the bride and groom's age grade the dominant feature of the marriage process is the opportunity to storm the wife-giving family and village in an act of solidarity and demand that they be given a number of

*Okeokpa*: Live cockerel

yams—symbolized as 'vagina yam' (*ji ikpu*)—from the groom, and a healthy live cockerel—'vagina cock' (*okuko elu ikpu*)[30]—from the bride's family. With these items, the bride and groom are 'given *ngozi*'—that is, ritually blessed to succeed. The metaphor of *igba ngo*—literally, mixing up sexual body fluids or sleeping together and having sexual intercourse—is captured and highlighted through calculatedly positioned fertility jokes and affirmative responses chorused in unison at the instant the blessings are given. Stated in the blessing is the wish that the new couple will succeed in bringing forth a child in the next nine months (*onwa ituolu, bere onwa ato n'afo*—a bouncing baby to the community of the patrilineage).

This ritual raises some obvious questions: Why do the Igbo choose yams and a live-cockerel as items to represent the feminine sexual organ? Further, why is the penis silenced in comparison to the attention given to the vagina? The answers to these questions need to be unraveled in order to bring out the underlying cultural idioms, metaphors, and symbols associated with male and female sexual relations at this stage of the marriage. I will, therefore, explore the issue of why the

*Christian wedding and cake rite*

vagina cock and vagina yam ritual is a central feature in the rite of taking a bride home.

The Igbo regard yam (*ji*) as a male crop, as opposed to cocoa yam (*ede*), which is considered a female crop. The Igbo yam deity is known as *ahiajoku* or *ajoku*, from which many Igbo names, such as Njoku and Nwanjoku, are derived. These names convey specific meanings to both those who call them and those who answer to the call. Many ritual ceremonies revolve around the planting, tending, and harvesting of yam—a major crop in Igbo—and key ceremonies, such as bridewealth and other forms of individual and collective events, are dignified with yam. This highly respected root crop is a symbol of prestige associated with masculine features.

Informants reported that using yams in the ritual of taking a bride home is deterministic because it constitutes part of the cultural scope of bestowing masculinity on a man at the moment in which he settles social debts through honourific rites. Further, these informants argued, since the suitor pays out bridewealth as a show of attainment and masculinity, it follows that the yam, rather than cocoa yam, bestows honour and dignity upon the groom's maleness. Therefore, they inferred, the Igbo marriage rites include yam and not cocoa yam. Cocoa yam enters the picture only after the payment processes are over, when a bride's family may resettle their daughter with various farming crops that include cocoa yam. As they explained this to me, I realized that the yam symbolizes obtainment, holding, getting, keeping, and continuing. In that sense, then, using the yam in marriage rituals is entirely appropriate as the yam seeds the root of obtainment and progression. That is why, the informants said, it is called *ji* (get and hold). Various forms of yam go with this semantic appropriation of gendered crops as a cultural yardstick.

Secondly, the yam, the informants explained, resembles the penis in its shape and thus conveys an expression of the power of the husband. During the going-home blessing rite, the groom's age grade and peers will usually invoke the shape of the yam while referring to the groom's sexuality and power of *igba ngo* (intercourse).

As a food, yam is very nutritional and consumed regularly by the vast majority of people. It is also a social food that embodies respect and honour, and delight is taken in the serving of it. Important ceremonies are marked with cooked or uncooked yam delicacies. In contrast, cocoa yam (*ede*) is rarely involved in public ceremonies, which suggests that Igbo rites of passage such as marrying are, in a sense, the crowning of the male conqueror (that is, the *di nwe emume alualu*). Cocoa yam is associated with the female buttocks (*ederi, ike*), similar in shape to the low mounds of cultivated soil the crop is planted in. Yam, in contrast, is planted in high, pyramidal mounds, signifying the protruding penis of masculinity versus the coco-yam shape of femininity.

Calling the yam 'vagina yam,' in context with the marriage-blessing ritual, suggests that masculinity focuses on penetrating femininity with the power of the sexual muscle and invokes the bone imagery of strength—man being the bone factor and woman the flesh factor. Levi-Strauss' theoretical explorations in binary oppositions such as *The Raw and Cooked* (1969) [31] make sense here in terms of understanding how symbols are played out in traditional marriage process thought patterns and practices.

'Fertility cock' or 'vagina cock' refers to the imagery of sexual appetite and the skills embodied in the cockerel (*okeokpa*). The Igbo leave their domestic fowl free to roam about and cater for themselves, thus the sexual lives of these fowl are openly witnessed on a frequent basis. Usually, the cock pursues a hen and displays its sexual skill before it grabs the hen and mates with it. Onlookers are excited by such demonstrations (although older women and men often chase the fowl away), and it offers them a chance to talk openly about the skill and insatiability of the cock's sexual habits. Similar imageries, such as those inspired by dogs (*nkita*) and Billy goats (*nkpi*), apply in the same way. As part of regular discourse, this cockerel sexual imagery (*okeokpa nchu*) is also appropriated to male sexual power and skills. 'Vagina cock,' therefore, is used in reference to the frequent displays of sexual interest and fertility that are, for the most part, common to all men and young people.

Both vagina cock and vagina yam are metaphoric and symbolic of male and female sexual responsibilities. The sexual advances incorporated in the cock imagery are representative of the expectations a groom places on his wife and vice versa. When considered together, the imagery of the vagina, yam, and cock is appropriated as a reflection of gender relations and power, fertility, and birth, which conjures sensitivity to marriage and rites of empowerment. Yet, when the Igbo refer to the vagina, they speak about *elu* (above) rather than *ime* (inside)—for example, *okuku elu ikpu* and *ji ikpu*. This again shows the binary relationship of symbolic items as they are considered as inside and outside, face to face with, and above (*elu*) and inside (*ime*) respectively. These particular binary opposites are also representative of the bride and groom's possession of one another—both inside and outside of their marital lives and their everyday regenerative gender experiences.

One more striking symbol of the Igbo duality of marriage rites is emphasized in the unfolding of events in twos and fours (parity and fourity), which is central to the social organization of gender and community. Cosmologically, in reference to the 'above' and 'below' of the vagina-yam and cock, the Igbo think in terms of 'above' (*elu*) and 'below' (*ala, okpuru*) in worldly dimensions. Here also appears the duality of male and female relations, which systematically evolve into husband and wife and son and daughter, suggesting further symbolic embodiment of underlying structural relationships. The male/husband figure as 'above' (*elu*) in contrast to the female/wife of 'below' (*ime, mgbada*) in the hierarchy of symbolism points to a pecking order and power chain devised of oppositional principles of organization. It is fascinating how this underlies Igbo references to metaphors such as *elu* (above) and *ime* (inside or below) in light of the hen and cockerel images of masculine and feminine elements of relationship and power.

People in the Umunumo Mbano area of Igbo, where the use of vagina cock and vagina yam is highly pronounced, enjoy gender relationships through sexual jokes evoked by this custom.[32] Such relationship dynamics in marriage rites are powerfully manifested as a necessary expressive process of gender assertiveness. Evidently, creative symbolic devices and identity reinforcement are gained through this very figurative rite of taking a wife home (*ihe nkporo*). Unique in their observation of this rite is the fact that the bride's family provides a 'fertility cock' rather than a 'fertility hen,' which, in a biological sense, would appear more logical. The groom, on the other hand, provides the 'fertility yam,' which is expressive of his masculinity and power to 'get' and to 'hold' (*ji, jide*) life and family together.

In observing the contrast between the practices of these customs amongst the Igbo, one cannot help but become aware of the strong play of the gender-identity juxtaposition of power. This contrast further suggests that the forces of gender symbolism at play run deep and go beyond the ordinary level of human perception and expression such that they are better understood metaphorically and symbolically in terms of how they categorize and reinforce the power of ritual moorings. Viewed in this light, the bride is both vagina yam and vagina cock and so valuably ties together the locus of belongingness, patrilineage, and humanity, thereby maintaining continuity and growth of the male holding force, principle, element.

## Shedding Tears and Going to Marital Home: *Ibe akwa ila ebe di*

The ceremony of *ihe nkporo* (final take-over) of a wife and the move to the patrilineal home is marked by an outpouring of concrete emotions. Tears shed by the bride, her sisters, her mother, and even her closest friends, are plentiful. The father, in a show of masculinity, generally displays a manly nodding of his head to the left and right and gnashes his teeth rather than shedding tears in public. The following questions arise: Why is there such weeping and sobbing if the marriage is truly a matter for great celebration, as attested to by the observation of so many accompanying ceremonies? Why this last minute crying as the bride finally leaves her parent's home? Are these tears of joy or some other culturally symbolic and meaningful expression of an emotional departure? Or could it be part of the biological characteristic of emotionalism often associated with the female gender?

*Giving blessing and shedding of tears*

Informants told me that weeping is both symbolic and understandable in that this is the moment that the bride comes to the full realization that this marks the end to her life as a free woman in her natal lineage. From this moment on, in order to visit her natal home again, she must seek the permission of her husband and the patrilineal family. And even if she is permitted to visit she cannot stay any longer than the period that has been authorized. Simply put, the bride sheds tears because she will be cut-off from the village of her youth and will miss her peers and her home. She also cries, however, because it is expected as a sign of respect to her parents and kinspeople. Should a woman fail to shed these symbolic tears she becomes the object of ridicule and people perceive her as 'running' to her marriage or husband (*igba oso di*). In modern times, as previously explained, *ihe nkporo*, whereby the age grade of the groom storm the brides family and lineage in order to take the bride home, is combined with the wedding eve. The shedding of tears, along with other forms of symbolic expressions of family and patrilineage ties and separation, are embedded into the gender-storming, high-jinx, blessings, and support that mark the continuity, and change, of marriage traditions.

## Symbolism and Marriage: *Omuma na alulu*

In this section, I will attempt to explain the meanings of some of the symbols that are useful in understanding Igbo stages of traditional marriage. The most obvious questions are, what is symbolism and what role does it play in marriage? Finding the answers to these questions guides the structure of the brief analysis provided here.

According to Gioia *et al* (2005:641)[33] a symbol is referred to as "a visible object or action that suggests some further meaning in addition to itself." Symbolism is an important aspect of procreation beliefs, and is used to define what males and females represent in society. Symbols carry secret codes, and are multifaceted political, ritual, cultural, and social objects of communication. They have the unique ability to refer to things that are either absent or present—to what is 'here' in addition to what is 'there.'

Symbols are designative, denotative, connotative, and ostensive in definition and meaning. Turner (1967)[34] theorized that symbols are effective because they combine ideological meaning (arrangement of social values and norms) with sensory meaning, which arouses desires and feelings (Morrison and Wilson 2002:67).[35] Furthermore, Turner sees ritual context as a major initiator of symbolic action and reaction in that ritual contexts constitute dramas in which the characters are in one situation at the beginning of the enactment and in another by the end. As such, ritual transformation is achieved through the dramatic sequencing of symbols and

Market stall for food trading is a common survival business married Igbo & African women engage in (Photo, courtesy of G. Offoaro 2005).

often through the dramatic participation of those who transform themselves and their world. In the case of marriage, the status and identity of the bride and groom are transformed through their initiation into wifehood (*onodi nwunye*) and husbandhood (*onodi di*) through rites of gender that are symbolically and culturally ordained and guided.

As White (1949, 1976, 2004)[36] said, symbols help articulate human behaviour into two ways—through the symbolic and the non-symbolic. The non-symbolic refers to bodily gestures that express what otherwise would have been spoken orally; for example, the 'thumbs-up' sign, generally means that things are 'okay' or going well and implies an appreciation for what is being observed. In voicing this same thought, one might say, 'right on.'

In contrast to non-symbolic behaviour, White explains, symbolic behaviour is radical in that it empowers us to express human feelings, thoughts, and actions in everyday life that could not otherwise be effectively articulated. He argued that other primates are incapable of this kind of abstract representation that humans create with the use of symbols. Therefore, he contends, the basis of human culture emerged from a world of symbolic interaction and the transmission of values, identity, and culture through symbols. Thus, symbolic cultural experiences are a natural component of 'humanness,' and the appropriation of suitable cultural symbols are dependent on a faculty that humans alone possess; that is, the ability to use symbols in organizing beliefs, society, marriage, family, kinship and lineage, and religious, economic, and political practices. Symbols serve to capture abstract realities and make them real on the level of everyday life experiences, and understanding symbolic beliefs and practices requires not only endogenous skills and contexts but also cosmological and epistemological strategies, abilities, and social expertise.

With access to symbols, humans have become more eager to learn and understand their surroundings via the creation of symbolic values and significations. As such, the most important form of symbolic expression in marriage, and other rituals of everyday life, is articulate speech. Articulate speech refers to the clear communication of ideas, some of which are embodied in the symbols familiar to a society. In addition, these ideas create and preserve tradition through accumulation and progress. This, in turn, produces and reproduces an extra-somatic, cultural order in gender relationships.

An important point here is that marriage is a symbol of society in which kinship is produced and reproduced. It is also a symbol that is marketed and challenged by cultural change and gender politics, as is the case today with the existence of feminism and the feminist movement. For the Igbo, traditional forms of marriage are symbolic expressions of their cultural values and system of knowledge. As we have seen previously, each stage of the Igbo marriage process is linked to checks and balances that foster the appropriate knowledge and lineage understanding involved in the transactional exchange. As a result, the institution of traditional marriage remains popular, although the pattern of mate-selection has changed due to adaptations to modernism.

The pairing of couples, in what is commonly referred to as 'match-making' in global popular culture, symbolically involves the families of both the young man and woman and their extended relatives. Symbolically, this demonstrates that marriage is aimed at achieving economic and political lineage alliances. New in-law relationships are formed, and these are symbolically expected to last forever—or, at the very least, as long as the players involved can take responsibility for the relationship and maintain its stability.

**Change and Diversity in Partner Selection**

From a cross-cultural perspective, there are several methods of finding a mate that are historically and generally accounted for (Ingoldsby 1995, 2004).[37] In the system known as 'marriage by capture' (*ijide nwanyi n'aka ike*),[38] men have simply captured women and taken them as their own. In another system, men have received women as gifts or as plunder from war. In a third system, a woman is impregnated by a man outside of marriage, or is raped, resulting in a forced marriage (*itujuro nwoke nwanyi, inyaba nwoke nwanyi n'olu*). The reasons for the creation of the

*In-laws with bridewealth gifts*

conditions that would lead to this type of marriage, according to informants, range from the man's 'inability' to wait for the fulfillment of his sexual desires, to his being unable to afford the bridewealth that would allow him to be sexually active (*ichi amu n'aka*) within a legitimate marriage relationship. Seizing women forcefully, under certain circumstances, may also be construed as an expression of masculinity.

Symbolic images that appear in the above examples of marriage portray the fact that it is a form of the language of power, gender, and sexuality. When designed and practiced properly by the society, however, marriage fosters dignity, honour, and cultural responsibility.

Another common form of marriage is that known as the arranged marriage. Cross-culturally, this appears to be one of the most common methods of partner selection. Under this model, as the Igbo marriage system illustrates, the parents, often with the help of relatives, choose a spouse for their gentleman. This form of marriage is often a mechanism of ensuring social payment, such as with the bride price. The purpose of this transaction is to start and legitimize an alliance with the family of the bride for the transfer (not the loss, as incorrectly asserted by some authors) of her services. Given that a bride, within this type of marriage system, continues to assist her family after marriage, and sometimes becomes their main source of support, the linguistic use of 'loss' to describe this situation is inappropriate and illogical. In fact, in societies where marriage payment is the norm—as with the Igbo—Stephens (1963)[39] recasts Murdock's Ethnographic Sample as follows:

Bride price is found in 260 societies; bride service occurs in 75 societies; dowry exists in 24 societies; gift or woman exchange takes place in about 31 societies; and no marriage payment surfaces in about 152 societies. This symbolically illustrates that marriage is a transaction between communities and families that is focused on as a measure of the cultural and social order of gender relations and kinship production and maintenance. In addition, anthropologists tell us that, world wide, there are 140 nations that believe in and practice polygamy and only 40 nations that favour monogamy. Incidentally, it is within polygamy that African societies—the Igbo in particular—find, both socially and symbolically, their ancestral *mis–en-value* and status.

One of the senses of the underlying symbolism of marriage (see also the subtitle: symbolism and marriage) is that marriage is a function of organized social and gender relations in which systematic forms of transfers are negotiated and enacted. The Igbo practice of marriage tradition shows that they do not view marriage as a function by which they incur human or material losses. Rather, both people and goods are culturally and symbolically considered, by both the wife-givers and the wife-takers, as extensions of the alliances that are formed to support, and share in, the honour of the bride and groom. The time has come for anthropologists to reframe the point of view that suggests that these types of marriages create losses. The Igbo data clearly depicts that this is not the case; for them, marriage is simply a transfer of daughter from father to husband, which bestows honour on all involved rather than fanning the flame of loss. Neither is the physical separation of parent and child that results from marriage considered or calculated as a loss. Rather, it is considered a gain when a marriage is successfully carried out. In fact, having an unmarried daughter is a sensitive matter, and such families run the risk of dishonour and ridicule. So it is that the Igbo would view the unmarried, rather than married, daughter as a loss. Hence, the message of folklore in reference to being married versus failure to marry (*oto n'aka nne*). That is, a loss in terms of marriage market dividends (*usu ahia*).

Even after the physical separation resulting from marriage, women do not discuss issues in their marriage-family without some useful input from, and inclusion of, their natal family members when it touches the bride's welfare—and this remains true throughout life. Unmistakably, marriage brings two families into a permanent unity, or oneness (*ogo na ogo bu otu*), for as long as the marriage remains responsible to the purpose of securing family, kinship solidarity, and reciprocity. Marriage is essentially viewed as a productive affair, which incurs many benefits as opposed to losses.

Finally, there is the form of marriage that takes the free-choice approach to mate selection. This approach is popular in the Western world and, due to multiculturalism and globalization, has become a pattern for marriage in the majority of societies world-wide. This marriage model symbolically illustrates a shift from kinship and economic to personal motivations. Individuals, rather than their parents, are considered to be best equipped to decide whom they wish to take as a partner. Currently, there is a controversy that arises out of this due to the convergence between heterosexual and homosexual relationships. It must be specified, however, that 'free-choice' does not imply that an individual is free to marry absolutely anyone—the rules of endogamy (marrying inside the lineage group) and exogamy (marrying outside the lineage with wife-sharing groups) restrict individuals from making certain choices in regard to mate selection and the preserving of the kinship cultural order.

Okonjo (1992) revealed that in the changing society of the Igbo about 55 percent of marriages are arranged, while the remaining 45 percent are free-choice unions. She argued that the fact that the majority of the latter involved younger people indicates a move away from arranged marriage to free-choice unions. Indeed, this is a trend we see in much of the modern world (Ingoldsby 2004:362). Furthermore, Okonjo stated, this movement of the Igbo toward the free-choice method of mate selection is based on 'falling in love,' as opposed to the pre-colonial and post-colonial experience of arranged marriage up to the late 1970s. It should be noted here, however, that the changes that occured in the 1970s through to the 1990s were also characterized by the system of finding a wife for someone else (*ihutara madu nwanyi*).

The various patterns of arranged marriage among the Igbo are now falling into disfavour with those at home, but are shifting to those in diaspora. Obviously, there is more to this trend than can be explained by the issues explored here, and further investigation is needed before this point can be properly understood. This would include studying the socio-culture forces that have undermined, or changed, the traditional forms of marriage that encourage more stable unions and have brought about this preference for free-choice unions. A deserved gender response to feminist movements and modernism cannot be ignored as a part and pattern of culture change in the new age.

Having explored the diversity in partner selection methods, I believe that the Igbo display significant symbolism that is appropriate to marriage as a rational means for securing the continuity of family and the patrilineage society. Whereas male to female marriage is the most common model, female to female marriage also exists and creates a circumstantial and symbolic variation on the cultural marriage pattern. We saw that Amadiume called females that marry their own wives 'female husbands' (*nwanyi di*). These are male daughters and female husbands who take on the male role to ensure that the family line survives. The most typical change in evidence in Igbo society today is that of a daughter being caught in a family situation where there is no male child to continue the family line. A daughter in these circumstances will, before marrying outside of the family, marry another woman, and call her her wife (*nwuye m*). Symbolically, this female-husband could then, within the rules of exogamy, marry from outside after ensuring the security of her own patrilineal line. Daughters who take on this role stand in between two different worlds of social obligations, and in between two different gender roles. Should they be considered male or female members of society when it comes to such issues as making social contributions and paying levies? I believe that this area of Igbo life and culture needs to be examined further in order to better understand the specifics of male and female symbolism in marriage identity, roles, status, and representations. More research in this respect will expose what cultural alternatives the Igbo have in place.

In the traditional stages of Igbo marriage, the symbolism of the vagina yam and vagina cock are important in that the ceremony of taking a wife home is equally characterized by an emotional impact that results in the shedding of tears. Understood in conjunction with one another, all of these things signify that marriage is both a realization of dreams and a struggle. The Igbo explain all of these facets of marriage metaphorically and, indeed, symbolically.

**Chapter Wrap Up**

It has been shown in this chapter that the tradition of marriage, amongst the Igbo, is a strong one. Men and woman alike consider it a grand event and engage in negotiating the best marriage opportunity for their sons and daughters. Not only does marriage offer the opportunity to fulfill kinship obligations but it also fosters social solidarity and gender inclusion. The processes of negotiating bridewealth have been discovered to be multifaceted, and each stage illustrates the dignity and honour involved in sharing and building alliances. Marriage is, in no way, viewed as a loss. Rather, it is the mutual creation and sharing of honour. To negotiate marriage is to create a powerful covenant, and all kinds of secrets are excavated in order to ensure that trust is built into the solidarity between wife-givers and wife-takers. Although modernism has influenced the Igbo society in various ways, a very strong cultural continuity in the belief and value of marriage, and the symbolism of the intrepid efforts that are made to secure a good marriage for daughters, signifies the abiding relevance of kinship. Fertility cock and vagina yam are significant in that they emphasize the degree to which sexual bantering is relished and valued in everyday lives. They also symbolize the importance of gender relations and sexuality in the functioning of families and society as a whole.

I will now move to the examination of the meaning of poverty and its impact on life and gender and class relations through marriage and other societal institutions.

# Chapter 6

# Sensitivity to Poverty and the Poor

In this chapter, we will examine who the poor are, and how they are defined—both by themselves and by others. The etiology of poverty will also be examined, as will the fears around marrying poverty and successive programs intended to alleviate poverty in Nigeria. In addition, the impact of the poverty debate on the female gender will be highlighted.

**Defining and Explaining Poverty**

Determining who the poor are is not as simple as it may seem. In the Igbo of Nigeria, the poor are easily identified by both appearance and behaviour. When I talked to the poor Igbo, one of them said to me, "Do you need a book to define me? Just look straight to me and at me—my home, the food I eat, the water I drink, the track road I walk down, the farms I cultivate, the markets I go to, the churches I pray in, the health facilities I use when I fall sick. I keep goats and sheep and fowls. I cook with firewood I fetch from the bush. Kerosene? No! Gas? No! Electricity? No! I roast my corn and peas in the hot ash (*ntu oku*). I crack palm kernels (*iti aku*). I wash in the river (*iyi*). And I chew sticks (*atu*) to clean my teeth. When the seasons change

from dry to wet, I live in fear of the rain and wind destroying my thatch hut. Worst of all, local financial contributions are killing us (*ntuntu, tukiritu egbula anyi*) because more people are dying and we are obligated to bury them. It is sad in this leadership world of Obasanjo." (That is, the poor leadership of the present administration, led by President Olusegun Obasanjo.) This reference to the name of Obasanjo also implies a spreader of evil or bad things in the local parlance of this informant.[40] So, defining who the poor are and how they feel about their poverty begins with listening to their voices. These voices were also recorded by Isichei, who was once counseled by a 95-year-old poor informant to write his statement down (*dedata ya*) (Isichei 1976).[41]

In the effort to understand who the poor are, or who is likely to be poor, there is a sense that the poor can be targeted as a specific group of people who are deprived. That is, those who cannot afford the basic necessities of life such as a good education, occupational skills, appropriate information, housing, food, health care, social mobility and active mainstream political participation. Poverty is often a life-long state, commonly characterized by distressing unemployment and underdevelopment of social skills and cultural or learned competencies.

In his discussion on the ways of understanding and breaking the vicious cycle of poverty, ill-health, and underdevelopment in Nigeria, the Minister of Health, Prof. Eyitato Lambo (see *The Guardian*, January 14, 2004)[42] brought to light some of the conceptual vignettes of poverty as it affects families, life, and culture. He noted that in Sub-Saharan, Africa, about 45% of the population live below the

*Women and Children Facing Rural Economics of Poverty Struggle*

national poverty line. While poverty can be defined as a condition of restiveness and deprivation, it also consists of being in a position where one lacks the capacity to respond to basic needs. The poor are often incapable of generating, and keeping, the socially accepted amount of money and/or material possessions required for living a meaningful life. The World Development Report (1994) identifies the poor as "those who are unable to consume a basic quantity of clean water and who are subject to unsanitary surroundings, with extremely limited mobility or communication beyond their immediate settlement."

The story of development in Nigeria is far from straightforward due to various ruthless military and civilian profiles. Statistics show that the population of the poor rose from 18 million in 1980 to 35 million in 1985. In 1992, there were 39 million poor, and this once again rose to 67 million in 1996. In the period between 2000 and 2004, this number was reported to be even higher—71 to 80 million.

What this demonstrates is that poverty, which encompasses about two thirds of the population, has continued to increase rather than decrease, and has made deep inroads into the lives of millions of ordinary, unsuspecting, Nigerians. Survival circumstances in the country have taken a turn for the worse with each passing administration and year. Massive looting of the public treasury and alarming squandering of the country's wealth has affected the well-being of men and women at large since 1980 right up until the present.

On March 1, 2004, Laolu Akande reported, in *The Guardian*, that, "It is greatly instructive that just a few days ago, the UNDP Resident Representative in Nigeria, Mr. Tegegnwork Gettu, while launching the Osun State Chapter of the Human Development Fund (HDF), actually made it known that the percentage of the poor in Nigeria has grown,

in what he termed a very negative trend, from 66 to 70 percent of the population, over the past six years."[43]

Women in particular should no longer, in my humble view, wait to rescue Nigeria and position the genders, since men have consistently failed to make any strides with their poverty reduction programs. Admittedly, though, the situation is frustrating since reform strategies linked with the International Monetary Fund (IMF) and the World Bank (WB) would require constant renegotiating of debt repayment, leading to cutbacks on social empowerment. The obligation for governments to budget for, and implement, strategies that would result in positive change is further hampered by the tendency of key players to siphon capital into their own personal interests. In all of this, women and children are the first to feel the direct negative impacts.

Hagberg's (2001) study of poverty in Burkina Faso has shown how the local people, in multiple ways, represent the realities of poverty that are equally true for Nigeria. Hagberg emphasized that the anthropological contribution to the study of this area provides an important context to understanding it, and pointed out that a narrow definition excludes many of the people who are perceived as poor. He argues that poverty must be treated as contextual, situational, and relational (Hagberg 2001:7). Poverty, therefore, is an important category of gender politics that builds first on kinship, class, and society. However, defining poverty is fraught with both structural and behavioural models of explanation that have been previously explored (Gordon & Spicker 1999, Pinker 1999, Anderson & Broch-Due 1999, Hagberg 2001).[44]

On the other hand, the poverty level, as it is considered in the global scene, refers to the income- and consumption-based level of well-being that falls in line with a standard accepted by, and applied to, a population group. The international poverty line, it is important to note, stands at a *per capita* average consumption of one 1985 USA dollar per day, as adjusted for the difference in purchasing power between countries. The global poverty line is currently about 12 dollars per day, whereas 'absolute poverty' entails living on less than one dollar per day (The Guardian, Jan., 14, 2004). The poverty cycle has, in itself, become almost a matter of 'destiny' in that the existence of life stressors—such as increased birth and death rates, environmental, health, and well-being issues, and other unavoidable poverty challenges—have created a situation about which the government of the day cares very little, or not at all.

In Nigeria, the number of people afflicted with poverty is estimated to be between 70 and 80%—a very serious situation indeed. Women are trapped in poverty more often than men, and also appear to suffer more than men in relation to economic and gender inequality. An important aspect of the poverty in African regions, therefore, is the plight of Nigerian women. Poverty in women is expressed in a number of ways, as the 1995 United Nations Human Development Report (UNDP 1995) revealed. Gender relations are also an important part of this equation because of their affect on certain sectors of poverty indicators. In particular, rural livelihoods and environments, economic and political reforms intended to address poverty issues, the decentralization of institutional structures involved in poverty discourses and initiatives, education and training for empowerment, and, finally, health and social services[45] are all impacted.

The poverty line and its implications have been continually stressed, and the UNDP report has also addressed the feminization of poverty as a component part of the problem. It has been pointed out that women comprise 70% of the world's poor. Yet, the government's poverty reduction program has failed to have any impact on the situation in Nigeria—particularly as it pertains to women in both local and urban areas. So what is going on here?

Gender-based differences and imbalances in terms of access to, and control of, economically productive resources are important considerations in the issue of poverty reduction. Constraints that are placed on women's participation in development and large-scale intercultural economic activities arise from certain notions and ideations of women from one society to another. Poverty reflects an inability to afford basic needs, a lack of control over resources, a lack of education and skills, poor health, malnutrition, a lack of proper shelter, poor access to water and sanitation, vulnerability to shock, violence and crime, and a lack of freedom, choice, and voice (cfr. Lambo 2004, OECD 1996, Hagberg 2001). However, measures, indicators, and determinants of poverty vary, as do the intervention methods used to reduce or eliminate it.

Many terminologies have been used to refer to poverty: 'income or consumption poverty,' 'lack of basic needs,' 'human under-development,' 'lack of capacity and functioning,' 'isolation and social exclusion,' 'relative deprivation,' 'vulnerability,' 'disempowerment,' 'powerlessness,' 'livelihood unsustainability,' and 'ill-being.' Thus, poverty is seen as a multifaceted metaphor regarding the condition of life. More noticeable is the increasingly feminist profiling and feminization of poverty. This is likely the case because, in the effort to understand gender and unequal balance of opportunity and rights, vulnerability to labour exploitation, sexuality, skills markets, and social status and identity inventions, the infantalization of poverty has been forged right from ideological devices to economic and technological conundrums.

The commonality of the human experience of poverty stems from the fact that it is both locational and social-group based, which apparently produces and reproduces themes of hunger, deprivation, powerlessness, violation of dignity, social isolation, resilience, resourcefulness, solidarity, state corruption, arrogance of service providers, and inexorableness of gender inequality (Nayaran *et al* 2000:3, Hagberg 2001:31).[46] In all of these, gender relation is a central issue around which poverty is critically excavated.

The Igbo do not shy away from saying that poverty is *oria* (a social sickness) and is feared (*itu egwu, ujo*), although it is often unavoidable as a subculture of the civilization process. The culture of poverty serves as an adaptive function of survival whereby poor people cope with feelings of hopelessness and despair that arise from their inaccessibility to greater socio-economic success. Poverty breeds social isolation and exclusion from social-mainstream thinking and events. Although culture mediates peoples' adaptation to the environment in which they live, it at the same time creates both physical and social distance between the 'haves' and 'have-nots.' Thus, the factors that lead to and perpetuate poverty have become a cause for vigorous debate and concern for gender-relational abilities.

**Etiology of Poverty and Targeting the Poor**

Hopker, in *Woodfin Camp* states "…it is clear that programs of research and extension designed to deal with the problems of poverty, lack of food, overpopulation, and pollution rarely meet their objectives" (cited in Greenwood and Stini 1977:7).[47] It is also argued that development policies rarely remain neutral in regard to cultural differences in the etiology of poverty. Regardless of the development base culture, such development policies are inevitably brought into place because they contain a vision of the kind of society developers are attempting to bring about—and this vision is often startlingly ethnocentric. A poor society, as Greenwood & Stini (1977:8)[48] argued, must not only adopt the technology and skills offered, but must also come to share certain cultural orientations with its benefactors. Development thus becomes an agent of cultural dislocation and, by extension, a cause for frustration in terms of gender equity and effectiveness.

What causes poverty in itself is a generative explanatory debate. Some say it is individualistic, others argue that it is structural, and the rest opine that it is cultural. Other hypotheses include the diversity of classes among poor people—namely, the working poor, the new poor, the disadvantaged poor, the truly needy and so on (Jenkins & Miller 1987).[49] All of these conceptualizations of poverty are associated with three approaches— assimilation/integration, human capital and structural profiling of opportunity, and access to wealth creation and participation in social service issues. Whatever the case may be, I would argue that one's survival is largely dependent on the larger trends in society. The 'need of achievement,' a theory preached by American psychologist, David McClelland, in the 1960s and 1970s, as the reason for people's failure to become rich is questionable in that the poor also exist in societies where people's cultural orientation is marked by a strong sense of achievement, an innovative spirit, a propensity to risk-taking, and entrepreneurial skill. Such is the case, for example, among the hard-working and positive-risk-taking Igbo ethnic group in Nigeria. The poor exist, I contend, due to the socio-economic structure imposed by the emergence of state bureaucrats and political foragers; therein lies the creation of an uneven distribution of wealth and power. Inequality is very real in the class-based political and economic system of the society, although both gender and classism, independently and collectively, successfully maneuver through the economic, political, and social-capital resources that are available. The powers-that-be, however, exploit and deprive those with unequal opportunities, skills, and strengths, and poverty is systematized.

As Karl Marx pointed out, in a capitalist system work is organized in such a way that economic surplus ends up in the hands of the bourgeois class. Women's groups influenced by psychoanalysis and Marxist theory, and thus involved in gender and socialist politics, have apparently questioned the relationship between women's attitudes and the actual patriarchal structural conditions in relation to the legal, political, and economic basis of gender oppression and poverty dynamics. The question is whether feminine nature, sexual desire, and approaches, have drawn women into oppressive relationships and, therefore, led them to accept and tolerate unequal economic, legal, and sexual treatment as a whole.[50] The implication is an ever-widening gap between capitalists and the peasant labouring class—the latter being condemned to distressful poverty given the forms of sexual organization of labour.

On the other extreme, Bourdieu and Passeron (1977)[51] used the term 'cultural capital' to refer to social and cultural cues. The fundamental elements of cultural capital range from personal lifestyle, linguistic competency, familiarity with elements of high culture (such as books, music, or art) to technical, economic, or political expertise (Quadagno & Fobes 1997, 1995).[52] They emphasized how this cultural capital can be negotiated in transforming poverty, gender, and classism. One of the dimensions of the theory of cultural capital is that it serves as a basis for exclusion, or inclusion, in levels of self-concept, society, jobs, resources, and high status self-control and equability. Social and cultural boundaries, as Nash (1990)[53] and DiMaggio & Mohr (1985)[54] claimed, are simply constructed around the possession of cultural capital, which is transmitted across generations through the family and maintained by sociopolitical forces. The key to the emancipation of women and the poor, then, is to be found in this premise as it applies to the ideology of the culture of poverty. Thus, it is surmised, liberal leadership would dismantle the notion of women and the poor as helpless and passive, thereby breaking the cycle of deprivation and inequality that typifies their existence.

In considering the question of who the poor are among the Igbo of Nigeria, those that readily spring to mind—and who require the most help in terms of poverty alleviation—include widows who lack any form of social support, orphans, the critically ill, the socially, mentally, or physically disabled, and the disengaged and isolated elderly. Others are the urban poor, persons displaced due to environmental disasters and political troubles, and the unemployed who have no means by which to rectify their hopeless situation. The next group to spring to mind would be the retired, or disengaged, workers. The plight of this group is particularly frustrating. Many are the heart-wrenching stories of retired workers standing under the heat of the sun in endless lines as they wait to receive their meagre pension allowance. These pensioners are treated as if they had never served the country, and the institutions they worked for, as normal, credible people. Successive governments have refused to take pensioners seriously and treat them with dignity, respect, and honour. If the present administration is to address the issue of poverty, it must squarely face all of the groups outlined above rather than speaking of poverty as if it is something that exists 'elsewhere.' Indeed, poverty is very real and exists with those people who face daily challenges that they do not have the capacity to resolve. Pensioners need a regular payment of their allowances, and investments into a pension development fund would go a long way to ensuring that an establishment would not fail in addressing this area of poverty.

The next critical group is the unemployed and retrenched workers. There is a need for the development of a social fund that would be committed to addressing the problems of unemployment and lay-offs.[55] Job creation and assisted-support initiatives for those who wish to start their own business would surely embolden people and encourage them to learn skills, diversify into other areas of service, and launch their own cultural, social, and economic ventures. New skills acquisition programs and centres aimed at forestalling retrenchment would inevitably support people and give them new opportunities to become self-sufficient and support their families and communities.[56]

The strategies mentioned above, with regard to helping the poor find meaning in their lives, are all workable given good policy determination and consistency. Indeed, they have been working well ever since Oscar Lewis conducted his ground-breaking study of the culture of poverty in the developed societies. Lewis recommended the creation of job centres and reinforcement agencies that would offer the city-poor he studied the opportunity to learn new skills and search for jobs in centralized job-banks. Providing training and support helps people resolve the trauma of being unemployed, and also assists them in coping with the challenges that are unique to the uncertainty of poverty. Financial help may also be needed to alleviate or cushion the effect of their misfortune.

Anthropologists offer glimpses of the struggles of poor people in less well-off places and show how little they have, as I have pointed out through the definition provided by the Igbo I interviewed. When the poor themselves speak out, they generate simple ideas of what they need to get back on their feet and make advances. Using 'cultural contacts' that embody direct, extended and comparative interests (cf. Middleton 2003:3) shows how concrete social development and global economic strategies for better understanding the poor and addressing their needs rest on effective anthropological approaches. Three such approaches rise out of the concept of security of the poor people of the world, security representing healthcare, a place to live, and a life free from the inability to effectively deal with dieases that are treatable and curable and the threat of war and terrorism.

Taking an active interest in providing security for those who don't have it is a critical human-rights issue. But in order to provide security, we must understand the people we are trying to help, which is effectively done through cultural contacts. The culture of the poor must be studied and understood in any developmental effort, particularily in terms of gaining security through development and accessibility to relevant healthcare needs. Security is only one small part of what the poor need to face challenges and make advancements in the mainstream social, economic and political realms. But without security, their situation will become much worse. For example, a sick person cannot think as well or do the ordinary things a healthy person can do to help himself or herself. Good health and accessibility to medical care and health-enhancing information and awareness will help the needy support themselves and move on. The saying that 'health is wealth' is an indisputable fact when it comes to achieving and maintaining a good quality of life in society.

The second step is providing the poor with the opportunity to change their situation. Poor people are helpless to change their situation in the challenging global economy if they cannot go to school or obtain the right quality of education, training, and experience. Lack of education and poor quality of learning are disadvantageous to achieving competence and enhancing capacity building. Nothing perpetuates the cycle of low paying jobs like the so-called 'survival employment,' or 'whatever a person can do to eat and pay the bills' that people must engage in so they won't have to resort to illegal activities. The consequence of this is a situation in which the inability to access education and training to elevate skills and opportunities for growth is invariably the cause of wide-spread poverty. In the age of technology, information is power. Linking the poor to global economic information will help them use their educational skills to fulfill the next aspect of addressing poverty, which is empowering them and giving them a voice (cf. World Bank Report on the Poor on Poverty 2000).

Thirdly, getting the right quality of education, and therefore the chance to access the global economy, will ensure that their empowerment is result effective. In this way, the poor will learn that there is room for interaction with others in various forms. Enhancing interaction opportunities for the poor is a means to an end in itself, and growing and expanding beyond poverty will re-create pathways that encourage them to think boldly and do things differently. The concept of global economy supports the obvious fact that the poor are not separate from what determines the global society. By giving the poor a place in that economy and the ability to maneuver within it, they will experience the importance of being connected to a previously unconnected global economy on their own terms such that they can make positive changes in their affairs and become equipped to break the cycle of poverty. There is every evidence to support the idea that linking the poor to others and to resources will provide them with useful opportunities for capacity building and exercising their voice in matters that affect them. The poor will not only gain the ability, and therefore power and empowerment, to determine the course of their own lives but also the ability to capitalize on their self-confidence and security and become a key part of a sustainable society.

Poor people are aware that for their voice to be heard and actions taken they must organizine themselves and define their goals in order to be listened, and responded, to. To ignore the voice of the poor is to deny them political and social power. Through advocacy training and intiatives, the poor can mobilize and create opportunities for themselves. The point remains that while people who are impoverished need work, they also need the security of healthcare and opportunities to gather and share experiences that will remobilize their world so they can meet their goals. By providing simple services, such as education and a better and more accessible health care system, and using international global policies to reinforce local and regional ones that connect poor people to technologies and markets, change and growth will certainly start to occur in the efforts to break the vicious web of poverty. This also entails and extends to informed assertiveness on the part of women. When cultural changes occur that support movement away from the poverty line, people will start feeling more secure and in control of their lives. All of this suggests that development can never be imposed or forced; it can only be facilitated.

Before proceeding to the investigation of issues particular to the poor, we will briefly explore Oscar Lewis's theory of culture of poverty in respect to who the categories of the poor consist of.

## Oscar Lewis and Culture of Poverty

Oscar Lewis (1966)[57] conceived the term 'culture of poverty' in the 1960s in his publication, *La Vida: A Puerto Rican Family in the Culture of Poverty—San Juan and New York*. What can be deduced from that research report? Mangin (1970)[58] concludes that culture of poverty is a contextual fact in that the poor in any given country have more in common with their compatriots in that country than with the poor in other societies. Lewis' thesis portrayed how different families were organized around a conceptual framework, which he called the culture of poverty. Oscar Lewis focused first on family and life in the society of the time, and argued that poverty breeds family disruption, violence, brutality, poor quality of life, lack of love, education and medical awareness, and mental cruelty—in short, a picture of incredible deprivation, the effects of which cannot be wiped out in a single generation (Lewis 1966:xiv). Lewis further contended that people who live, or are made to live, in capitalistic societies in slums, ghettos, and squatter settlements develop similar structures, interpersonal relationships, and value systems that transcend national boundaries. Poverty is a phenomenon, and what is most worrisome about it is the development of female poverty as a cultural system.

The culture of poverty is seen to flourish in societies that exhibit certain features such as high rates of unemployment and underemployment, which result in idleness, low wages, stress on accumulated wealth and property, and personal inadequacies and inferiorities on the part of people residing in poverty-shaped societies. The implication is that the lifestyle of poverty breeds self-perpetuating and self-defeating cultural approaches to gaining emancipation due to the fact that people who live in poverty have a mental structure that resonates with that of those who are governed by hopelessness and despair. The inability of the poor to delay the satisfaction of their immediate desires in order to effectively plan for the future corroborates the fact that the poor concentrate on what can alleviate their condition in the short term rather than concentrating on a long-term, systematic solution. In order to challenge poverty, cultural capital[59] must be distributed to men and women in such a way that it creates competencies. Employment, gender engagements, and a desire for a sense of competency are emphasized as the vehicles for upward social mobility. The poor differ with respect to their need for activity, freedom, independence, and social contact. The fear of poverty and a low status quo are, therefore, tied to a loss of vitality in role-playing.

Lewis's theory of poverty suggests that if a culture of poverty is lived among the poor it is probably an essential strategy for coping with their poverty and cannot be, by itself, the cause of poverty. Although the 'culture of poverty' accompanies the poor, it does not exist in the same measure in every region of the world. Here two questions can be asked: Is it the fault of the poor that they live in poverty they did not initiate, cause, and sustain? And, who is sustaining poverty as a way of life for the poor? While there is some validity in the belief that poverty is perpetuated throughout generations, it is equally true that in Igbo, and by extension, Nigeria, it is sustained by the very leaders and bureaucrats that immerse themselves in the problem and play to the gallery as if they intend to offer concrete, effective solutions and then fail to do so. In the end poverty remains in place, untouched.

I will expand on this further when I show that poverty alleviation programs in Nigeria, from the 1970s until the present date, have been introduced to the detriment of gender relations. Before I turn to that theme, however, it is worth mentioning that Oscar Lewis identified over 70 traits that characterize the culture of poverty and categorized them into four groups as follows:

i. *The relation between the subculture and the larger society:* This involves the disengagement and non-integration of the poor into the major institutions of empowerment of the larger society. It also pertains to ethnic segregation, discrimination, fear, suspicion, and apathy. Other factors are a lack of effective participation, chronic unemployment, inadequate education, and underdevelopment; also, I must add, are the factors of high migration to other countries and the inverted priority of 'brain drain.' These features are true for the Igbo, and they point to the fact that a culture of poverty is institutionally made and remade for the poor.

ii. *The nature of residential community:* This focuses on areas of residence, most of which are characteristically depicted in slums and ghettos, such as poor housing conditions, over-crowding, and social aggression—all of which impede development. The solution to this, Lewis argues, requires only minimal input into re-organization from those outside of the nuclear and extended family system. The urban-poor in Nigeria are relegated to slum life by systems such as *Ajegunle* in Lagos and the various *Sabon Garis* (strangers' quarters) in the different cities of Nigeria where most Igbo people initially live. A single room may be occupied by a family with three to five children. What sort of life and health does that afford the occupants? And how does it assist those occupants—particularly the women—in thinking and acting effectively? Low income and inconsistent maintenance of basic infrastructures and facilities such as sewage, water, electricity, roads, and bridges are common issues that deny the inhabitants adequate sanitation and decorum. Street hawking is an exceptional occurrence championed by the Igbo in all Nigerian cities. What does this systemic ethnic and gender poverty show about the construction of poverty patterns for the Igbo?

    iii.    *The nature of the family:* Here the author argues that family and marriage instability is a common result of poverty. And, unless the issues underlying poverty are addressed, family commitment and solidarity are reduced to mere lip service. How does all of this come into play in the syndrome of poverty in Igboland and Nigeria, and how does it affect the progress of family unity? Is the quality of marriage, therefore, determined by the level of bridewealth obtained?

    iv.    *The attitudes, values, and character structure of the individual in society:* Here Lewis pointed out, once again, that individuals who grow up in a culture of poverty have strong feelings of fatalism, helplessness, dependence, and inferiority. Therefore, there is the threat of weak ego structures and confusion of sexual responsibilities and, by extension, the danger of contracting sexually-transmitted and potentially fatal diseases such as HIV/AIDS. Blood rituals for money, crimes such as home and highway armed robbery, and violence add to the insecurity of family health and community survival. Moreover, these events reflect the implications of deprivation.

Taken as a whole, how is poverty expressed within the policy programs in Nigeria's successive administrations, and how are those programs affecting the Igbo and other ethnic societies? This is the issue I will now explore.

## Gender and Poverty Reduction Programs in Nigeria

Recognized poverty programs have thus far lacked specificity, although they are popularly addressed in speeches and debates about gender relationships in Nigeria. An overview of some of these poverty-policy strategies will help describe the Nigerian experience of governance and poverty, and the impact that that has on gender-building capacity.

Beginning from General Yakubu Gowon's military regime after the civil war (1967-1970), the poverty program focused on rehabilitation and development. Gowon's response to poverty, gender, and development was aimed at what was called the National Accelerated Food Production Program and the Nigerian Agricultural and Co-operative Bank, and was devoted to agriculture and the improvement of rural life (see also Maduagwu 2000).[60] This program had little impact as it did not go beyond providing the opportunity for the awareness that poverty was real, and made worse by the war. As such, it did, however, magnify the important fact that it is the responsibility of government to design programs that address poverty. At that time (1972-1976), the oil economy and foreign provisions and food importation formed the basis for the Nigerian view of the culture of poverty.

Next came the infamous 'every man and woman must go to farm' policy known as Operation Feed the Nation (OFN), imposed on Nigerians by General Olusegun Obasanjo in 1976. Some critics have branded this economic policy as 'Operation Fool the Nation,' which began as military-based agriculture and progressed to ex-military civilian politics (see also Arowolaju 2004).[61] The administration was so occupied with teaching local areas how to farm that it failed to develop any professional farming methods that might have achieved results. Local farms, as we know, exercise peasant agriculture, with the first of the harvest intended for consumption and the rest intended for sale at market. The fact that Operation Feed the Nation was a misplaced tactic brought the noble intention to failure only after huge sums of money had been wasted. The program failed to correctly target the poor, and this continues to be a problem. What made things worse was that the necessity for importation of the basic needs of life was not curtailed in the least.

Following the fiasco of Operation Feed the Nation was Shehu Shagari's Green Revolution Program of 1979. In this strategy, reducing food importation and boosting crop and fibre production were the main objectives. However, rather than the program rewarding the poor for their efforts, the upper echelon soon cashed in on the fortune to be made by acquiring land for the purpose of obtaining farming grants and loans. When the program came to an end in 1983, huge sums of money had once again been wasted.

The story continues in the regime of General Mohammed Buhari, whose poverty program was given the name 'Go Back to Land.' This was followed by General Ibrahim Babangida's Directorate of Food, Roads, and Rural Infrastructure for Rural Development— DEFRRI. Feeder roads, electricity, potable water resources, and proper sewage systems for local dwellers were the main focus. Again, those highly connected to the government of the day cashed into the program and foraged from it whatever they could. For example, Community Banks and People's Banks cropped up everywhere, and investors took the opportunity to make and remake themselves in the setting. Even more blatant was the bogus actions of Mrs. Maryam Babangida, who swept her way into the poverty program gold mine with adjunct programs such as Better Life for Rural Women. Nigerians quickly realized that this program was, ironically, a circle for rich urban women rather than the poor. The problem here, again, was the inability of the policy formulators and strategists to target who the poor that needed to be reached were.

General Sanni Abacha's regime then had its turn and proceeded to introduce yet more social programs for the poor, the Family Support Program (FSP), and the Family Advancement Program (FAP). Not only were the Nigerian poor once again taken for a ride, but this regime magnified the use of the rhetoric of the plight of the poor to serve the bureaucrats, politicians, and rich in society.

Another form of poverty adjustments that brought to bear on the huge population of the poor was the infamous 1986 SAP—Structural Adjustment Program. This program further worsened the condition of the same people whose economic structures it was intended to adjust as the poor continued to be victimized by economic policy decisions made by those who had high connections to the government of the day. SAP increasingly became a program of settlement that served the purpose of 'getting what you want where and how you want it,' to the exclusion of the poor. The program symbolized the art of 'swindling,' and was summarized by the slogan 'don't get caught.' The implication was that the top to bottom approach of depriving the poor is permissible, and the government of the day will close its eyes and ears to one's dealings as long as he or she is not exposed. Given those conditions, how could the poor have joined in the battle? And who was the battle intended to fight?

By 1989 through to 1999, the looting war expanded into households and villages, and a phenomenon of elaborately designed scams designed by gangsters emerged. Petrol became a metaphor for 'blood' and 'high-sea-killing' a metaphor for schemes that cheated people of huge sums of money. This was the infamous '419' (four-one-nine), which shot itself boldly into local and international business communities with ploys designed to plunder the finances and treasures of all categories of unsuspecting investors.

In the history of its development, corruption has never, to say the least, resolved the problem of poverty, particularly when it is composed of policies of economic violence, intimidation, and usurpation. In his article, "How Kleptocracy Kept the People Poor" (*www.naijanet.com*, July 1, 2005),[62] John Vidal comments that Nigerian leaders have officially stolen over 220 billion pounds of sterling from the country—an amount equal to all of the Western aid to all of sub-Saharan Africa in the last 40 years. Vidal then questions how Nigeria can be one of the poorest countries in the world—with an average income of less than 4 pounds a week, with every second person living in absolute poverty, with one in five children dying before the age of five, and with the most dangerous slums in Africa—while it is, at the same time, touted as having the greatest natural resources on the continent and the most potential for development. That Nigeria can be both rich and poor at the same time can be explained by the oil economy. Oil was first extracted in the Niger Delta in the 1950s and is now increasingly pumped from off shore. Oil revenues, since Nigeria's independence in 1961, have divided the nation and created poverty

for the greater majority, particularly women and children. Successive military rulers exacerbated this through endemic corruption at every level of life. With the introduction of democracy, it is hoped that conditions in Nigeria will change, given the connections it presently shares with the international community.

It is significant that in the present administration, led by President Olusegun Obasanjo, the crusade against poverty and corruption is emphasized. Alleviation of poverty has been placed on the top political burner, and critics observe and analyze daily whether anything worthwhile is emerging. How far this government will go with their poverty alleviation program initiatives is a matter of hot debate. In the meantime, the poor in Nigeria, including the Igbo, remain among those who cannot afford to forage the means for a decent quality of life.

Accurately targeting the poor necessitates examining the sources of crisis and crime eruption that cause wholesale harm to others. For example, religious and ethnic conflicts that have become sources of economic and political rituals in the North of Nigeria are an issue that must not be ignored in planning poverty alleviation strategies. In these yearly rituals, Igbo people are displaced, maimed, and killed after working hard to establish businesses and other activities that aid their survival and assist them in their fight against poverty. But the displacement of these successful entrepreneurs automatically places them on the level of poverty, if not chronic abject poverty. So, in managing poverty for the Igbo, poverty alleviation programs in Nigeria must pay attention to the existence of events that promote frustration and elevate, rather than reduce, poverty. In the fight against poverty and corruption, the eruption of crises in ethnic rivalry and religious wars, which are known to have become systemic in Nigeria, must not be allowed to continue to thrive. This, by extension, includes the crises that erupt during political elections, in which large numbers of people die or are injured so severely that they are burdened by the struggle for survival under the chronic culture of poverty of the Igbo, and Nigerians in general.

Having said all of the above regarding poverty and gender, there is a strong belief that bridewealth patriarchal structure and politics diminish women. Women, however, testify to their immersion into bridewealth as a means of overcoming poverty. They have ensured that the bridewealth device is complicated as a way of 'forcing' men to acknowledge their value. At the same time, however, they appear to play to popular opinion by challenging and ridiculing poor men and poverty itself. In their desire to shun poverty, sometimes successfully and sometimes unsuccessfully, women are ambivalent in the discourse of bridewealth power dynamics. Social and development commentators, such as the former Dean of the Faculty of Law of the

University of Ibadan, Mrs. Adefoluke Okediran, the Chairman Development Policy Centre, Prof. Bimpe Aboyade, and the Oyo State Commissioner for Establishment, Mrs. Esther Adesanya, have all called for an integrated effort to tackle widespread poverty in the country, irrespective of indigenous economic and social devices that have not aided the situation. In particular, Mrs. Adefoluke Okediran said, in a recent workshop on localizing the Millennium Development Goals in Ibadan, organized by the DPC, Ibadan, and the African Network of Urban Management Institutions, that Nigeria, which was ranked the 23rd poorest nation in the world, might not meet its goal to eradicate poverty by 2015 (or even 2030)[1] unless all stakeholders renew their efforts. She called for the creation of more sustainable indigenous and modern intervention programs, credit schemes for the economically- marginalized groups, and plans for the sustainability of public transportation systems— especially urban mass transit. She also canvassed for the development of more educational programs to promote literacy, the revamping of small-scale industrial-credit schemes, and the expansion of the agricultural-financing plan. Social and economic empowerment, in allowing for a degree of independence, will help women in their efforts to realize a quality of life. Strengthening the communities in which the women live will, likewise, enhance their capacity for development and empowerment. It is also important to note that since Nigeria's resource base is mainly oil and gas unless, and until, Nigerians jettison the idea of oil and gas resources as 'freebies,' the country will continue to wallow in poverty and crisis.

Subsequently, training women to cultivate the habit of scanning the environment around them as men do, and making firm decisions to be part of the solution rather than victims of the environment, has been argued, by the Delta State Development Commission (NDCC 2005), as one step in alleviating in poverty.[63] The Coordinator, Omawumi Urhobo states unequivocally that one of the ways poverty

---

[1] Words in italics are mine.

can be given an up-rooting in order to reduce hardship in the country is through a process of psychological rejuvenation. That is, a process through which rural womenfolk could be assisted to change their circumstances and break away from the circle of ignorance and invented poverty imposed on them. Thus, psychological emancipation, if enacted, will change the attitude of depency exhibited by rural women. As such, women have to make the decision to lift themselves out of poverty, beginning with establishing a balanced psychological drive to access credit facilities and awareness programs for self-improvement. The message is clear enough, but how are world leaders seeing and reacting to poverty and feminist movements? In seeking to answer that question, I will advance and highlight the role of the G-8 political and economic class on poverty and development reforms.

The genesis of the G-8, which actually began as G-6, dates back to 1975 when it was first initiated by the then President of France, Giscard D'Estaing. Given the socio-political and economic plight of his time, D'Estaing pointedly reasoned that in order to tackle some of the global economic issues facing the modern world, the leaders of the most powerful nations needed to discuss the issues and come up with a strategic plan of action based on an adequate understanding of the situation. With that goal in mind, D'Estaing reached out to selected powerful leaders and the celebrated G-8, as we know it today, took off.

**World G-8 Spotlight on Poverty and Development Reforms**

Historically, the position of women in society, and the impact of economic, commercial, and technological development have become increasingly associated with changes to divisions of labour and access to income, property, and markets beyond the traditional household. Also entailed in this is the diverse ways in which local cultures, governments, and planned development interventions for empowerment affect women's participatory abilities. There is, however, no universal pattern for changes in cultures because different cultures and governments face specific gender challenges as their social and economic interests develop. Apparently, the promise of prosperity for developing countries has not come to fruition and, as Haviland *et al* (2005:188) argued the 'have' and 'have not' gap between nations and

Source: Dose Daily Magazine        *Distressed by poverty*

genders continues to grow. The point is that the important process of understanding local gender ideology, and of viewing gender as a negotiated process, is reshaping the role of international organizations and fixers of world economies, such as the G-8

authority and the influential Paris Club of Creditors alliance. The G-8, a group of the eight most highly industrialized and richest nations of the world, from time to time conducts a summit with the purpose of discussing issues of mutual interest, one of which is the condition of poverty experienced by less successful economies in parts of the world, particularly Africa.

Opportunities for each gender to contribute to, and benefit from, G-8 intergovernmental and corporate development policy supports will necessitate continuous renegotiation in response to changing market opportunities and interaction with state and local configurations of gender and power. It is now well recognized that poverty is a predictor of poor health and the inability to make sound decisions.

The G-8 summits are lobbied by developing countries for an increase in foreign aid and debt relief, cooperation in development through favourable markets, and support for social and institutional empowerments. All of the G-8 members (Canada, United States, Japan, the United Kingdom of Great Britain and Ireland, the European Union, Germany, France, Russia, and Italy) agreed on proposals that would target some useful percentage of their GDP for the fight against poverty. Unfortunately, the percentages committed so far are far less than what is needed to meet the severe need. Sir Bob Geldof, the organizer of the Live 8 Concerts, which coincided with the G-8 summit of 2005 (July 6-8 in Gleneagles, Scotland) and were designed to boost poverty awareness, is tactically pressing G-8 governments of countries such as Canada to assign 0.7 percent of their GDP to foreign aid. With the exception of the European Union and Norway, this has not happened. British Prime Minister, Tony Blair, in canvassing for the G-8 summit, said of Africa that "Africa is a wonderful, diverse continent with an extraordinary, energetic, resilient people. But it is plagued with problems so serious that no continent could tackle them alone."

Bob Geldof's anti-poverty crusade consists of fundraising concerts and powerful messages about the severe poverty faced by many parts of the world. In particular, the threatening issues of African debt, African poverty, and AIDS are concrete developments that demand that critical decisions and solutions be reached and carried out by a collective force. The concerts' main goal is to influence the G-8 leaders to respond to global poverty. Many of the world's presidents and prime ministers theoretically believe in, and claim to support, the idea of committing a larger percent of their GDPs to foreign aid. At the same time, however, they express fear of their governments' ability to keep such promises; such is also the case with promising debt relief to African countries that are on the path to reform. Donor nations are constantly encouraged to double their aid to the poorest African nations, including targeted institutions and structures that help women develop their skills and opportunities. As a consequence, the New Partnership for Africa's Development (NEPAD) was initiated and adopted in

*Children Challenged by Poverty Use a Broom as Available Playing Toy*

2001 to control irresponsible governance linked to de-development in Africa. Its main purpose is to address poverty, particularly through reforms acceptable to

reviewed standards and international measures. In effect, this would result in what Pantaleon Iroegbu and Matthew Izibili, in their book, *Kpim of Democracy: Thematic Introduction to Socio-Political Philosophy*, call "enwisdomized governance" (Iroegbu & Izibili 2004: V). This is, by all means, not only implicit to wise governing, but is also understood to mean the governance that is executed on wisdom. The mobilized people within the new African political leadership must not only give special consideration to, and think forthrightly for, their own country but must also reach out to the international community in an effort to improve their circumstances. African leaders have been increasingly challenged to demonstrate results and continuity as a prerequisite for receiving ongoing benefits from G-8-assisted development through reform programs. It is hoped that consistent democratic policy reform efforts will ensure good governance in regard to development, and that creative measures will increase the equality of opportunity and reduce the poverty gap between genders.

General reform schemes—for example, Nigeria's implementation of its home-grown reform program under the International Monetary Fund (IMF)—have intensified surveillance as a legitimate instrument that fulfils the requirements for debt relief and policy support. The good news, in this regard, is that Nigeria has been granted debt relief by the Paris Club of 15 creditor nations in the amount of 60 to 67% ($18 to $20 billion) of its $34 billion debt, including $6 billion in arrears.[64]The debt burden was caused by political dishonesty, bad governance, abuse of office and power, criminal corruption, mismanagement and waste, fiscal irresponsibility, and a community that was openly tolerant of corruption and illegal methods of accumulation. In that sense, the debt burden is a threat to the peace, stability, growth, and development of Nigeria. On the other hand, debt relief means that the country will have debt service funds available for use in education, health, agriculture, water, and power facilities—areas related to millennium development goals and crucial to the well-being of the people of Nigeria. President Olusegun

Obasanjo, in April 1999, initiated a relentless campaign for debt relief, with the goal of re-creating opportunity and empowerment for Nigerians. The reform process leading to the recent debt relief was led by an Igbo woman—Financial and Economic Minister, Dr. Okonjo-Iweala. The initiation and implementation of an economic reform program provided the anchor for the government's renewed efforts to persuade creditors to consider Nigeria's case for debt relief, as well as the cases of 14 other poor African nations who were also granted debt relief by the G-8 in 2005. The measure of granting debt relief is said to represent the creditors' contribution to Nigeria's economic development, as well as its fight against poverty (*The Guardian Online News*, Friday July 1, 2005).[65] Critics of the government still view the government's macroeconomic policies with suspicion because, notwithstanding its success in gaining debt relief, ordinary people in Nigeria have yet to feel the benefits of reform.

The most recent development is an effort to enhance Africa's rapid and consistent integration into the world's political economy, a goal NEPAD is vigorously pursuing. It cannot be claimed, however, that NEPAD's development policy formulation and process, with regard to gender and equality, has been well received on all fronts. Randriamaro Zo, in a paper contributed to the World March of Women, stressed the women's concerns regarding the 'marketization of governance' at the expense of gender opportunities and empowerments. She argued (Randriamaro, p.2) that, within the new framework of NEPAD, the state has simply rolled back and reorganized "in the form of deregulation from public interest to regulation in terms of private interests…" Furthermore, gender equality advocates have underlined that "current trends indicate that states are being re-organized to serve the interests of market forces, and these interests do not coincide with those of the dispossessed." As well, the reality of the hardships faced by poor women across countries, and in Africa in particular, reveals that the re-organizing of the state holds little relevance to NEPAD in that it is likely to perpetuate the economic and social exclusion of poor women, while further entrenching patriarchal patterns in politics.

All said, G-8 leaders, such as the former Canadian Prime Minister Jean Chretien and his USA counterpart, President George Bush, told African leaders in the Ethiopian capital, Addis Ababa, that Africa is a continent on a historic journey of renewal and if her legacy of pillaging and decline is to be reversed it will occur only within a secure world. Shaped by Africa's experience of plundering, looting, hardship, poverty, unstable political circumstances, and non-sustainable development, her painful past begs for positive solutions and meaningful action. Peace, security, democracy, good governance, human rights, and sound economic management are prerequisites for ending the economic marginalization of the continent. An empowerment policy aimed at providing equal opportunities for women and men in all respects is, of course, equally important. NEPAD is a 'two-way-street' partnership with the G-8 authorities of the West, and the expectation is that both sides will candidly demonstrate their commitment to reciprocal and integrated obligations. So it is that, in the global conditions of the day, the reality of the situation cannot be construed or exaggerated. Any deceptions will be discovered, resulting in the loss of any benefits other than those that are developed and reinforced through strong commitments. The time has come to remove all barriers to the integrated development of mutual and cohesive relationships in a secure world, gained together.

I will now concentrate on further implications of NEPAD by highlighting some of its important features. NEPAD is considered a vision and strategic framework for Africa's revitalization, the renewal of gender relations, and negotiated empowerment for all aspects of growth. NEPAD originated with a mandate to develop an integrated socio-economic development framework for Africa, which was given to the five initiating Heads of State in Africa (Algeria, Egypt, Nigeria,

Senegal, and South Africa) by the Organization of African Unity (OAU, now called AU—African Union). The 7th Summit of the OAU/AU in July, 2001 formally adopted the strategic framework document, which was subsequently well-received by the G-8 Governments in 2002 when it was presented to them as a new vision to support their collaboration with Africa's collective, concrete path to development.

To a large extent, NEPAD was designed to address the current challenges facing the African continent. These issues, such as escalating poverty levels, underdevelopment, and the continued marginalization of Africa, demanded that new, radical interventions be spearheaded by African leaders in a mobilized effort to develop a new vision that would guarantee Africa's Renewal (see KAIROS Africa 2001, 2002).[66]NEPAD has since served the goal of reinventing Africa, thus placing her on a path to sustainable growth and development. In the international community, NEPAD is celebrated as a model for international cooperation, and its plan of action and process is lauded as being authentically African in design and implementation.

G-8 leaders and civil society participants, among others, continue to assess NEPAD's implications and how best to ensure its appropriate implementation (Randrianmaro, in: KAIROS Africa).[67]The acceleration of the empowerment of women is one of the central primary objectives of NEPAD. Indeed, all of NEPAD's principles and objectives, such as the objective to implement peer-group democratic governance assessments, development reviews, and correctional methods, are laudable. Other objectives include the reduction of extreme poverty by half by the year 2015, and the development of a sustained average gross domestic product (GDP) growth rate of above 7% per annum, to be realized for the estimated period of 15 years.

The whole issue again raises the matter of liberalization and an open economy being forced on Africa through the ability of the strong economies of the

West to advance their own pressing interests to the detriment of the weak, thus introducing new forms of poverty reinforcement. Yet, it is worth noting that these current challenges will persuade Africa to seek self-reliance more than ever, while still cooperating and partnering with the global community on her own terms and implementing strategies of empowerment that extend from region to nation, individuals to communities, families to groups, and male to female genders. Certainly, development initiatives in Igboland must recognize the differential impact of an economic policy of bridewealth power on women and men in light of the development of official development assistance. An empowerment-based approach, when viewed from the perspective of human rights, must be the framework of bottom-line discourses concerning Africa's development strategies to challenge material- and mental-poverty situations. An in-depth gender analysis, based on issues such as bridewealth power, is a step in the right direction as far as ensuring women's participation economically, socially, and politically. That participation must then be reflected in development policies, programs, and projects of awareness and social empowerment.

However poverty is viewed, women are significantly impacted. As women seek modern-lifestyle goals, interesting strategies for evading poverty through marriage develop. How these strategies are expressed within the goal of finding a marriage partner are expanded on in the following section as I present what I discovered through internet chatting. These discoveries help to clarify the strategies and cautions women employ in their efforts to control their own destinies in regard to marrying wealth or marrying poverty.

**Marrying Poverty and Online Chatting**

Considering the above notions of poverty and its metaphors in life, I extended the research approach by engaging in a wider network through internet chatting with Igbo women and men in the urban and diaspora areas. I wanted to hear more opinions, from those directly involved, on the issue of women and poverty as it concerns bridewealth. With this goal in mind, I asked the people I was talking to, "Would you marry a poor man or woman?" The findings, which are the result of chatting with sixty-seven men and women, are reflected here. Although this random number of subjects is very small in relation to the huge number of Igbo people in urban and diaspora areas, it does provide a representation of how the Igbo feel about poverty and marriage in relation to bridewealth. To the Igbo, collectively, poverty also refers to those who have neither the voice nor the material capacity to act either for themselves or for the community (*ogbenye enweghi onu okwu*). Conversations online make this even clearer.

Women stated that it would be foolish to think that a lady would want to be poor and wretched all her life. If a woman had two suitors, for example, she would naturally favour the rich one, who could guarantee her comfort—this would also, of course, be expected of her socially (*Daily Independent Online*, February 24, 2004).[68] The men had this to say: "If you are in love with a woman, she will co-operate for as long as she doesn't know much about you. The moment she realizes how much you are worth financially and how much money you can commit, she will reconsider the relationship." This raises a point concerning a vital cultural behaviour central to the Igbo that must be emphasized regarding gender relationships and the level at which 'secrets' are communicated. For the Igbo, secrecy between men and women is a part of daily life. Apparently, though, men prefer to keep their financial secrets to themselves. This would imply that men don't always give their wives a true picture of how much they earn, or how much they have in reserve. Thus, economic secrecy among the male gender leaves women to guess at the true financial wealth of their partners. This secrecy on the part of the men is considered, by them, a way to keep women loyal, respectful, and hopeful. Also, it is suggested, in situations where two families, or sometimes co-wives, may struggle for access to a man's wealth, family stability is served best if the interested parties have little knowledge of the true financial situation, thus lowering tensions between them.

There are, however, some indicators that not all women are after money at all cost. Some men are so powerful, or so dangerous, that a woman might run the risk of being turned into a slave by the husband's family members should she enter into a relationship with him. Informants do generally agree, however, that money is an important factor when searching for a mate as it is a practical tool for providing material and physical comfort. Yet it is also argued that wealth and poverty can be relative since the opportunity and capacity to keep and acquire wealth are not placed on the same footing as actually owning present wealth. One informant stated that a man may be rich in one thing and not rich in another. This would suggest that differing viewpoints are culturally and socially acknowledged. The question is, how can a man's wealth be quantified in terms of its ability to attract a serious relationship such as marriage?

Responding to the above question, women stressed that a suitor could be observed, and recommended, as being 'nice,' but that is certainly not the only thing that matters in terms of mate selection. If such a man is poor, the future he can provide is uncertain. I was told that parents warn their daughters to shun any qualities in a man that will not offer them a good chance at a comfortable life, and to avoid selling themselves to men who are 'not worth the trouble.' Marrying someone who is jobless, broke, and hopeless is a matter that leads to serious disappointment on the part of one's family and kingroup. The major emphasis, when it comes to finding a mate, is placed on one's future happiness and capacity to help others in the community. In this respect there also emerges the desire for a mate who is healthy and has the ability to create reciprocal relationships. Parents and peers fuel the fire of these kinship social obligations based on what women describe as 'material rewards' as opposed to 'genuine attraction.' And what it all comes down to in the end, following this common pattern, is what women stand to gain in terms of material rewards versus intangible assets that a man may possess, such as attractiveness or social grace.

In these conversations, people also pointed to the fact that men and women sometimes lose potential partners they had hoped to marry to other men or women, even after the relationship is significantly advanced. The opinion was offered that some men and women, once they have 'made' it in life, or have become successful, forget about those who have raised and supported them. This unpredictability of men and women is a serious issue that sometimes leads women—or even men, if they are in a tight spot—to resort to the services of healers in an effort to secure a relationship rather than face uncertainty, failure, or disappointment. This whole issue will be analyzed more in depth in chapter ten.

Through the chatting, other informants emerged who talked about praying and asking God to intervene and bless the opportunities and choices that they make when choosing a partner. In summary, bridewealth cross-cuts every decision that young men and women make, both in urban and diaspora settings. It is not a matter to be taken lightly, and people negotiate daily for the best possible future for themselves and their immediate and extended families. It is generally believed that marriage can protect women from poverty, so the women focus great effort on earning, sustaining, or renegotiating opportunities for better identities, roles, and statuses. Fear of poverty motivates women, the elite in particular, to go to extraordinary lengths to meet their aspirations, and this is well expressed in the changing notions of bridewealth and its power. This issue is explored further in Chapter 8, where the impact of diaspora is considered, and some further related issues are explored in Chapter 10 within the context of the dialectics of ritual and power in negotiating gender. Prior to entering into those discussions, however, it is necessary to explore bridewealth within the giving and receiving theory in order to explain the underlying dynamics of power and their impact on marriage and gender relations.

# Chapter 7

# Theory of the Gift Swap-over of Bridewealth

In this chapter, I will briefly explain the theory of gift giving and reciprocity in the context of gender and power relations. As it applies to kinship relations, bridewealth is theorized as a mechanism of power of gender stratification, which is more visible among the Igbo after marriage. I contend that bridewealth is an economic transaction with benefits that are enjoyed by both men and women. At the same time, however, it also serves as a patriarchal tool to edit women's status and power base in society. Marcel Mauss and Pierre Bourdieu's conceptual theories of gift exchange are concerned with exploring and analyzing the concept of the power of bridewealth as it relates to gender-based kinship.

## Power of Giving and Receiving

To give and receive constitutes the heart of all relationships. Giving may be used benevolently to strengthen existing relationships or form new ones, or it may be used aggressively to 'fight' or 'flatten' such relationships. Position and prestige are often gained through the act of giving. In addition, gifts may be used to place others in debt so that the giver can demand the loyalty of the receiver (Mauss 1950, Bourdieu 1980, Cronk 1996). Strings, of some nature or another, are always attached to gifts and the act of gift giving, and these strings affect how people and groups relate to each other. In every instance, giving and receiving positions offer glimpses into relationships—and nowhere more vividly than between the sexes. Giving positions may generate relationships, class differences, power, authority, control, and the balancing of household and community order. Bridewealth, for example, always carries the personality of the giver, reflecting his persona. On the one hand this promotes solidarity, but on the other hand it reflects a sense of power—never more pervasive than when it is linked to the colonial inventions of 'male' and 'female' (Oyêwùmí 1997). Therefore, calculation is insipient to marriage wealth,[69] and this is true both historically and presently.

## Before and After Colonialism

In pre-colonial times (as is still the case today), bridewealth was comprised mostly of goods and services. Only a small fraction was paid in cash, even though academic discourse has made much of the element of monetary payments (Ekejiuba 1995: 148-149). In theory, a man's wealth, through the so-called *aku eji eme ogu* (ties of in-lawship), is transformed, via the female body, into social relations. Services are rendered to the bride's home, their nature varying to suit the circumstances. A widowed family, for example, might perceive the son-in-law as being the 'husband' of the household. This type of service relationship was intended to establish and stabilize the supportive tie between two families in such a way that the long term interests of both families are protected. Generally, the Igbo regard in-law families as one; what affects one one, affects the other (*ogo na ogo bu otu, ihe meturu otu meturu nke ozo*).

The forms of service and labour provided by men were dramatically influenced by changes instituted by colonialism. Historically, a suitor would farm, mend the house, and labour for his mother- or father-in-law.

The present economic system, however, no longer places such an absolute premium

*The Youth dancing after a wedding*

on keeping young men in the village community and there is an increasing movement toward the cities. As a result, bridewealth is more often paid in cash. However, echoing Christian beliefs and sentiments, the Igbo say that bridewealth is never fully paid until death (Uchendu 1965:53). Thus, despite its tendency to evolve towards a purely monetary system—and its accompanying values of inflation—the original meanings and implications of bridewealth remain the same. Money is but the symbolic representation of services rendered.

Mauss (1950) and Bourdieu (1980) have discussed the power and inequality expressed through obligation. Some aspects of bridewealth can be understood in terms of their logic:

i. it is a gift to the in-laws (*ihe a na-enye ndi ogu, oke ndi ogu*)
ii. it is a prescribed obligation for any suitor (*iwu ihe ndi ama ala na-eri n'aka ndi ogu*)
iii. it is a compulsory exchange (*o bu nmanye omenala*)
iv. it stimulates reciprocity (*iweta nmashi na nkwwughachi ugwo*)

A woman, in this sense, is *ugwo* (a debt). It is reasoned that 'a woman is not reared for the free taking by any man' (*azughi nwanyi ka nwoke ozo kporo na-efu, ma o bu ka agbaa eron*); rather, she embodies an obligation. Refusal of the obligation is not an option; to accept the marriage is to accept the obligation. And, as the Igbo say, '*a na-eji olu oma a ga-ndi ogu*' (in-laws are always to be approached with a 'good voice'). This implies that marriage is one long exercise in reciprocity—realized with promises, expressed by social payments, and demanded as bridewealth.

For Mauss, mutual, but asymmetrical, obligation is stressed when exchange occurs; for Bourdieu, obligation involves a "struggle for distinction."[70] Both of these explanations stress the value of a gift, its utility and power in the materialization of the 'pre-existing system"— that is, the system of deep normatives—and the practices that reiterate it.[71] (See also Goody and Tambiah 1973). In wife-taking, obligations and reciprocities follow from the imperativeness of gifts. Power and dominance are inbred into the system by the asymmetry or balance of resources. As Bourdieu points out, "interest and strategy" mediate the objective—an improvement in economic conditions, the division of labour, and the symbolic conditions of prestige. This constellation is what constitutes marriage, particularly bridewealth marriage, relationships. Although Mauss and Bourdieu argue that bridewealth is part of a struggle for male prestige and distinction (for men to prove themselves as men among men), historically, before the effects of a cash-economy were felt, Igbo marriage was not an inflexible, mystical 'force.' According to Amadiume (1987), it was actually an open and flexible patrilocal system of interpretable normatives. Men remained on patrilineage land and guarded their property. They sent their daughters off as wives elsewhere—though never too far away. Non-lineage women (also from not too far away) were brought in for regeneration of the family line and domestic and economic labour. Upon marriage, a woman's husband's lineage acquired rights over her sexual services, reproductive capabilities, and labour power. At this point in history bridewealth was, strictly speaking, 'childwealth' in that it legitimized the children born to a woman and could be terminated only by divorce, at which point a woman's patriline was obligated to repay the bridewealth. When a woman was married, her patriline did not give up the right to protect her—in fact, it was her brothers' duty to do so.

A man who owned an abundance of land required an abundance of labour. This problem was solved through the expediency of polygyny and the possibility of strategically maneuvering daughters into good marriages so that they would remain loyal and grateful. Rich and powerful women could, as well, take on this role and created master/servant relationships by undertaking to pay bridewealth. In this way, a large labour force was created. 'First daughters,' referred to as 'male-daughters' (*oke ada*) by informants, who had no male heirs in their families, were groomed to 'stay-back' and play double gender roles—both that of a man and that of a woman. As such, they were permitted to marry other women. These woman-to-woman marriages legitimized the children born to the 'wife' through her lover(s).

Thus, prior to the effects of the cash economy, men and women were both actively involved in marriage practices, and exchanges were enacted in ways that were ideologically and socially situated. In particular, as the example of women-to-women marriages shows, it was the institutional, organizational dimensions of

*Gathering for the reception of arriving in-laws at a civic centre*

bridewealth that were important, not the bio-moral and consumerist logic with which modernism and Christianity have imbued it.

# Chapter 8

# Diaspora, Trendy Cash Economy, and the Impact

Up to this point, I have been exploring the ideology of bridewealth power. I now want to examine it further within the context of migration. Thus, the main focus of this chapter will be how life in diaspora has influenced bridewealth and power in respect to the trendy cash economy. The chapter will also show how, given that the state of being married is still of the utmost importance in Igbo society and to be unmarried is to be subjected to taunting and humiliation, women are taking actions to secure their own marriages as a response to the changes in society. The experiences of these women demonstrate that achieving the goal of marrying into wealth, rather than poverty, requires hard work and strategic planning.

**After the War**

Since the end of Nigerian–Biafran civil war in 1970, the Igbo have regained their cultural appreciation for the value of migrant life. Migration to the western world has increased as various opportunities for survival are explored. This became especially common in the late 1970s, and intensified in the 1980s, when the economic and political climate in Nigeria turned sour. A high rate of unemployment forced people to remain in school longer, and those who migrated did so with a good education and high hopes. Following from this migration was the desire of men and women in diaspora, after having settled well in their new countries, to seek marriage partners from back home. Prior to this development, there existed the seeking of marriage between urban and rural dwellers. The cultural expectation for those living in the city, however, was that they would return home to marry. This was particularly true for men, as women who lived in cities were seen as wayward and lacking in virtue. (This bias was overlooked as far as men living in the cities were concerned.) The ideal woman, therefore, was to be found in the locales. The ideal husband, however, was more likely to be found in the cities, gainfully employed in business and, therefore, having the means necessary to provide a generous bridewealth.

So, as migration moved from urban Nigerian settings to international domains, these same cultural ideological beliefs followed. Male suitors, particularly those from the USA, Canada, and Europe, along with their relatives at home, devised a system for having their wives 'mailed' to them. This system is described by the Igbo themselves as 'photo-mail partner choice' (*di foto*) and 'phone-call into marriage' (*di fone*). Literature (for e.g., www.brides-4u.com, www.msncache.com, and www.theoque.com)[2] refers to this development as the 'mail-order bride' system. This phenomenon is not new to the Western world; when European settlers, the majority of whom were men, began colonizing the American continent they were often unable to find brides locally and would write home to Europe with the hope of securing a mate. During World War II, the practice of writing letters to women with the intent of maintaining a long-term relationship was pronounced. Marriages have been successfully arranged in this way for thousands of years, and that success has continued into the electronic age.

It is within the last century that the 'mail-order bride' became a part of the Western lexicon as settlers moved west, where traditionally men outnumbered women in the population. Marriage by proxy, or immediately upon the bride's arrival

---

[2] Or in some cases the mail-order groom is shipped to order.

to her new home, was equally part of the order of the day. Popular social slogans such as 'find me a find and catch me a catch' and 'I will bring the veil and you supply the groom' evolved as a popular local-culture message for seekers and makers of marriage deals.

In modern-day society, people quite commonly pay fees to match-making agencies with the hope of finding the 'perfect' mate. Globalization, through efficient transmission of electronic information and transportation, has increased the

*Author discussing issues of bridewealth with a paramount traditional ruler, His Royal Highness, Eze T. Ogoke*

network for seeking brides and grooms and moving them from one culture to another. The introduction of the internet in the 1990s revolutionized the mail-order system as a popular means of meeting people as this form of culture change evolved from an age-old marriage custom. The phenomenon has become further commercialized through online websites as men and women 'advertise' themselves as mail-order spouses. This development has become especially predominant in Thailand, the Philippines, Africa, Asia, Russia, and Eastern Europe. Westerners 'buy' brides from these supply sources with the hope of gaining a mate who will provide them with loyalty, caring, and domestic stability.

Increasingly, while Western men are turning to marriage agencies or introduction services to find spouses from preferred parts of the world, African men and women—and the Igbo in particular—rely on their cultural networks to achieve the same end. In practice, this system consists of the relatives of the male involved seeking marriageable girls in their homes and schools and then proposing marriage to them while showing them photos of the 'hopeful husband' (*di ebu m n'obi*). These girls, in turn, have telephone conversations with the men they are interested in. The final decision, of course, rests in the hands of the male as he is the one who ultimately sends the money for bridewealth if an agreement is reached. The mail-bride system has had a significant impact on the mate-selection process in terms of choosing between a home- or diaspora-based suitor. Negotiating gender skills and patterns changed as enormous pressure was placed on men to seek opportunities for migration so that they could better their chances of securing the 'best' women at home for marriage. These same men, now from abroad, seek elite women and that, in turn, presses on the women to pursue a higher education so that they might have a better chance of being selected. Thus, the diaspora marriage culture has become a new direction from which the fortune of the bride's family is changed.

To the traditional and socioeconomic factors that women consider in seeking out a husband who will enhance their prestige, status, position, and role are now added such things as high educational attainments, prestigious employment, and the ownership of material assets such as attractive houses and automobiles. This change that has marked male and female relationships is acknowledged by community members as being related to new cultural values that have emerged from globalization. The emergence of this socioeconomic environment encouraged and persuaded men and women to seek more resourceful partners from wherever they could be found. Increased emphasis was placed on wealth and the mobilization of the kin-network and one's circle of friends to assist in the achievement of a 'good' marriage. Given that in order to meet a mate of the desired profile and status one must seek for them in the places that they live and work through a network of relatives or through visiting and/or meeting them at schools, workplaces, and social events, it is not surprising that busy social calendars have become trendy. This change also marked a point where men and women no longer needed to wait to be introduced to a recommended partner in their father's homes at an arranged time. One outcome of this development, in terms of its affect on those unable to marry, has been the widespread sex-related street- and night-life in major cities such as Benin, Lagos, Onitsha, Enugu, Owerri, Awka, Umuahia, Aba, and Port-Harcourt.

The existence of this scenario for all these years has had a dramatic impact on the reinforcement of sex and gender power, class, and the opportunity for evading and reducing poverty through marriage-wealth and related matters. On the side of people in diaspora, the scenario has changed somewhat since the mid-1990s, when men in diaspora adopted a preference to return home for the purpose of seeking out, and appraising, a woman for marriage. The impact of the global community has become more obvious in that distance is no longer an accepted excuse for partners to be 'parceled' to one another.

In pre-colonial times, women were articulate in the practice of a flexible system, and participated fully in public life—they were not mere objects circulating among, or acted upon by, men. Women took on political tasks through their familial roles—as a daughter controlling a funeral, or as a wife controlling fertility ceremonies for instance. Even though the ideology was inherently patriarchal, embodying anti-female rules and practices, it was always flexible enough to accommodate female strategies (Amadiume 1987: 70-1; 86). With the historical impact of colonialism and the influence of a cash economy, however, all of that changed. Initially, patriarchal ideology could be justified by neo-traditionalism whereby old structures stayed in place but were solidified. The binary logic of colonial gendering, along with the distortions wrought by the circulation of money, however, transformed women into objects circulating around and through the male sphere (as in Mauss' description). The 'inherent' power of bridewealth (i.e. its patriarchal structure) provided the basis of, and reinforced, male dominance. As the cash economy began to disimbed and dislocate the organizational institution, so too bridewealth became increasingly disproportionate. Bridewealth, always known as 'suitor brought-in wealth' carried the power to dominate the productive and reproductive power of women. In this context 'regeneration' became defining. But, contrary to Mauss' conception, there is nothing 'magical' about bridewealth exchanges in and of themselves.

Along with gaining independence in 1960, Nigeria's economy officially became monetary-based, resulting in the commodification of everything, marriage included. Cash, in large quantities, began to flow into, and articulate, bridewealth. Between 1962 and 1987, marriage payments inflated to excess. At present, it costs between N50,000 and N500,000 to marry a woman in the central Igbo area, one informant said.[72] Again, the expectations and type of goods and services asked for vary according to whether the suitor is at home or abroad. The farther away from home a suitor lives and works, the greater the bridewealth that is likely to be expected from him. As a result many local communities, the Pentecostal churches, and state legislatures have pushed for a fixed cash payment of N60.[73] The *National Concord Newspaper* (Oct. 14, 1987) reported on communities that fixed all expenses at N1,000 (cf. Ekejiuba 1995: 152). Other communities, such as Arochukwu and Onitcha for example, have fixed the bride price at N30,00—excluding listed gifts and services. In the central Igbo areas (Mbaise, Etiti, Mbano, Orlu, for example), although the practice of high bridewealth is quite conspicuous, its nature is contested both in the media and through various spokespeople of the communities.[74] Increasing costs of marriage place so great a burden on the people in Igboland that it impairs their lives thereafter. Mr. Okechukwu Nkume, a forty year old informant said to me, "*Ndi ogo m chara m olu, ha shiri m onu n'ala, naa m elu na ala.*" (My in-laws gave me cut-throat, they really showed me, asking for heaven and earth).

Comments such as these are very common.

Within this monetized economy, the Igbo woman has ideologically become an 'object of exchange' (as anthropologists say). This has led to women's permanent and absolute absorption into, and exclusive transformation by, male normatives. Because marriage and kin responsibilities are supreme values, women have lost their voices in the proceedings. Whatever is offered determines a woman's worth and fate. Women thus became ensnared by the machinations of bridewealth. No longer can there be any pretence to *iha otu* (equality). Rather, marriage is now associated with *inye aka* (support), and women have become *ikporo* (taken over) by men and 'settle' (*ichiba ukwu*) with them. As such, wives are seen as *ndi inye aka* (helpmates' organized by the power of bridewealth). So bridewealth has not only served as a social transaction but has equally come to imply ownership (in the modern sense of possessing and holding) of a woman after marriage.

If a woman fails to marry, society virtually excommunicates her. If she is divorced or separated, she becomes an interloper (or refugee, an uncomfortable stranger) to her kinfolk. Families and close kin members prefer for a woman to stay in a marriage, no matter how difficult her circumstances may be, rather than have her return to her parents and siblings. Women are not entitled to pieces of family inheritance, and no property is ever to be allotted to a woman should she leave a marriage. Rather, she is expected to inherit property in her marital family. In extreme cases, returning home after marriage may be accepted, but only as a temporary measure until any misunderstandings have been cleared up and the couple has reconciled through the mediation of elders and in-laws. Of greatest significance is the fact that, at the onset of every marriage, both the intending bride-to-be (*nwunye ohuru*) and the intending husband-to-be (*di* or *ogo nwoke*), are instructed to check and examine themselves and their consciences because, once they agreed to the marriage and have accepted it before the kinsmen, it is expected that they will behave properly and live within the norms of responsible marriage and 'good' family structures. It is hoped that no subsequent trouble or shame will be brought to the sharing communities through irreconcilable misunderstandings and separation. The point is that, with the payment of bridewealth, a bride's family relinquishes her. The Catholic Church has tried to ease the situation faced by unmarried women by making celibacy a virtue (Uchendu 1965:187-97). An unmarried Igbo woman still, however, remains a sign of social anxiety and disaster—the female equivalent of poor, male, Igbo 'trash.' It is impossible to diminish the blatant patriarchal structure and meaning with which bridewealth has come to be endowed.

To a limited extent, wedding gifts are important in leveling social power. These gifts are equivalent to the 'dowry' common in other cultural areas, such as various parts of Africa such as Kenya, India in Asia, and Baghdad in Iraq of the Middle-east. The dowry is instituted according to specific rules of the wife-givers and wife-takers. Usually, a portion of the bridewealth is redistributed for the purpose of acquiring the items that constitute the wedding gifts. Wedding gifts, or the dowry, may be given in the form of cash, various household utensils, furniture, electronic devices, appliances, and agricultural items such as yam, cocoyam, and pumpkin seedlings. They may also take the form of a sewing machine, bicycle, motor cycle, or even a car or house. These modern household items replace the traditional wedding gifts—such as a stove or 'gas cooker' replacing an 'iron tripod stand' (*ekwu igwe, ekwu ato*). Offering a dowry to the bride and groom, besides symbolizing a bride's family inheritance, is presumably intended to 'soften the blow' of excessive bridewealth. But softening the blow is not the only intent. When *aku eji due nwanyi ulo* (wedding gifts with which a bride is bid farewell and resettled in her new home) are offered, they have a subtext of overt reciprocity—this, however, is a short-lived and superficial effect. What lives in the minds of men, in the patriarchal construct, is simply the amount that one paid for a wife. Wedding gifts are quickly forgotten, and referred to only in the context of public reception and collective momentary appreciation and representation. Bridewealth valourizes male institutional and organizational power; the obliquitous and obligative 'force' of wedding gifts is negligible in comparison to a paid out bridewealth (*pace* Mauss).

**Tensions and Reference to Bridewealth**

Contemporary Igbo women may be often reminded of the bridewealth, or 'expenditure on her head' (*icheta ugwo isi*) that they represent. For example, a man may cry out, in profound anger and exasperation, '*O bu m luru gi*' (I married you!). Exclamations such as this are common in daily life, and their mood is echoed in the following situation:[75]

> Emeka is a young man of thirty-six. Employed in civil service, he has an annual income of N50.000. He has just finished paying the bridewealth for his wife Adaku (*Adaku* - 'daughter of wealth') to his in-laws. He laboured and saved for ten years to meet the required payment and, upon paying it, was reduced to poverty. He does not want his parents-in-law to intrude into his family, and keeps his distance from them. He resents them and feels economically dragged down by marriage. In consequence, he barks out orders to his wife and in-laws, and complains that all his marriage amounted to was social payment, and that it is destroying him. Each time he has problems with his wife he reminds her that she was married to his wealth—the same wealth that has now led him into such dire straits economically.

In the past, Emeka would have had a lineage standing behind him to help with the bridewealth, but the standards and values have changed in such a way that he was forced to gather the bridewealth alone. His anguished utterance, 'I married you,' carries all the weight of unevenly distributed responsibility. Clearly Emeka wishes to be married to a woman of appropriate status for his position, but the bridewealth, with its changed conditions and shifting normative structures, has economically crucified him. The impact of this on the relationship after marriage is disastrous. 'Gift and its obliging relations' has become a matter of unquestioned loyalty and obedience to the giver. In other words, 'I married you' translates into 'I paid for you,' and entraps and entombs the wife, excluding her from anything beyond her husband's will. Such is the space created by contemporary bridewealth; a woman is limited to the domestic sphere and must submit to her husband and obey him unquestioningly. The woman's independence is surrendered, and the man controls everything. Herein is the key to the male authority of bridewealth. At one time bridewealth was a system of flexible strategies linking lineages, now it constitutes an unspoken unilateral, dictatorial power. A conversation between an Igbo man and his wife from Mbano is revealing:

> "... imagine! This is the woman I married with my money and here she is messing up! I don't need to say what you should do. Return all the bridewealth and go your own way!" Retorts the woman, "With two children in hand I don't blame you for feeling the way you do. I would go at once if you could put me back into the shape I was in before marriage."

Although marriage reduces a woman's authority and value, what could be gained by her leaving the marriage? It seems to be a dead-end street; leaving the marriage and returning the bridewealth is not a fair deal for the woman, for not only has she already lost her 'youthful charm' but she would lose her status as well. For both partners, the marriage is a trap. Women are constantly reminded that their place is in the kitchen *(usekwu)*, and often face physical violence as well. As Babangida (1991: 8) wrote:

> ... whatever the cultural ethos, whatever the traditional idiom, the essence of keeping women virtually unknowable in political life is part of the universal patriarchal construct.[76]

Regarding alliances based on diasporal suitor expectations, the scenario plays out differently. A male coming from abroad with the intention of marrying must indicate interest and make some of the money allocated for bridewealth available to the bride's family. Once the initial social payments are made, it is hoped that the rest will follow in regular intervals throughout the lives of those involved. Linking with a family in diaspora in an obligatory kinship relationship is much sought after as it results in the forming of networks that offer the greatest chance for successfully negotiating the new realities of migration and the dollar economy. While some women refuse to marry a husband based at home, others devise strategies by which their suitors are enabled to pursue their studies abroad, thus establishing a life in diaspora. In this way the woman is afforded the opportunity to have a husband in diaspora.

28-year-old Udoaku testified to having persuaded her parents to sponsor her fiancé's studies abroad as a way to ensure her a happy marriage—a condition her parents also viewed as quite acceptable. Soon after a traditional marriage was carried out, it became apparent that Nnanna, Udoaku's fiancé, was obliged to seek admission into a school at overseas in order to meet the conditions set out by the wife-giving family.

While this type of arrangement works out fine for some, others suffer long waits before realizing their diasporic marriage dreams. In the prevailing circumstances, many women are trapped rather than being liberated, as they had initially hoped. Cases showed a huge number of complicated marriages that were distorted, and even ruined, by the distance between the wives at home and their husbands abroad. Only rarely would a husband wait at home until his wife could join him in diaspora. The existence of absentee wives or husbands marked a moment in gender negotiations that either fostered or devastated relationships. The following case is illustrative of this:

> 36 year old Chikeremma recounted how she remained at home after her wedding and spent 15 years waiting hopelessly to join her absentee, American-based husband. After a 15 year marriage, with the husband in the USA and the wife at home, she queried, what excitement could possibly remain?

Chikeremma is not alone, and reflects the plight that the majority of diaspora-based marriages face. When these situations continue over a long period of time the women, at some point, become stigmatized, as in the following case:

> 38 year old Amarachi Chinyere was married for three years before her husband migrated to the USA, with the hope of bringing her to join him, as had been negotiated. Eighteen years passed by without her stepping a foot into America. She noted that she had given up all hope of joining him and had gotten down to the business of living her life, and raising two children, without his presence. Strong in spirit, she prides herself for the way she handled the situation; as long as her husband continues to send her and her children money so that they can afford the essentials, it no longer matters to her whether she ever sees America. She stressed that this dilemma that arises out of the 'diaspora deal' can only be truly understood when one is personally faced with the fact that there is nothing more she can do to change things, at which point she must simply accept her fate and go on. Others, however, frequently refer to Amarachi, and point at her as an example of what can go wrong in these types of marriages, and her presence fires up people's probing and social anxiety.

Of recent development, mainly among European business tycoons and fraudulent entrepreneurs (419ers),[77] is the marriage deal called 'one at home and one away.' For the purpose of this discussion, I will refer to this as the 'checking-out syndrome.' In these scenarios, the focus of bridewealth, upon the migration of one partner, shifts from that of achieving an ideal marriage, to that of gaining the maximum material and social benefits. Men and women can easily negotiate to have the male live abroad and marry someone who will facilitate his remaining in his new country of residence and his economic and social survival. The women are left at home to fill their customary roles as wives, raise the couples' cultural off-spring, and maximize their power as wealth-keepers and kinship-connectors for as long as their husbands send them the material necessities. The husbands will pay occasional visits home in order to reintegrate, appraise things with their wives, or perform some other useful economic activities. They then return to their extra-cultural homes and their invisible 'away-wives' if they have not finished with them yet. In this gender politics of survival, polygamy, rather than bigamy, exists and is reinforced from an ideological basis as a strategic way to fashion out survival during difficult economic and political times. It is clear that gender is a shifting concept, and people carve out ways to accommodate their needs and expectations by playing the ideological prisms and symbolisms in new ways—challenging the modern gender ethos through kinship forces of survival.

This form of gender sexuality negotiation for social status is well known among the Igbo, and, in the USA particularly, it is referred to as *akata* relationship phenomenon. *Akata* culture originated in the era of slave trade, and is a manifestation of the crucial necessity to remain liberated and legally able to work in the USA. In other words, *akata* shapes gender behaviour in such a way as to negotiate sexuality while also earning the status required to have a decent opportunity for survival in the USA social and political economy.

The word *akata* is derived from an Igbo medicinal plant called *akataka* (*akata* for short), used to treat difficult psychological and psychiatric imbalances.[78] Appropriating the symbolism of this plant to describe migrants facing the difficulties of settlement reveals the urgency and pressure of life in diaspora. This scenario places pressure on both genders—the man in diaspora to maintain two homes, and the wife at home to ensure that her husband is still connecting properly.

Another approach being adopted can be seen in the craze to have one's child socially adopted by the child's country of birth. To achieve this end a husband will do whatever it takes to raise the money to economically support his pregnant wife while she lives abroad until she gives birth. Wives are rushed overseas to countries that have favourable terms according to the couples' wishes, such as Britain, the USA, South Africa, and the Republic of Ireland. Once the child is delivered abroad, connections form and an investment is made into the child's future.

As commodifications, women have become ever more feminized and infantilized. Male ideology is well illustrated through men's discussions about women. Distinctions, though not overtly derogatory, focus on mental capacity and culture-nature in what are clearly colonially-derived categories. Women symbolize nurture and food, but are also the gender that is 'moveable' when necessary. For example, a man working in town may live with his family and, all things being equal, life remains manageable as long as the man's income is sufficient to pay the rent, purchase food, make social contributions, meet responsibilities in the village, and tend to the general health and well being of the family. However, if the man should lose his job or become ill and is no longer able to meet those responsibilities, the living arrangements change. Women are often sent home in order to lessen their husband's burden; the common view is that such women will face less anxiety struggling with their in-laws than they would trying to cope with the high pressure imposed by modern and urban life. In the case following, an informant who spoke on this issue had a word of caution:

> 41 year old Doris Anyanwu shared how, in times of difficulty, she was twice sent home from towns in which she lived with her husband. She advises women to discuss issues with their husbands more critically rather than

taking on passive roles. She advocates women working together and taking bolder steps when their husbands are failing. Role and identity, she inferred, should be concerned with the challenges that each of the genders face, and the contributions that each can make as they strive for a better life together. Marriage should no longer be a one-sided affair, and women who have let it remain as one have always experienced lower status positions and placement in terms of decision making and problem solving.

Women are also regarded by men as 'noise-makers'—talkative, less thoughtful, instinctive, and irrational. They talk before they think, act before they reason. On the other hand, men see themselves as those who think before they speak, who make less noise and are therefore rational and more ancestrally-endowed. The women they marry are merely containers for men's biological genes and the regeneration of society. In consequence, women—'for their own good'—must be confined by men to the domestic hearth, where they will be compelled to concentrate on maternally bonding the male genes (*mkpuru, akuru, omimi nwoke*), and guarding men's reputation and privacy. Boundaries between female and male domains must also be controlled—once women are successfully relegated to the interior sphere of life, they are invariably less polluting to male space and power (Douglas 1966: 145; Dubisch 1986).

Women are also considered impossible to please; if a man offers gifts and services to a woman, she might reciprocate by preferring another man. This all too easily occurs if a woman sets her mind on someone else. Thus the Igbo emphasize that 'whatever you do for a woman, come what may, she will determine her own preferences' (*a na-emere nwanyi, ya na-emere onye ka ya mma*). Consequently, women must be controlled. Bridewealth then, as it entails belonging to a man's 'family space' (*ama onye ozo*), is an effective tool for chaining a woman to the hearth-hold and holding her fast to the social rules and reciprocities that are expected of her. Women are both sources of wealth when properly cared for and of turmoil when they are not. They are avenues to distinction, power, and the solidifying of social relations and integral kin networks, which are the aims of a good marriage. If a woman fails to marry, or turns out to be a 'bad' wife, she undermines this system and throws everything out of kilter.

As bridewealth strengthens, male attitudes encourage women's submission to male desire (Nader 1989: 323-335). 'Gender' thus transforms as a relevant schematization that intensifies inequality both in domestic and political realms (Modjeska 1982; Ortner and Whitehead 1981; Schlegel 1977; Strathern 1982). Status, being both essential and a cause for obsession among the Igo, determines male and female strategies and behaviours. Bridewealth is only the beginning of this disaster; after marriage it only gets worse.

# Chapter 9

# A Changing World

This chapter further examines the traditional expressions of bridewealth, and explores the meaning of bridewealth in the context of change and continuity. This will demonstrate how women, in both local and urban centres, are taking measures to effectively face those changes and attempting to create new forms of social power and inclusion in the patriarchal society.

**Changing in the Cutting and Trailing Edges of Change**

Despite the patriarchal ideology, despite the effects of Christianization, colonialism, and the cash economy, women are, nonetheless, constantly developing imaginative and innovative ways to cope with their circumstances. This is not simply a question of educated, professional, middle-class men demanding educated wives; it is also a question of women taking matters into their own hands. The traditional female husband in a woman-to-woman marriage (Amadiume 1987; Ekejiuba 1995: 48) is but one example of this.[79]

Uchendu (1965, 1995: 69) uses the term 'gynaegamy' to describes woman-to-woman marriage, widely practiced throughout Africa. In a gynaegamous marriage, Uchendu says, the biological father of the child is irrelevant. An *iko* (lover, male-concubine, service man) is chosen by the woman, and a child resulting from that union would, under no circumstances, ever identify with the *iko*. Such children are not illegitimate, for they are defined by a legal marriage. A 'bastard' (*onye na-enweghi nna*) in Igbo is one who has no official father, but the role of official father is taken on by the female husband in a woman-to-woman marriage. These marriages are perfectly legal in Igbo culture, and are completely devoid of Christian and colonial 'lesbian' implications. Igbo civilization affirms that a wealthy and respectable woman can be a social and legal husband (Uchendu 1995: 70). In this respect, women have appropriated the norms of bridewealth as the means by which to legitimize a marriage. Bridewealth has never been, and is not now, just a patriarchal practice.

In modern times, women 'boundary-crossers' are often highly innovative. One example of this is the urban 'female husband.' Because cities have no traditional ancestors or common bloodlines as do villages, women are ambivalent in this environment. As women are no longer the representatives of traditional values (which have 'eroded'), urban cosmology takes over—urban wealth and social position become their primary focus, and indigenous ways are shunned. Salaries are earned in modern and state enterprises, corporate values become 'local culture,' and cash is prestige.

*Igbo quest for wealth versus poverty and gender positioning*

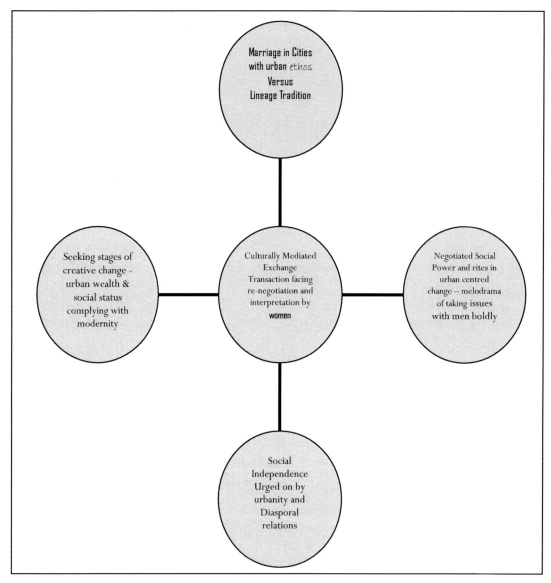

*Figure showing change and curiosities within tradition and mordernity*

Within this urban culture, women take titles and join clubs and ritual societies. Some invest part of their wealth in paying bridewealth in order to become female husbands—others buy a husband (cf. Uchendu 1965; Amadiume 1987; Ekejiuba 1992; 1995: 53). Economically-active, urban women who do not broker these types of transactions leave themselves open to the accusation of having a 'catch a man obsession.' That women take issue with their treatment at the hands of men, which leads them to creative changes that are reinforced by education and employment opportunities in the urban setting. However, the need to avoid being accused of an inability to marry still prevails so, for *acada* (university elite) and working class women, 'marital deals' become a common strategy. Above all, the unbearable insults that are a part of unmarried life are to be avoided. Informants say that "it does not matter whether a man has married before or not" because the woman retains her independence while conforming outwardly to the role of a 'married women.'

Other women who are critical of male control tend to go out of their way to avoid bridewealth. High bridewealth, which is now pricing women out of the market, was

*Cross-section of women negotiating with men during their Association's Orie -Market-Day Meeting*

commonly considered to make wives less 'proud and cheeky' (Mitchell 1957: 25). But, as one informant said, "The world is changing and no positive thinking woman will stand for being fed and jilted. What men are doing is so blatant that women are carving their own way out." Some families have started to refuse bridewealth (though not communal gifts) in an attempt to reduce, though not eliminate, the husband's control. In a survey of fifty couples in Mbano, Mbaise, and Etiti—areas in which high bridewealth is paid (*ugwo isi nwanyi*)—three of the couples had dropped the tradition of bridewealth entirely. Together with the independence of urban women, a fight against bridewealth has emerged as a form of social solidarity. What follows is another example of an innovative strategy that some women resort to in order to avoid being construed as living under a marital-curse (*azi di*):

> Ogechi is thirty-six and, having graduated in economics in 1990, is now a civil servant with the Ministry of Education. Though she had several chances to marry in the past, she 'missed the boat' because of the high bridewealth demanded by her parents and kin. Bridewealth in her area was too high for potential suitors and, moreover, her being a graduate placed too high of an expectation on potential suitors. Eventually, gripped by frustration, she considered two options: 1) join a Pentecostal Church or 2) take the next man who presented himself regardless of whether he could pay the bridewealth. She joined a Pentecostal Church and, enabled by the Church's rule of low bridewealth, married in 2001, thereby saving face. To her kin, however, Ogechi was a deep disappointment.

This practice of joining the Pentecostal Church is on the increase as more women protest the contradictions of bridewealth. Since the development and elaboration of charismatic and Pentecostal movements, women have been able to identify easily with them: one, as means by which to reject, or at least soften the effect of, the socio-cultural status quo and escape marginalization in the patriarchal bridewealth market setting; and two, the new movement provides cover for ambitious young women seeking to break away from the traditional bonds of family ties and wealth distribution. The argument is that this type of institution aids women in achieving a flexible economic, social, and political independence. The culture of the church tends to offer women the concept of social ties with other 'born-again' believers, empowerment as believers, and the personal and community strength necessary to overcome hardships. Moreover, it attempts to foster secure socio-economic independence, and a new social category of 'believers' once the membership and identity of participants is officially acknowledged. As Spinks (2003:22-23)[80] points out, women are increasingly attracted to Pentecostal movements because of what they offer: opportunites that elevate the role and status of participants, participation in worship and entertainment, social support, the challenging of the dominance of male elders, and a means by which to make friends and promote match-making so that women trapped by socio-cultural factors within the traditional marriage setting are enabled to overcome their bonds. It is believed that the new faith and social opportunities offered by the church empower women in both the short- and long-term course of gender identity and struggle, as well as enhancing social tools that they can use to overcome subjugation through religious equality and forms of displaying equality before God.

## Eaters and Keepers, Producers and Bringers

In the Igbo collective register, women are dependent on men and are called *oriaku* and *odoziaku* (eaters and keepers of husband's, or man's, wealth). Such semantics are, however, being transformed. Some spokeswomen contend that women are growing beyond being mere 'eaters and keepers,' and that perceiving women through such terminology leads to a misconception. Women themselves claim that, rather than being 'eaters and keepers,' they are 'creators and bringers' (*okpata aku*) of wealth. The underlying question is a legal one: whose wealth is it that an Igbo woman 'eats and keeps?' Changing semantics and legal categories may have a dramatic effect on the nature of bridewealth. Clearly, women themselves are receptive to changing circumstances. One informant argued that unless women embrace change they will remain within the realm of denigration.

> In a marriage ceremony that took place between Amaobi and Ogonnaya, the chairman of the occasion and his wife were introduced as Chief and Lolo Moses Igwekala. They were ushered to their seats to supervise the pouring of the marriage palm wine (*igba nkwu*), and the master of the ceremonies subsequently addressed the chairman's wife as the 'eater and keeper' of wealth (*oriaku and odozi aku*). The master of ceremonies called on the chairman (*onye isi oche*) of the occasion (*emume*) and his wife, whom he addressed as *Lolo* (a praise title-name given to a crowned chief's wife), and added to her accolades 'the *eater* and *keeper*' of the chief's wealth. The chief's wife stood up and seized the moment to assert herself and reposition women, stating that women should no longer be viewed as 'eaters and keepers.' Gone are the days, she said, when women accepted and rejoiced in such male gender bias and labels, and it should be clearly asserted that women are, rather, '*producers* and *bringers*' of wealth, and should be addressed as such. She argued that women are no longer found working only in kitchens, cooking and caring for children. They do all of this and still work in offices, engage in trade, win contracts, go to school, participate in politics, travel abroad, and make money just as men do. What else, she queried? Clearly, we, the women, she asserted, are calling into question the naturalness of our social placement, given that we increasingly enter the labour force, support and raise our families, and sometimes taking over due responsibilities. A thunderous applause followed and the ceremony continued.

In light of the above, we can understand that gender ideology assigns women the role of eaters and keepers of wealth, and holds them in a supportive status (*inye aka*), in spite of their economic contributions (Brettell & Sargent 2001:249). That this ideological gender economic arrangement assumes that men are responsible for economic provisions and women are responsible for domestic labour and nursing (cf. Lips 1988:260) suggests that Igbo society measures the worth of the male gender by viewing their wives as eaters and keepers. The identity and symbolism of the provider role demonstrates ideological age economics of lineal reciprocity, primarily revered as purposeful and meaningful

*Kanu weds at Imo Concorde. Photo: The Champion Newspapers Ltd.*
*The modern day professional sports person and his image in society at home in a public wedding are illustrative of the so-called gender power. Hence to give is to hold the loyalty of the receiver - materially, professionally and symbolically.*

through the title-names given to women. This indicates not only the widespread acknowledgement of the denigration of women by bridewealth, it also indicates how some powerful women are trying to redefine the situation. If the designation of women as 'eaters' (*oriaku*), is to be replaced by women as 'bringers' (*okpata aku*), this necessitates the re-definition of women. It requires regarding a wife as an equal partner in generating resources and in taking responsibility for matters both inside and outside of the home. Thus, there are signs that, in the *longue durée*, bridewealth is changing through colonial binary logic (solidified by the cash economy) from a patriarchal, but flexible, ideology into a new kind of flexibility in which the commodification of women is repudiated and a new role is created for them.

**Matrilineal and Patrilineal Faces**

Cultural forms and constructs used within the Igbo kinship system in the description of marriage and kinship continuation appear to be complex. Deep-seated and interesting kinship group organizational styles are situated in three primary corporate modes; as previously pointed out in Chapter 3, the lines used for tracing genealogy include the patrilineal line, the matrilineal line, and the uterine group. Here I will highlight the difference between matrilneality and patrilineality as it relates to the cultural and kinship mechanism of bridewealth. In everyday conversations regarding marriage, procreation, and childbearing and rearing, Igbo women, in particular, tend to stress their multiple kin-connections rather than just focusing on their husbands' patrilineages. They also seem to invoke more complex ties, mainly in identifying instances of misfortune that may pose a risk or require intertwined sacrifice, such as avoiding incest while seeking a bride (Feldman-Savelsberg 1996:178). This is important because the role of kinship involvement in marriage and procreation reveals the gendered experience of kinship power and social belonging (ibid: 1996:179). From the perspective of matrilineality, the uterine, or 'heart and kitchen,' site places emphasis on a woman's role as not only mother, but also wife and head of the *nkpuke* (uterine womb) force, also called *nkpo-nne*, subsisting under *obi-nna* (the father's significance as the vital blood link in the household).

At first glance, the Igbo are mainly patrilineal, but literature has consistently shown a matrilineal norm in a few of the communities in Arochukwu that share borders with the Cross-Rivers State, and there are also community areas in Afikpo that are known to practice matrilineal gender relations. Matrilineality is characterized by tracing descendants through the female line, the female-residence rule of matrilocality, and a pattern of living whereby a husband settles with his wife's kinspeople. This is contrary to patrilineality, in which kinship is traced to male ancestors, residence rule is governed by patrilocality, and a woman lives with her husband's kin. Property and inheritance follow the rules of residence in both systems—in matrilineal society children gain inheritance through their mothers, whereas in patrilineal society children gain access to resources, rights to and over property, bridewealth, and power through the father. In other words, descent-group membership, social identity, rights to land, and succession to public office are all inherited via one's mother or father (Brettell and Sargent 2001:347). Basically, this cultural appropriation of kinship authority initiates and restates a sense and pattern of human rights that are exercised and facilitated in institutions and manifested societal structures of manhood and womanhood (cf. Gilmore 1990).

Beyond the contouring of kinship human rights, as Foucault (1978) suggests, these structures are precincts of power: "where there is power, there is resistance [and invariably] this resistance is never in a position of exteriority in relation to power." Of course, it can be argued that, based on accounts of women's experiences of bridewealth power, lineage kinship systems that negotiate gender with bridewealth operate within structures of patriarchy irrespective of the language of matriarchy. The tactics women adopt in dealing with men are revealed in their private behavioural practices, which often differ from their speech and actions in the public sphere (Menon 1996:132). There is a matrilineal puzzle that cross-cuts patrilineal devices of bridewealth in that women cherish the idea of their suitors being challenged with social payments, and take pride in themselves when that occurs. There is a prevailing view that the challenges of bridewealth payments will bring men to the realization that women are inevitable partners in their pursuit to 'be a man.' In other words, the ability to marry is central to defining one's manhood and the genuine kinship that is connected with an evolving responsibility in society.

As Schneider (cited in Bolyanatz 1996:81) affirmed, matrilineal descent and strong bridewealth payments are understood to have at least two functions: first, to promote solidarity of the lineage as its members work together to pool their resources so that individual members can marry and, second, to reinforce the marriage brought about by the bridewealth payment. This reinforcement occurs when a wife-giving group applies pressure on their sisters, or female relatives, to 'stick with' the marriage and, in

**Groom giving ring (ola) to his bride**

Network doing so, ensure that they will not be obligated to refund the bridewealth. Bridewealth, as a consumable, bonds people together in lasting kinship relationships in a structure of related power, loyalties, and idiosyncrasies.

According to custom, it is the norm to refund such payments as a bride price should divorce (though few and far between) occur. One is socially expected to conform to this kinship tradition concerning debts and obligations, and informants stated that failure to conform is viewed as a serious infraction that results in cultural forces intervening to worsen the condition of a divorced woman's life—

*A Titled Chief Offering Rite to a New Couple*

misfortune, illness, disability, or even death are among the dangers waiting to befall her. The culture does offer some sort of cover in that, when a woman remarries, the proceeds from the second marriage are appropriated as repayment for the debt incurred in the first marriage. However, families that are capable of repaying the debt prior to a divorced woman remarrying are liable to do so in order to reduce the ill-feeling that the debt may generate in the communities involved. Repayment not only marks the cutting of any final ties, but also brings to rest any psychological implications that may have been elevated along the way.

The impression garnered from high bridewealth payments, as they have been explored here, is that they are expected to promote both marriage and lineage solidarity. The paradox then is this—while bridewealth systematically reinforces marriage, it also adds force to the descent-group power exercised by men in respect to it.

Counter-intuitively (Bolyanatz 1996:84), there is a structural conflict of 'gender power relation' inherent in bridewealth. In the complex social process of making and unmaking gender power relations in the Igbo cultural nexus, bridewealth power constitutes the basis of relational structure, as well as depicting Igbo socio-cultural forms of gender identity and normatives.

# Chapter 10

# Gender, Sexual Power, and Healers

This chapter looks, once more, at the issue of negotiating gender, sexuality, identity, and power. It vigorously explores the genuine desperation women experience when it comes to finding a mate, and discusses the senses behind the strategies women adopt and share with one another, such as consulting healers. It is argued that healers are an important link in negotiating gender, marriage, and sexuality. The chapter also maintains

*Healer in his consultation hut*

that gender is an aggregate that draws its sensibilities from other sectors of society, and finds its resources in the content and course of gender action.

**Why Consult Healers**

Negotiating sexual power through Igbo healers (*dibia*) is a common custom aimed at achieving one's end. As such, the negotiating of desired opportunities does not happen solely in the public and kin-connected realms, but often also mobilizes

*Healer Opara explaining issues related to marriage, fertility and life with Ezumezu or complete body symbol*

other cultural resources such as the field forces of land, water, air, and forest. This is popularly referred to as *isi ofe ala, ide nwoke obi, iku aka nkpuke, igba aju, ima akpu love, isi ofe eju* etc., which provides an approximate portrayal of the specific cultural devices some women access through the services of healers. The goal is to engage

*Healer Iroabuchi and tradition of solving gender related problems*

and ensnare their preferred mates through socially-viewed love petitions and other such devices. Women, when unsure of how to succeed in securing the particular male that they would prefer as a life-mate, are prompted to have healers prepare 'love potions' (*ogwu lovu*) that will help them achieve their goal (see also Bell 1981).[81]

Such 'love-medicine' customs, as Hamilton (1981) suggests, compose a mechanism with which women challenge the ideology of male pride and perceived superiority. In the face of circumstances where central-decision making exists in the realm of men, these love rituals are also viewed as love 'magic' or 'enforcement' that assists women in negotiating, utilizing, and maintaining sexuality and the marriages of their choosing through ritual tactics that foster their power and social standing (Bell 1981:322).

As previously stated, the pressure to marry comes from several sources, such as parents, peer groups, colleagues, in-laws, kinsmen, and *umuada* (married daughters). Economic factors and social expectations also add to the perception that marriage is imperative if one is to truly 'belong' to the cultural mainstream of community fulfillment. If the suitor is well off, poor parents may see marriage as a bridge to prosperity. Women, themselves, consider themselves as 'flowers' intended to bloom for a limited time in a limited place.

Angela Anosike, 28, expanded on this further when she stated that women are marketed by age and body-shape—and aging is not a friend to ladies. After women have completed school or learnt a trade, they are under pressure to settle down and rear children before menopause sets in and they employ all possible means of meeting the social expectation to marry properly. Some commit the issue of marriage to God in prayers; others employ the more practical approach of dressing attractively, behaving 'nicely,' and flirting. Yet others resort to the use of love potions in food and on their bodies to get their suitors to yield to them. Rich ladies sponsor men or assist them in establishing businesses, with the expected return of marriage. The use of sex as a ploy to trap men works for some women, and does not work for others. When getting a suitor to succumb becomes a pressing issue, women resort to stronger means, such as going to prayer houses or consulting healers.

## Exiging the Patriarchal Dominance

Common rituals are followed as prescribed by indigenous love therapists. Counseling is an important part of the process, and women are generally questioned to ensure that they are positive about what they want before they challenge male dominance and target a mate. Cases show that many women have been successful in the use of ritual prayer houses and healers as a means by which to secure a marriage. In sharing confidences with one another, women discuss how they go about the business of trapping men into marriage—apart from allowing pregnancy to occur, which is often unsuccessful. The men most often targeted are those who are already successful or show promising potential, as this offers the best guarantee of a rich bridewealth and a comfortable financial state after marriage. The following case dialogue illustrates this point:

> 29 year old Nnenna discussed openly how her friend pursued, and won over, Uche, who resided in Holland. Uche, 34, was among the successful 419 entrepreneurs, and his fame spread quickly through his home town and amongst young females hunting for this class of prosperous men, otherwise referred to as 'those who have made it.' Ngozika, Nnenna's friend, confided in us when we approached her for suggestions and advice on what strategies women might employ to negotiate their way to success with a targeted man. It is, she stated, a matter of taking useful risks and remaining focused. Further, she declared, one has to do whatever it takes to trap these men—because they are very powerful and rich, they can easily jilt any woman at any given time and get away with it with no questions asked. Pointedly, she said, 'beating them'—that is, winning their loyalty and commitment to marriage—it is a struggle, because there are many girls going after them at the same time. In order to facilitate one's chances, it is necessary to consult a strong healer who can do something about it. "Look," she emphasized, "I am a very beautiful girl as you know and see me, but that is not simply all that these 'money-boys' are out for. Being beautiful and flashy are important entry points, but to sustain their interest after taking you out for 'good-times' and sleeping with you for a number of times 'is just another show' (*nke a bu ihe*

*ozo*). So it is that, at this point in time, there is a need for strong medicine, *juju* ability, and ritual enhancement from a strong *dibia* (healer) to 'smoothen things out.'" (Iroegbu 2004).

Evidently, according to this testimony, there are critical moments where

*Bridewealth feasting and guests*

women feel they need to take action in order to design for themselves the life they desire. Negotiation of sexuality and gender is achieved not only through physical attraction, but also through the use of facilitators, agents, charms, and rituals. This also reveals a culture-specific way in which women explore sexuality in both short-term and long-term relationships. Women and men's behaviour, when they wish to catch, and sustain, attention from a member of the opposite sex, consists of important acts—displayed and approached differently from culture to culture—that relate to the construction of sex and sexuality, marriage, and social expectations. Moreover, the specific behaviour of these women underlines the use of eroticism through rituals in order to enhance the connection between sex and the brain and impact bodily emotions and reactions. It also points to how people learn these behaviours, and how sexuality acts as a construct to identity and social position.

It must be noted that biological research in terms of human sexuality is complex in that it involves continual intermingling of mind, body, and experience. Because lust (*idara madu n'ihunanya*) is triggered and functions biochemically, love-potion rituals tend to work for both women and men. *Time Magazine* (Feb. 9, 2004)[82] explored the variety of love potions that have been advanced by modern science as ways to enhance sexuality between women and men. It is important to acknowledge that indigenous medical practices play a significant role in helping women and men improve their opportunities and achieve their desires in regard to marriage, fertility, identity, and status.

Researchers, such as Masters and Johnson, once believed that women are sexually lineal. Rosemary Basson, of the University of British Columbia, however, has subsequently found that both women and men operate circularly rather than lineally, and inevitably take extra measures to empower themselves and enhance their lot. The implication of this, in the framework of the Igbo, is that women in particular experience a strong desire to marry as a result of context, how they feel about themselves and their partners, how safe they view a situation to be, and their perceived possibility of success in any given circumstance. Risking the loss of an opportunity to attract a good marriage is to risk an assault on one's dignity, so women employing the services of healers—including spiritual houses that specialize in such gender and sexuality activities—amounts to skillful handling of their negotiating power-base and capacity for control, thereby increasing their chances of success. These tactics help women broker their circumstances and gain access to their socially-expected wishes.

My contention, therefore, is that women are usually sexually assertive when it comes to achieving their goals—irrespective of the submissiveness that is expected

*Healer Dibianta Iheanacho explaining the power of roots and ancestral knowledge in dealing with health and social issues in society as it affects women and men.*

of them by the male gender. Following MacKinnon (1994:257-263), it is important to remember that sexuality, in a feminist light, is not simply a separate sphere of interactions, feelings, sensations, or behaviours, in which pre-existing social divisions may or may not be a dimension, in which gender occurs and through which gender is socially constituted. It is also a pervasive and invasive dimension of social life that permeates the whole of social-gender differences and dominance (MacKinnnon 1994: 260). What happens to women, and inspires them to 'hold men' through love rituals, is the result of their particular experience of social arrangements. Women are conscious of male qualities—including their 'slippery' nature prior to being 'tied down' and committing to loyalty to, and respect for, a particular woman. These qualities are socially created and reinforced on everyday levels of sexual and gender negotiations. For itself, male dominance is also a sexual gender theory of some sort, and male or female power takes the form of males or females' socially ascribed expectations of the opposite sex.

In capitalist countries, as in the Igbo republican view of life and status, wealth is central to power. Masculinity consists of 'having it and showing it' through bridewealth. On the contrary, femininity, in many instances, consists of 'not having it.' This leads to women submitting to bridewealth and designing ways to enter into 'having it.' Negotiating sexuality and gender through bridewealth defines the tensions that exist between having, and not having, a socially-dignified gender identity and power. The fact that gender power is ideologically restricted must be recognized, as must the stereotypes accompanying the positioning of men and women. Gender and sexuality, as it is framed in rituals, is all about power confrontations in which one either wins or loses.

As customary as it may be for women to employ ritual devices to trap men into marriage, thereby creating gender identities and roles out of necessity or choice, the conceiving of those ritual acts as the means to an end is not a hostile action. As to gender negotiation, it is sexual attraction and demands from families and friends to marry that most essentially evolve as unequal in the social lives of men and women. The cultural significance of the female need to cope with social expectations is simply a normative of gender bias and power.

At the moment, I will not discuss the various forms of female-gender sexuality rituals in depth. Suffice it to say that some of the more important methods involve cooking meals with love potions, concocted with prescribed vaginal fluids, on certain Igbo market days (*eke, afo, orie* and *nkwo*) of the week (*izu*). Other rituals are tied to particular circumstances, and are aimed at challenging patriarchal authority or bending gender power through other means available to women.

Okeke (2001), among others, has described and analyzed how women among the elite in postcolonial Nigeria negotiate social independence through 'bottom power'—a common phrase in influential and educated Nigerian circles that refers to any use by women of their sexuality to gain and appropriate men's favour. Okeke addressed the issue of how the dynamics of gender relations are changing among elite women who use this 'bottom power,' both as individuals and as authorities with access to social opportunities. They do so, she argues, to enhance their negotiating skills and achieve upward occupational mobility and status (Okeke 2001:234-235). This gives the impression, as informants also clearly noted, that the degrees of success that women seek through the dispensation and use of healers and love rituals vary (cf. Bell 1981). In light of this, it becomes even more significant and interesting to see and understand how women and men apply sexuality in creating opportunities to meet their plural, socially-expected needs and roles—and the issue of bridewealth is a large part of this social and cultural dynamic. Okeke's view on the notion of 'bottom power' in negotiating social independence not only widens the interpretive net, it also intersects the cultural inventiveness and underpinnings of the idioms of the everyday gender world in local and urban lives at home and in diaspora in which, gender-wise, the so-called 'sexuality matter' fosters social engagements and empowerments that belie the cultural facts of social bridewealth power. This is, as one may infer, significative of, and expected in, the complex backgrounds of gender struggle, mobilization of cultural resources, and changing social opportunities.

Furthermore, I concur with David Gilmore's account of the qualities of conventional analysis of gender, sexuality, and power when he writes that "sexuality is a form of social power" (Gilmore 1987:4-5).[83] He reminds us that women carry an immaterial or conceptual resource—their chastity and sexuality—arbitrarily elevated to a central position as an exchange value for men. Within the paradox of chastity and promiscuity, men objectify female sexuality, not only as a libidinal goal in itself, but also as a contentious and arbitrary social index for masculine power. Challenging that power and defining feminine identity, roles, and other advisable gendered attributes in society has been the goal that women employ their sexuality to attain. This suggests that, when deeper attention is paid to everyday negotiations involving men and women, a range of variant identities, relationships, and power may emerge. A useful transaction logic related to this can be found in the question raised by feminist scholarship, "what difference does difference make in power relations?"[84] Sexuality and gender analysis should provide insights into the differentiated effects of patterns and social spaces that men and women share when power is negotiated and used to achieve ends, as well as insight into how an unequal relation of sexual power is bargained, and how it may find expression within family development and community bridewealth policy outcomes.

**Social Independence and Empowerment**

Of further relevance here is the discourse of social independence and empowerment as viewed by both Okeke and Gilmore. The question suggested is this: Is empowerment equivalent to independence? Wouldn't empowerment or independence become critical for women and not for men? Randhawa (1998:415) and Hall (1992) have analyzed 'empowerment' as a construct, showing the dimensional models of gender construct that women face. Hall proposed an identity-empowerment theory, the premise of which is that "women's behaviour and quality of life can be changed by increasing their awareness of the strength of social influences and of the interplay between intended and unintended consequences of women's decisions and actions" (Hall 1992:2). While it is important that women engage constructive changes to improve their status and social independence, the empowerment theory speaks specifically to identity empowerment as it is represented through concepts such as self, dyad and triad, family, religion, definition of the situation, reference groups, class, culture, and society. The impact of experience in the context of bridewealth power will surely lead to an awareness of the roots of empowerment, and therefore create conditions conducive to the reduction of the inhibitions and entrapments endemic to women's gender, age, controlled independence, and social class. In any case, perceived forms of control unleashed by the power of bridewealth cannot be disregarded as a matter represented by the internal and external continuum of gender relations. In other words, as Randawa (1998:415) explains, the emergent conceptions of the empowerment theory reflect paths to autonomy, liberation, and entrapment in the internal, external, and rationalistic dimensions. The theory of empowerment in respect to the gender question suggests that the act of empowering or state of being empowered exists in opposition to independence, which refers to exercising a right of reason, choices, and preferences, free from any external influence, to dominate in matters of ethics and governance of one's own decisions. The idioms of empowerment and social independence, in feminist theory and social psychology, as well as by Rappaport's notion of multilevel construct (Rappaport 1987), clarify the fact that women's status has been defined and controlled by constructs that intertwine their strengths and competencies.

In regard to means of empowerment, Melenyzer (1991) argues that empowerment is manifested in the ability of women to relieve themselves of the oppression of low income-earning capacities, invisibility, and lack of representation in decisions that affect them. Empowerment, she suggests, must conform to a "power with" (see Randawa 1998:418). In addition, Melenyzer (1991) suggests that the controversy over the means to empowerment borders on concerns regarding the relationship between gender and school, patriarchy, hegemony, and androcentricism orchestrating inequality. Melenyzer also charges women with the task of disclosing disempowerment; that is, women must struggle for critical and democratic relationships with their own colleagues, and must root out the sexism and discrimination expressed in institutional structures and in daily-life practices (Melenyzer 1991:417). In the analysis brought out, one can see that empowerment relates to self-efficacy in terms of the ability to produce and reproduce personal and social change when people are equipped with cultural-awareness skills in a changing society.

I will now turn to the consideration of gender implications for development in the decades to come.

# Chapter 11

# Gender and Development in Decades to Come

As chapter ten examined how women establish, negotiate, and challenge male dominance using the power of sexuality, this chapter will focus on the forces of gender development. We will explore how development focuses on women's issues in such a way that it encourages women to take up those issues themselves through policy mobilization and negotiations. The mobilization effort, thus far, has resulted in various feminist workshops and conferences that currently promote gender causes and processes, including advocacy for women's rights to security versus insecurity, opportunity versus lack of opportunity and lack of power and voice (the voiceless poor) versus hearing their voices and empowerment (cf. World Bank Report on Poverty 2000).

**Critical Development Debates and Women**

To say that there is a male bias present in scenarios of development involving women is inarguable. The fact is that development has been pursued in an androcentric or male-centered way, resulting in women having been adversely affected by that development. The implications of this fact have thereby delayed opportunities for raising the profile of gender equity issues. Above all, gender inequality has been recognized as a serious constraint to development and there is a need to focus on new critical policies, and reinforce existing ones, that make gender equity a consistent and progressive goal of development—a purpose with the expected result of transforming the concept of critical development itself (Miller *et al* 2004).[85]

Awareness of debates about gender was introduced to the Igbo through political, educational, and developmental pathways, including the "dancing women's movement" and aid programs that stretch back to colonial times (Green 1964 [1947], Leith-Ross 1939, Afigbo 1987, Bastian 2001, Okeke 2001). It is important to note that, soon after the Igbo women's war in 1929, Green and Leith-Ross were granted Leverhulme scholarships for the purpose of studying Igbo women in their native environment.

*Elder Stateswoman, Margaret Ekpo*

Leith-Ross (1939) concentrated on describing some of the main rites of passage in life in the four areas she focused on, one of which was how the organization of institutions of bridewealth was changing from a primitive to more westernized form. Green's attention was focused on providing an anthropological analysis of a small Agbaja village in Ehime Mbano, part of the central Igbo area where the research for this book took place, with strong emphasis on the role of women and women's organizations. Meek's book, *Law and Authority in a Nigerian Tribe* (1937), also points to the role of the Igbo Women's War in shaking the British administration out of its state of apathy.[86] Lackner (1973) and Amadiume (1987), among others, have expressed strong concerns about the existence of gender and racist attitudes in reports, from the 1930s and 1940s, on Igbo men and development.

So, just as the process of development once climaxed in the historical Aba Women's confrontation with the colonial forces in 1929, women continue to challenge policy issues. For example, Chief Margaret Ekpo, who was thrust into the political struggle due to the litany of complaints her husband put on the table and also by his giving her the chance to assume a public life he could not engage in by himself, was a giant of the 20th Century Nigerian politics and a pioneer activist of women's rights in Eastern Nigeria. Margaret Ekpo's political giftedness and the leadership risks she took for the sake of women remain invaluable, and she needs be afforded a central position among those involved in gender analysis and power.[87]

Van Allen (2001) notes, of Igbo women in the context of colonialism, development, and the global economy, that the Aba Riots, or Igbo Women's War, basically arose out of the fact that women were 'seen but not heard.' Ideologically, the colonial practitioners and 'fixers' of gender calculated that listening to the confronting women would undermine the complex ideological organization of society's political view of women as invisible in terms of their inclusion and exclusion. Women in the culture were paid for and acquired by their husbands in the armpit of bridewealth and that included their voices. This calculation arose, quite simply, out of the observable position of women in visible political culture. The calculation, however, proved wrong, and resulted in women being treated severely in the legendary riot that ensued. Not withstanding the traditional Igbo society complex, women did not occupy political roles equal to those of men, and this has manifested through the years in women's issues, other than the ones attributed to them from men's ideological and cultural point of view, being ignored.

The evidence also suggests a general pattern concerning women's political organization and levels

*Okada Culture and Challenge to Poverty*

of the involvement. Prior to colonial penetration and ideological incursion, gender relations in indigenous cultures appear to have been organized along parallel lines of complementary cosmological gender forces. In his article, *Thinking about Women and the Origin of the State*, Rapp (2005) shows that prior to colonial penetration of the culture men and women had distinct, but equally significant, roles in production, distribution, and ritual activities. Taking note of substantive ethnographic histories from Africa, Asia, and the Americas, this suggests that patriarchal, colonizing powers effectively dismantled the native organizations, political structures, and ritual contexts pertaining to development, gender, and power relations. Consequently,

*Uju-Ngozi Development Forum in Ehime Mbano L.G.A. since 2000 emerged through one of the Integrated Development Initiatives of Fr. Prof. P. Iroegbu. Uju-Ngozi in particular operates a micro-credit financing, agricultural and trading activities in addition to social collateral solidarity enjoyed by members and the associated communities*

leadership and authority were designated as male activities, while female tasks and roles were devalued or obliterated (Rapp 2005:308).

The ease with which women are ideologically marginalized and deferred rests on the lingering existence of bridewealth in life and thought processes. Hence, cosmological changes in bridewealth, influenced by migration, are developmentally ideological precipitates of structural tensions that now exist between women and men and between communities.

The Nigerian-Biafran war from 1967-1970 and beyond has also stretched Igbo women into multiple gender roles and resulted in the development of self-help initiatives.

Thus, a self-conscious awareness of global perspective has developed into increasingly diasporal behaviour with the aim of achieving a change in gender-value status. Women's, gender and development issues are, by and large, not only locally derived but also conflated with images of, and influences from, migration.

In regard to Igbo women, European colonialism, and now Americanism, are all embodied in the undermining or elevating of the development of women's economic position. In 1970, for example, when Boserup (1970),[88] in her work, *Women's Role in Economic Development*, discussed the question of women and development roles, awareness of the issue increased. In addition, anthropologists focused on, and intensified, the intriguing gender issues involved in development and its impact. Critically planned development interventions, it is argued, are intended to positively affect women's ability to participate in, and benefit from, developmental change and, as such, are constitutive of different cultural and modern state's competencies in facing specific gender challenges as economies and social-processes develop. As the economy, including marriage and bridewealth, becomes more and more commercialized, gender inequality has, at the same time, become increasingly convoluted. Sponsored organizations that stress women's rights and the enforcement of collective rights through access to opportunities have not yet moved far beyond what traditional gender cosmology already offered. There is significance in the reifying of local gender ideology and the viewing of gender as a negotiated process (Jefremovas 2000),[89] even though women have been important traders and political forces in village and kinship stability since pre-colonial times. In Igbo society, as in other societies and cultures, gender is intimately related to production, reproduction, and consumption, each of which has a different complex impact on development. Opportunities, *per se*, in which women can contribute and benefit from economic and social development are cyclically renegotiated in response to changing cultural realities acting together with state and local patternings of gender and ability.

In addition, United Nations Conferences have had an enormous impact on women in regard to showing gender sensitivity and taking action.[90] Their aim has been to raise women's consciousness and encourage them to achieve 'equality' with men in all aspects of life—something that Nigeria, as a nation-state, is anxious to embrace in its efforts to improve its reputation in the international arena. The mobilization of the political 'first-lady syndrome' has been in vogue in Nigeria since the 1980s, and women today are crossing male social boundaries more than ever. While women are becoming more visible through political appointments to significant Ministerial offices—as the current Federal Minister of Finance, an Igbo woman, Dr. Mrs. Ngozi Okonjo-Iweala, shows—the chance of a woman winning a political election is still very slim. For example, the foremost Igbo female politician, Margaret Ekpo, shone in the first republic, and her efforts paved entry for women into the realities of colonial and modern politics of public life. Nevertheless, from the late 1990s to 2003, in the central Igbo area of Imo State, only one woman, Mrs. May Ezinne Agbiogwu, was successful at winning a Local Government Chairpersonship portfolio election in the midst of numerous Local Government Areas (L.G.As). Having accomplished that feat, Mrs. Agbiogwu was perceived as an exceptional character. Male chauvinism and political biases still blinded many people to her true nature; this is particularly true of her political opponents, who labeled her as a 'man-woman' (i.e. a man in a woman's body-person). Rather than crediting her as a female who possessed, in and of herself, sociopolitical skill, resolve, and ability, people seized the stereotypical political inability of women as an instrument for political aspersion. Others even perceived her as a political nightmare in possession of 'numinous intelligentsia,' and consequently charged and stigmatized her as a married woman using bridewealth identity gendering (*nwanyi alul*) to bring women down in the political market. The representations and realities of what women experience in gender struggles and power relations should capture attention and direct strategies in social-development policies. In the everyday political reality, feminist scholars are coming out with mounting criticisms of male-dominated mainstream political practice, and are targeting political action as an area desperately in need of more developmental reworking. It also must be acknowledged that, in terms of political activity and development, the reality of the political engagement of genders cannot be fully accounted for through a uniform history of male-dominated political worlds. Development processes can only rationally begin, survive, advance, and be sustained when it is realized that active participation and access to opportunities is dependent on both men and women's political engagement skills as they interact with society.

Various publications—for example <u>Better Life for the Rural Women, Women in Education, Women in Development, Commission for Women Affairs</u> (Acholonu 1993)—urge women to "think boldly." The central aim has been to make rural women aware of their subordination, and provoke them into doing something to rectify the situation; how this impacts bridewealth power and the position of women is another issue. The Igbo people are, thus, under pressure to play their part in portraying the image of modern Nigerian society.

The 1975 United Nations' Year of the Women and the 1995 Beijing Conference on Women fostered, among other things, a framework for exploring diverging conceptions of feminism and empowering women to rise to the challenges of development—a process that has continued on to the present platform for gender equity and a gender bill of human rights. Activities provoked by practical gender interests are diverse and take many forms. Women's collective history of gender profiling has been of importance to the Igbo since the 1929 Aba Women's colonial war led to subsequent feminist intellectualizations of women's movements moving from the local to the national and international gender-development arenas. Feminist movements must involve a feminist consciousness in issues such as bridewealth power positioning. When women come together to press gender issues, it is important to realize that gender round-tables or fora can accomplish several purposes *en masse*, particularly when strategic gender interests are broadly conceived, well articulated, and timely focused. In terms of strategies for seeking change and continuity in the realms of gender equality and bridewealth power equality, women can advance the frontier of knowledge by looking for baseline power, through massive bridewealth literacy campaigns and discussion of women's issues, to cope with difficult economic and social times in political transitions.

A gender/feminist consciousness can be produced and reproduced through interactions in women's organizations focused on responding to practical gender issues. What 'gender' means to the Igbo consciousness in positive political thought life must be highlighted differently and constructively in the geography of life imposed by bridewealth. The realization by policy makers of how important it is to learn from the paths women follow to shape their world, and of how different those paths are from the elite political-order level of occupation that men follow, is central to the ethnographic knowledge base of the gender condition. How one perceives the deepest aspects of a woman's world, as it is orchestrated by bridewealth power, is most often dependent on the social transportation and organization of political spaces and identity that one has. The public labeling of a woman as a 'man-woman' rather than acknowledging her for 'who she is' sheds light on the interface of political housewives and their participation in the mainstream male-dominated political lifestyle ideologized through bridewealth. This is not to say that there are any easy cultural generalizations that can be made about the nature or degree of women's political power. As we already saw, gender is a strong issue surrounding the assigned bridewealth code of action and political engagements; because of the numerous designative norms of bridewealth, women are afraid to take power because of a fear of divorce, which inevitably leads to political and social intimidation, poverty, and the woman's loss of her children. It is for this reason that women, for the most part, are not likely to assert their growing consciousness of gender power beyond that which is already accommodated by the politics of bridewealth. This situation suggests that there is a need to loosen the burdens and implications of bridewealth power, not only for economic reasons but also as a matter of political and development process, equity, and social empowerment.

One woman captured the sentiments of many Igbo feminists when she said "enough is enough of this savvy and heavy expectation (i.e. bridewealth)." The following also characterizes those sentiments:

> ... whether educated or not, mature or not, women are held to be *sold* in marriages at great expense resulting often in the husband working till a late age to obtain the bridewealth after which the married girl becomes imprisoned, sometimes tortured or made to toil through severe labours to obtain money for the family to repay borrowed sums for the marriage social payment (Ibah 1988: 4).

Notwithstanding the sweeping of bridewealth into cash payments, the complexity of bridewealth is equally noticeable in the sense of collective and individual modes of reciprocal concerns. Notably, nobody wants to severe social ties or 'lose face' in the community setting. The Igbo passionately regard bridewealth as an ideal form of collective sharing, not as an end in itself. While the contradictions of contemporary bridewealth are undermining it from within, it is also coming under fire from without. Bridewealth *per se* is not the problem—in fact, it can be imaginatively re-interpreted in many different ways using many different strategies. To speak of it, however, as though it were simply a traditional, mystical, static thing—'our culture,' or 'what the Igbo do'—would be a mistake. This would amount to empty talk, a mimicking of the colonial order, and an assertion of neo-traditionalism. Instead, bridewealth must be seen as a cultural container that is not empty of representation, and often, as well, as a signifier awaiting a new ideology. Perhaps the first step in this would be to deconstruct the history of colonial gendering, and its dialectical entanglements with prejudice and imperialism.

Many women interviewed suggested that it was necessary to curtail excessive bridewealth, and in some communities in Igboland co-operation with local leaders has resulted in stabilizing it into a nominal or token sum. This frees both parties from bridewealth constraints after marriage, transforms patriarchal structures, and aims to reposition those values, qualities, and forms of employment that have historically been considered 'feminine.' Myopically, this might be considered a challenge to the basis of Igbo gender cosmology. That, however, would require overlooking the fact that what has come to be regarded as a static Igbo cosmology is actually a recent invention that came about through the destruction of the Igbo ideology of motherhood (Amadiume 1997:198). As long as the social payments and expectations of bridewealth remain unmodified, even in new forms of diaspora transformation of gender relations, both men and women will remain enslaved to its colonizing, commodifying, and self-alienating norms.

As if the rising alarm about the plight of men and women in regard to the heavy expectations of bridewealth as a demonstration of wealth was not enough, the 419 fraud scammers, preying on both home and international sources of funding, introduced and characterized a new wave of bridewealth as a public spectacle in the 1990s through to the 2000s. Hyped by many Igbo as a social-consciousness milestone for wealth and status achievement, these spectacles consisted of women becoming mere objects traded in 419 exhibitions, shifting bridewealth from family and kindred households to a more expansive public celebration of the female body at local school fields, churches, and public civic centres.

The 419 syndrome continues to have a serious impact on women as many are trapped in a dilemma of wealth and social conflict in morally approved gender negotiations and business lives. This trafficking in female bodies—reproductive and productive—veiled by neo-traditionalist talk of bridewealth, and valourized by anthropological accounts of the 'imperative of the gift,' exacerbates the problem. To emancipate women is to emancipate the Igbo from these colonial and denigrating gender norms intensified by global gender inter-circulation, roles, and dollar identities.

As has been shown, both home and diaspora settings create forms of gender difference and dominance. And in the decades to come this is likely to remain the case as new forms, yet highly negotiable by both women and men, are created. The female gender is likely to identify even more signs and symptoms of complex multicultural conditions of powerlessness and orchestrate new ways, as yet unimagined, of fixing women's unequal economic conditions. In other words, gender consciousness will increase.

That being said, an upward movement by women in terms of life-conditions will not happen on its own, but will remain dependent on the impact of wealth and income. It is hard to imagine the existence of a gender relation that is not created, shaped, and defined by a traditional cosmology of ownership of means of production, such as in bridewealth devices. Thus, continuity is likely, which shows that the union of women and men results, and crystallizes, in a deep, inescapable cooperative gender partnership in which men win at some points and women win at others in regard to their designs for survival, life-paths, and self-concepts. This suggests that the concept of bridewealth is central to what happens after marriage in two senses: first, it is invoked as a means by which to explain male behaviour within the framework of bridewealth and, second, it is an important device by which to measure the prevalent degree of submissiveness on the part of female behaviour.

Informants consistently reported on the ways in which the effects of bridewealth can decrease stress and emotional frustration on the one hand, and increase the tensions men face in Igbo society on the other hand. There is much reason to believe that women caricature men who cannot, or fail to, payout bridewealth. Such tensions and clashes often go beyond the immediate daily life

*Mrs. B Ajonuma explaining the role of women healers in gender negotiations and ways to create and enhance gender relationships for the future.*

scenarios of the male and female and rest more on the impact of the failure to payout on the bride's kinsmen and women.

Besides witnessing an incident of exclusion and denial, we were also told of several related cases where participation in the community sharing of gifts arising from marriages was refused a mother or father whose daughter's expected bridewealth had not been fulfilled. In one situation, we spoke with Mama Cecilia, a woman of approximately 66 years of age, who provided details about how her kinsmen and women gossip about her, taunt her, and sometimes call her names, such as *"ori nke onye ozu"* (other's eater), due to the fact that her first daughter's husband had not yet fulfilled *ihe ndomi na ihe umunna* (part of the series of bridewealth payments customarily due the kinsmen and women in the community.)

Given that a person denied participation in the community-sharing of bridewealth receives treatment from the community that is equivalent to being ostracized, Mama Cecilia confirmed that she had obtained assurances from her daughter and son-in-law that that obligation would be fulfilled. Neither women nor men feel good about unfulfilled bridewealth obligations, and those involved are regarded as useless and undeserving of respect in terms of the social scale of contributing to the joy and happiness of other members of society. According to custom, in cases where a son-in-law has pledged to pay a part or whole list of materials related to bridewealth, as considered acceptable by the members of the sharing community, through a guarantor (*onye ina n'ebe*) it is expected that the go-between or surety (*onye ebe*) will keep demanding payment until it is fulfilled. In extreme cases, unfulfilled obligations may be settled at death before a community will fully honour, participate in, and accord a sequence of burial rites.

In fact, this woman informant stated, "what you are asking me to explain is a complex ancestrally conditioned and institutionalized issue of community essence. In deed, the only language the community understands is to have their share of the brought-in-wealth by the fact of marriage of their daughters to the outside lineage wife-takers who should well reciprocate accordingly." Although things are changing, everyone is still expected to contribute to the common custom of securing society's happiness by pressing on one's son-in-law to fulfill community demands of the bridewealth social responsibility.

Bridewealth certainly has its pros and cons. On the one hand, it is celebrated as a social payment which essentially establishes and reinforces the solidarity of the wife's and groom's sharing groups. On the other hand, it is fraught with anxiety in terms of fulfilling the demanded gifts and cash payments, and sets up the inflation of the difference between men and women in terms of power, opportunities, and social positions in the scheme of life after marriage. In one way or the other, bridewealth organizes a social code of denigration for women. Though its style is changing, massive education and strategies for controlling it are desperately needed among the Igbo as a whole. It must be understood and emphasized that being a woman is not a handicap, nor should it reduce one's chances of living a fulfilled life. Given that this point has been made, time and again, in different circles of women's emancipation program debates, it is surprising that many of the elite Igbo women themselves have continued to cling to fear and hopelessness when it comes to arriving at social, economic, and political equality. As Margaret Mead once told North American women, and by extension all women and Igbo women and men at home and in diaspora, the feminine hope is that "a range of opportunities was open to them, inasmuch as domestic social roles, usually the so-called housework and childrearing were not women's inevitable lot and that anatomy was not their destiny." The feminine hope is, indeed, all of this and more; it is also a one of a kind hope that grants human diversity a chance to reach for self elevation and to carry the society along in multiple changing ascribed and achieved roles and statuses.

**Gender, Health and HIV/AIDS**

Several questions about gender, health, wealth, and poverty concern the state of affairs of women and men in the wake of the development of HIV/AIDS. This theme will explore questions regarding women and health in relation to bridewealth. In particular, it will highlight the unequal access to opportunities that eventually places women in a vulnerable position and frontal line of tactics to defend themselves against HIV/AIDS. Nevertheless, after observing the rise in HIV/AIDS infection rates among women, it is necessary to emphasize several issues and questions concerning gender, women, and health. Primarily, the endemic HIV virus should be a matter of deep concern for policy makers and healthcare workers (see Iroegbu 2004). Attention must be called to how women and men are either genuinely or falsely represented, and to how they themselves presently think, feel, and act within the scope of the dramatic HIV/AIDS scourge. It goes without saying that this mammoth killer disease presents a deep worry for Igbo women and men and other members of society. An understanding of gender and health issues within Igbo society must inevitably incorporate bridewealth issues as well.

Medical anthropologists, in particular, often concern themselves with the question of how people conceive of gender, illness, and health from a cross-cultural perspective. They also attempt to play a genuine role in the understanding of health conceptions and healing systems. With regard to HIV/AIDS, health, and poverty in society, there are essentially five main areas that anthropologists focus on: the ways in which biological and social factors interact in disease causation, analysis of western and non-western health systems, illness and healing as systems of significance, the political economy of health, and the application of anthropological knowledge to improve health care in highly gender-based constellations. In effect, medical anthropologists study links between individual genders and health practices, cultural systems, and larger political and economic forces that shape gender and disease, such as HIV/AIDS. They show, for example, how holistic approaches to the concept and explanation of illness have been effective in relating HIV/AIDS to poverty and gender. As such, the engaging of anthropologists in the local understanding of HIV/AIDS and gender practices could help improve prevention and treatment programs, as well as gender empowerment and gender repositioning in society.

Further to the points raised above, most local and urban men and women in Nigeria tend to suffer from chronic illnesses, and die from illnesses related to poverty, inadequate nutrition, lack of portable water, crowding, and social and community stress. Others, who are wealthy, tend to suffer and die from stresses of affluence such as heart disease and social, economic, and political crimes. AIDS, however, knows no boundaries, and targets rich and poor alike. HIV and AIDS prevention is among the most important health issues facing young women and men today. Even though the struggle to gather wealth and payout wealth in view of marriage and social titles, the implications are in taking health risks in itself. In other words, to access wealth, both men and women take high social risk behaviours.

**Social Power and Safe Sex**

Engaging in high-risk behaviour in order to access resources is pronounced among women as they find compelling ways to negotiate sexuality with the men who control wealth and access to it. In this way, gender inequity is inextricably linked to the organization of society, and results in different life expectancies and experiences between genders in terms of age, sex, income, class, and occupation. Gender and health manifest themselves in cultural differences through such things as the varying methods by which societies establish gender relations and form gender rites and social empowerments. Both sexism and patriarchy are systemic in the Igbo-Nigerian health-force. This situation reveals the cultural complexity of patriarchy, with the gender ideology of male thinkers and fixers of society aimed toward the subordination of women.

Women and health in development processes constitutes a serious issue. Decisions pertaining to health and development are made in relation to norms of gender, values, procreation, and fear of disease as associated with males and females. In comparison to how serious the HIV/AIDS epidemic is, the acknowledgment of its danger is not nearly as high as it should be among genders. Since the campaign on preventing transmission of HIV/AIDS began, the choices people make in regard to engaging in sexual intercourse or other activities that involve the exchange of bodily fluids have changed a little. Most local and urban people interviewed seemed not to have experienced the disease personally but, at the same time, they talked about the various stigmas attached to it. In other words, HIV/AIDS, although

*A Travesty in Modern Nigeria Reported in Media*

thought of as quite present, appears to be invisible in terms of it being perceived as a precursor to death—hence, campaigns that caution against infection of the disease are, at that moment, proving incapable of making inroads. This is not to say that the stories about HIV/AIDS are unbelievable—as informants stated, they are quite believable. However, the people's behavioural responses to the HIV crisis are directed by their personal experiences, beliefs, values, and social impressions about appropriate sex relationships.

The social power to keep a chain of male and female friends, fertility, and marriage are all issues that conjoin in boosting one's measure of social success. In effect, the use of contraceptives and decision-making dynamics vary from one relationship to another, as does the importance and value placed on procreation. Decisions to use, or not use, preventive strategies in sexual relationships are strongly, to say the least, influenced by economics, the gender-dependency curve, and values about morality, procreation, and parenthood. In general, people usually consider sex before marriage immoral, and the strategy of using condoms is an effort to control the outcome of premarital sexual relationships. In a sense, the use of condoms indicates, for some, that the act of engaging in sex is regarded as typically immoral and directly opposed to fostering good spirits, cordiality, and natural pleasure.

It is important to note that science took over where the theology of health drew the line in terms of sexual behaviour. In the former, education about preventive measures such as the use of condoms and the deconstruction of HIV/AIDS myths have been the favoured methods of increasing awareness, and avoiding unprotected sex is considered valid. In the latter, however, sex is only considered valid in marriage, and morality is such that it is believed that sexual relationships must be controlled in legitimate social ways to ensure the continuity of kinship. It is equally important to note that the main issue facing health care providers goes beyond the biological functions of the body—they must also gain local knowledge, skills, and cultural competencies.

But where do gender and HIV/AIDS fit into the politics of bridewealth? This question in itself is a contentious one. But the fact is that this issue is closely related to sexual behaviours and the implications generated by the anxiety and power around the gaining of resources and the displaying of the grandeur of bridewealth within society.

**Sexual Behaviour Practices and Implications**

In-depth interviews and conversations showed that current sexual behaviour is having a much more negative impact on girls and women than it is on men. Physiologically, females are not equipped to easily escape infection, and many of them experience gender inequity in the form of sexual violence. Imposed sex, rape, and short-cut marriages (see Chapter 5) are common experiences for girls and women. Sex between older men and younger girls is well pronounced. 'Survival sex,' in which girls and women resort to earning money or gaining favours through sex, is also widespread. The high rate of vulnerability and poverty among women adds to the problem. Poor sex education, lack of adequate information, and limited access to health facilities such as sexually transmitted disease (STD) clinics constitute yet another problem that contributes to risky behaviour. The prevalent attitude is one of 'if sex happens, it happens,' and the possible consequences are only fully realized when it is obviously too late to do anything about it.

Yet another issue is that of poor life skills, which make it difficult for young people to negotiate condom use. Exposure to drug use and the occult, as well as high-risk practices aimed at survival, are all prevalent among youth who don't attend school—a social category that is not easily tracked down and, therefore, remains invisible until its members present themselves to the health-care system. In order to deal with the problem of HIV/AIDS, it is essential to emphasize the fact that it is not only a health issue but also a serious human-rights issue. Women and men are obviously entitled to basic rights that are denied by the presence of HIV/AIDS. The 'right to life,' which has now been abridged by HIV/AIDS, is a major concern facing effective gender relationships and survival. Gender relationships, already strained, become further stressed by the uncertainty that exists between potential sexual partners. Also essential, of course, is ensuring an adequate standard of living, including food, health, education, and protection from abuse and exploitation—issues that are an ongoing challenge in the face of poverty and other inevitable external forces.

**HIV/AIDS Prevalence and Fear**

HIV/AIDS in Nigeria, and by locality Igboland, is prevalent among adults (15-49), and UNAID, in 2002, estimated that approximately 5.8% of the population was infected. A total of 3.5 million people have been identified as infected, with the youth in general, and vulnerable women specifically, being the hardest hit. It is speculated that the HIV/AIDS' wave will strike 18% to 26% of the population by the year 2010. A sero-prevalence survey showed that young people are at the highest risk, with people from the ages of 15 to 24 accounting for over half of the infected persons (UNAID 2003). The epidemiological profile of HIV/AIDS in Nigeria has been offering a disturbing picture since 2004, when it showed that Nigeria is virtually the most affected area in Sub-Saharan Africa. This is particularly troubling because those who are infected are often unaware of their condition and fail to change their lifestyles. Knowledge about the availability of condoms is not an obstacle and, indeed, people do sometimes use them. The consistency of this use, however, varies, and people are often caught in situations where condom use is not an option available to them, as explained previously. For example, sexual crimes, armed robberies, and ritualistic crimes, often involving luxury buses and the like, are commonly committed along express-ways, and people fall victim to unprotected rape. Few people, especially women, feel they can speak out about these experiences or seek medical help.

The issues of women being included, or excluded, in health-care practice,

*Healer Rosana in Her Shrine Explaining Issues Concerning Women, Marriage and Health*

and their authority in terms of awareness of, and treating, their own health problems have a long history in the course of the gender struggle. The position of women in healing, and their authority to apply their gender knowledge, power, and competency to the practicing of medicine has never been the same since the writing of an official Catholic text on witchcraft, *The Hammer of Witches,* which led to an official state-sponsored witch hunt in Europe and elsewhere by two German monks, Kramer and Sprenger (see Ehrenreich & English 1973, 1979). The 'place' of women in healthcare and healing was further convoluted by the story of Florence Nightingale, referred to as the founder of modern nursing. Nightingale's model of the nursing profession supported the traditional stereotype of the physician as a father figure and the nurse as a mother, tender and nurturing.[91] Women were relegated to a subordinate position in the medical labour-force, and this remains the case today when it comes to medical issues concerning women, gender, and infectious diseases such as HIV and AIDS. The concept of women as the caring, tender, and nurturing gender is equally tied up with the ideology of women's roles and identity (cf. Reverby 1987; Growe 1991; Clarke 1996:332-338). Bridewealth relates to all aspects of female power and resistance. The sexism ideology is reflected in the specific roles and levels of roles, rewards, and working conditions—including those defined by bridewealth—that women and men can share.

Women and men in locales, urban neighbourhoods, and diaspora, as stated earlier, are all presently impacted by the existence of HIV/AIDS, and observation indicates that women are the hardest hit. The Nigerian Health Ministry has pointed out that the implications are complicated and serious in view of the sexual habits of Nigerian women and men. Cultural taboos, fear of mockery and discrimination, and the shame and stigma associated with HIV/AIDS result in people being highly reluctant to get tested or seek medical attention. The existence of injection-drug users is not acknowledged as it should be. Homosexuals, likewise, are spoken of far less than they should be, as homosexuality is considered a free-choice that occurs only in nations where such practices are permitted as a form of culture change and an individual's right to his or her own sexual preferences. The cultural assumption amongst the Igbo is that the practice of homosexuality is uncommon, and therefore taboo. On the contrary, homosexuality does exist, and, even among the heterosexual population unprotected anal intercourse, and other sex practices designed to preserve a woman's virginity prior to marriage, are not uncommon in Islamic communities. These are deep gender issues to which there is much more than what is ordinarily perceived, and further research is essential in these areas. Nevertheless, heterosexual practices, circumcision, genital mutilation, and genital cleansing and care remain hot topics of debate.[92]

HIV/AIDS adds to the changing danger-belief system affecting genders. Women are most at danger in conforming to the rhythm of the dangers of modernity due to the hybridization of sexuality, scientific development lapses, societal aftershocks, and vicious helplessness in dying. Sexual dangers and taboos are not new, and represent crucial points of entry and exit to the social body, gender power, identity, and roles that are organized and recognized by a society. HIV is a forerunner to the danger of gender disorder, deficiency, and death.

**Transmission, Gender, and Combative Methods**

The transmission of HIV/AIDS, in regard to women's sexuality, is a fatal frustration. Competing theories of the origins of HIV/AIDS date back to the 1930s or earlier, and have focused mainly on women, African Green Monkeys, and homosexual lifestyles in the USA. Sufficient commitment is needed from governments and individuals to address this issue through the creation of a 'policy of release' from the burdens and obstacles created by bridewealth, thus becoming effective as a symbolic load centre of democratic expression in this and other delicate gender-political issues.

In laying bare the impact of HIV/AIDS and its implications on gender, a minimal look at the nature and symptoms of the disease is telling. As far as it being a 'killer disease,' current reports on the massive world-wide population depletion resulting from AIDS are, in no way, exaggerated. HIV is an acronym for Human

Immunodeficiency Virus; a tiny blood-born germ that attacks the human immune system and, over time, tears down defense mechanisms and renders the body vulnerable to disease.

The HIV virus, like other forms of viruses, is a genderless microbe or pathogen that contributes to bodily-related illnesses; avoiding infection requires an understanding of the appropriate sanitary and safety practices for handling human bodies in cultural environments. Disease-causing microbes, or pathogens, require a host in order to grow and multiply inside living cells, as well as cause diseases such as colds, measles, hepatitis, and AIDS. 'AIDS,' as a word used in common speech, metaphorically implies that death is close at hand. What's more, it is a death transmission often based on gender power.

The impact of HIV/AIDS is currently discernable in gender relationships and survival patterns. AIDS leads to the dissolution of infected-gender households as parents die and children are sent to relatives for care. A decline in school attendance and education is also visible, as is the dramatic effect AIDS has had on the labour force, setting back economic activity and social progress (*www.avert.org*). The huge majority of the HIV/AIDS-infected population are within the 15 to 49 age group; this severely hampers the productive labour force and, in turn, Africa's—and particularly Nigeria's—ability to cope with the epidemic. Another impact of HIV/AIDS on gender is the stigma and discrimination foisted upon those who are infected, which results in a fear of testing and discourages sufferers from admitting that they have the disease and seeking treatment. All of this suggests that greater local and intercultural awareness is needed in order to change gender, age, and cultural mentalities and bring about a shift toward preventative actions.

When HIV adopts the human body as its host, it weakens and overwhelms the immune system by progressively destroying certain helper cells, called white blood cells or 'T-Helper Cells,' the result of which is a decline in health, strength, and vitality.[93] People infected with HIV, if left unchecked and untreated, progress to having full-blown AIDS, and eventually die from the disease. Infected people are prone to unusual opportunistic infections, including cancers, which they are unable to resist because of their compromised immune systems. Once HIV is detected, treatments and medications attempt to render it a long-term condition rather than a short-term death blow. In other words, palliative treatment to help the immune system cope with the virus, rather than a cure, is possible. This means that people who are HIV positive can live for many years before becoming ill, and anyone with HIV is capable of transmitting the virus to others through such things as unprotected sex, sharing needles when using injection drugs, and piercings and tattoos—basically, any activity that involves the exchange of bodily fluids such as blood, vaginal secretions, and semen. HIV is non-discriminatory when it comes to sex, age, religion, sexual orientation, and ethnicity. In this respect, everyone is affected by gender-focused intimate transactions and AIDS, which may lead to untimely death.

Given women's status and unequal share of economic and political power, women are more vulnerable to HIV/AIDS infection than are men. Women are much more likely to be in a position where they do not have the economic power and social independence that would allow them to make their own decisions in sexual relationships, and are vulnerable to the bodily whims of those in power over them. Women's liberation and empowerment in this regard will subsist in a combination of social and economic independence. The power to recognize the facts and the will and opportunity to act will go a long way to addressing gender issues—in particular sex, health, poverty, and rewarding status mobility. Modifying the present gender-based bridewealth politics would begin the process of a gender and power shift toward healthier, improved gender relations that would have positive results for kinship structure, the cultural nexus, and societal functioning as a whole.

In the following chapter, I will focus on feminist senses and shed light on men's sensitivity to feminist theory as well as exploring the debate about feminist movements and the underlying propositions for men and women.

# Chapter 12

# Male Feminist, Gender and Feminist Senses

There is a wide range of feminist movements, and a growing number of people, institutions, and agencies across the world are embracing, with varying degrees, the ideology of gender justness or equity. As Naomi Wolf puts it, "anyone who believes women matter as much as men do is unquestionably a feminist."[94] The question then arises: what hopes, opportunities, and benefits does feminism offer, especially to men? Why should men focus on feminist senses of bridewealth power and not on masculinist senses? To answer this question, it is necessary to briefly explore how male feminists sometimes feel about 'doing gender' from the feminist light. Robert Jensen writes in his article, "Men's Lives and Feminist Theory" (1995, 1997), that men should distinguish between "progressive male identity politics" and the "men's rights movement (*parri pasu*) with feminist senses." The goal is to find a way to persuade men that their patriarchal identity politics should be based on a feminist critique of male power and male sexuality, one in which systematic engagement with men's lives will bring about a commitment to real change. To persuade a patriarchal culture of this is, by no means, an easy task to advance. As Jensen further argued, this requires that feminism be seen as something more than a means for crude 'male-bashing' (Jensen 1997:421).

It must be observed that not every male or female may positively fathom feminism as a progressive movement in its own right. For some, feminism is perceived as a socialist evil. For example, a renowned U.S. Televangelist, Pat Robertson once said:

> "Feminism is a socialist, anti-family, political movement that encourages women to leave their husbands, kill their children, practice witchcraft, destroy capitalism, and become lesbians" (*Dose Magazine*, August 24, 2005).[95]

The women's liberation movement is, to people like Pat Robertson, a sad development in the new age that needs a re-sensibilization to root out its malignant cells. This puts forward the fact that not all people see feminist senses in the same light within the differing contexts of everyday lives and professions. The positions that people hold in society can obviously influence their perceptions of feminist thoughts and actions in certain ways.

That being said, having experienced bridewealth power and lived within it in order to understand it, it makes sense to me to argue that we also must engage in feminism in order to fully understand it and thereby find new ways to shape a progressive gender world in a changing social culture. The politics of male identity and feminist senses will likely continue to polarize the idioms of power and gender identity insofar as subjugation and exploitation underlie gender operations. With the powerful and the less powerful, constant pursuit of the common goal of emancipation will continuously connect men and women. If we can understand gender as a form of creating identity and distinctive roles, we can also understand that it results from the obstacles or privileges that the culture in which one lives attaches to one's biological and social characteristics. Male feminists acknowledge, rather than ignore, the pattern of those obstacles and privileges created by the power of a bridewealth culture of collateralization—that is, the ideological promises and practices of bridewealth as a measure for gender and security after marriage.

*Igbo Women in Ceremonial Outfits*

According to Jensen (1997:422), "the way in which societies value some characteristics of genders and denigrate others, and mores define those characteristics as male or female, more valuable or less valuable, is not merely natural, biological, or genially inevitable."[96] Jensen is, of course, correct in this statement and, when we read between the lines, we can say that his argument is suggestive of the fact that the way genders are 'made' can also follow a process of deconstruction in which genders are 'unmade' with the goal of achieving gender equity. Up to this point, the problems of kinship and structuring of gender upon marriage and residential relocation after marriage are to be found in some of the underlying ideological issues that still rest in a systemic practice of patrilocality or matrilocality. These traditional residential lifestyle choices are culturally strong norms that are essentially opposed to neolocality in urban complex community, a residential option seen only as peripheral to the local meaning and significance of the order of kinship settlement after marriage. Neolocality is not, so to speak, a choice in itself, but an adaptive response to urban extension.

Neolocality is expressed in the urban milieu, yet it is regarded as an extended pattern of kinship residence not unlike someone building a new home far away from one's father's house in the village. Igbo people living in the city experience neolocality while, at the same time, keeping strong ties with the village—from where, it is said, the real traditional cultures and values, in effect, feed those living in the cities. Neolocality is a point of conflict between traditionalism and modernism, and directly creates conditions that make culture change predictable. Paradoxes of home values and urban profiles arise that cannot be brushed aside. For example, how can the problem of kinship be addressed if a couple decides to breakaway from the culture by acting and living a Western lifestyle completely devoid of kinship normatives? Any attempt to answer this question must not lose sight of the fact that globalization and life in diaspora involves people moving and finding meaning in the predispositions of interculturalism. More often than not, as informants noted, deviation from one's cultural views and values are met with incessant gossip and ridicule. How would such gendering dilemmas be confronted in the struggle for gender equality? Would men and women not lose their cultural values, considered a part of their roots, to the urban culture? What sort of gendering will make sense other than that which is informed by the culture itself? Many of these questions are difficult to answer, as they point to the core issues that make identity creation such a complicated topic of discussion.

From another angle, if we contend that it cannot be assumed that gender can ever be unmade once it is made, we must at least recognize that it is the result of a combination of issues: historical, ideological, biological, social, cultural, and economical and political jingoisms of power and sexuality. And therein lies the bottom line. Hope of change still exists because culture itself is not a fixed concept of attitudes, values, and behaviours. Rather, it unfolds over time and change is inevitable—just as evolutionary cases of cultural changes have demonstrated. It is critically important to lay bare the facts of the 'unsaid,' in terms of how gender relations are experienced and lived in the present day, for the purpose of future analysis and the understanding of gender discourses and development.

At any moment in time and place, gender movements and struggles for rights may create conditions for change, and when the forces of change emerge the ability to resist masculinity or femininity will stress the uncertain and contradictory nature of initiated gender relations and power. Male feminists see the benefits that feminism offers in a diverse world, just as female feminists see the same through their own determinisms of gender reality. Feminism, it is argued, provides a better route for men to come to terms with their own lives. On a divergent note, feminism as a whole does not make it difficult to see and understand the fact of the (suppressive) nature of patriarchal values and structures, and the bias of sexism and male power. The contention is, rather, that feminism urges men as a whole to see and take feminism seriously by evaluating not only the politics of public patriarchy, but also their personal conduct in private, especially in the bedroom (Jensen 1997:423) and the matricentric homestead, in view of the grand design of bridewealth power.

Furthermore, feminism can help men answer many of their male-centred questions, relieve pain, heal wounds, and allow them to be not only gracious and courteous men, but men who also understand that feminism is not only about women's issues or gender relations but is also an explanation and critique of the domination/subordination dynamics that structure power relations. By allowing men and women to better understand the world in which they live, feminism invents, through the deconstruction of the male structures, insights that can be applied in other struggles of life. The power and status differentials society and gender principles create give men more choices in several domains on the one hand, and bestow some female-gendered dichotomized domains to women on the other hand. It is a fact that both genders react to the power that masculine and feminine profiling and controlling overpoweringly exerts. For example, a wife will react according to the masculine behaviour displayed by her husband and, likewise, a husband will react to feminine behaviour without consulting others as to what that reaction should be.

In gender stratified societies, bridewealth constitutes an economic politic of gender and transaction with which men maintain their masculine status quo. Through continuous creation of distance from women as *ndi alualu* (married folk), men place themselves above women by applying kinship cosmological values of patriarchy. What we see is a masculinist-imposed profiling of men over women in the patriarchal regenerative value system, power formation, and systemic structuring of gender identities and inequalities.

Feminist leftists have criticized the women's movement of being a fragmentation of the total whole, a view in which feminists have been accused of the inability to mount a frontal attack in deploying power, positive thinking, and strategy. The point from which to deconstruct bridewealth is not off-centre of, but aligned within, society. It can be inferred, therefore, that this view of feminism is not primarily the position of an imagined absolute outsideness, but an alterity that must vitally understand itself as an internal exclusion and inclusion. In part, this view may be asking that analysts reasonably state that feminist theorizing, taken as a whole, has gone beyond the male liberationist's focus on better sex. Regardless of that, it has hitherto shown understanding of, and sensitivity to, the structuring and regulating of women as a desire aimed toward economically, socially, and politically oppressive ends. That is why, in addition, there is a need to point out that feminists have also long argued that to demand greater sexual freedom is good, but without formulating that demand in terms of the transformation of the social relations within which sexuality is organized and articulated is to invite old constraints to be placed on women as a desire. This means that in order for bridewealth analysis to be understood as a critical centre of gender knowledge, in particular in connecting gender relations, sexual politics, and power, it must adopt pragmatic and concrete transformational essence equally and consistently.

The point is that feminist criticism is equally valuable, and can help elaborate the extent to which the phallocentric meanings and truths of culture subsist under the male patriarchal identity. On the one hand, women's silence and exclusion from struggles over how they are labeled and represented have illustrated the condition of humanist thought. On the other hand, knowledge of the female world has everything to do with the constitution of power in our world and, therefore, the economic and political devices expressed in bridewealth. The male-feminist discourse makes the body of bridewealth an object of knowledge, and that objectification of knowledge inescapably invests it with the power of celebration in protest to the patriarchal heritage. In analyzing bridewealth and the methods of deconstruction and reconstruction it is pertinent to adopt the use of critical modes to align gender equity and gender social correctness.

So, is feminist theorizing useful? It involves both emotional and motivational functions, such as centrally-embedded issues of communal prestige and honour and behavioural-support elements in society. Indeed, the theoretical significance of feminism cannot be over-stated. Like language, feminist theorization of society is a species-specific skill; feminist theoreticians engage in and perform cognitive tasks in an effort to analyze, evaluate, and manipulate the properties of gender representations in order to respond to gender movements. We generally benefit from feminist theorizing because it brings into bridewealth the analysis, and control, of important social bodies that are constitutive of gender inventiveness and struggle. Feminism makes evident our conviction—perhaps only a hope at present—that reconfiguring the norms and discourses of gender and body relations to forms of feminist competence in the emergent new-world order will obviate the simplistic advocating of gender stratification and neo-stratificationism. Put another way, male and female figural crossings are often juxtaposed, making the body contest a systemic binary facticity of sex that underlies the social constructedness of gender (Martin 1996:79).[97] Whether biologically or socially constructed, the concept of gender is a politicization of gender differences and characteristics such that the materiality of the body is entangled in its formation through social consciousness. To speak of male feminists in this context is to recognize the fact that more explicit desires for, and empathies toward, gender equity can best be reconfigured in the bodily gender through discursive re-significations (Martin 1996) in bridewealth power.

Central to these assessments and predictions is the fact that, in present Igbo society, it is unlikely that bridewealth power could be fully understood without exploring its qualities before, during, and after marriage, as has been attempted here. Bridewealth suggests that the multifaceted aspects of gender are woven around, and reflected in, opposition between male and female principles and relationships. Taking gender seriously requires understanding that it is about the cultural experience of being male or female—in this case, how men and women's lives are shaped through bridewealth after marriage. Through the application of more critical feminism, women and men in Igbo society, either at home and in diaspora, will enhance or challenge socially-defined gender conclusions, reminiscent of the implications of bridewealth and gender conflict, in a suspension of hostilities and a spirit of compromise.

Further consideration of bridewealth supports the fact that gender, as a principle of social organization of role, identity, and status in society, depicts strong mystified political relations of both genders within the constructed meanings of the Igbo world. The question of why women are the subjugated gender cannot be resolved by focusing only on the motive of bridewealth and its empowered intentions independent of the cultural constructs that inform gender expression. Because of the workings of gender identity in a changing everyday reality of migration and its influence on the local culture, an analysis of bridewealth needs to consider the values and conditions that define the sexes in Igbo, as well as the typifications each gender holds of the other.

Feminist senses contribute to making discourses on gender a lively experiential and intellectual debate and, in this context, to the conceptualization of bridewealth as a total whole. In doing so, both men and women have been privileged to recreate themselves positively by participating in the politics of identity and roles. Feminist senses have also assisted women in finding a starting point for equality by exploring and understanding, more than ever before, the ambivalent intent and purposes of bridewealth. In this way, the understanding of bridewealth, both generally and in its specific applications, can go beyond the empowerment of both men and women to 'play gender' with or without guilt to an acceptance of male and female bodies as screens and metaphors with which to construct knowledge. Changing the actual conditions in which the present gender normatives are embedded will affect gender politics of identity and power. This is much more than an emotional issue of women's yearning; women, as informants stated in divergent ways, want to 'be like' men (*o na-amasi umunwanyi ibu nwoke*). Why is this so? It would be a mistake to think of this as an empty desire or wishful thinking—clearly, there is much more to it than that.

Feminism encourages men to rethink their lives and their systems of relationships with women. Its goal is to initiate and enact a systematic intervention that takes bridewealth, as a whole, and the culture it exists in and examines them together in the light of the resulting changes that the society will have to contend with. On the interpretive level of feminist senses, one can postulate that they call for a move from the 'content issues' of bridewealth power to the 'process issues' of the harsh experience of women's daily life after marriage, with the intent of adjusting gender behaviour so that it is equitable to women. While this may be the case for interpretation and reinterpretation of feminist senses, males often view feminist resistance as being aimed solely at endlessly questioning and re-questioning the patriarchal conjectures and ideological strategic frameworks of social, political, and economic spaces of interaction. At another level of interpretation, however, feminists urge men to abandon the roles that result in them being perceived as puppets of patriarchal values and structures such as are systemic with bridewealth devices.

Furthermore, interpreting gender and bridewealth power entails not only delving into explanations that go beyond laic applications or uses of complex attitudes and experiences, but at the same scrutinizing the empowerment or disempowerment process between genders. To understand the dynamics of bridewealth requires focusing on not just the narrow issue of local conceptions, but equally on urban and international influences that foster the connections between bridewealth beliefs and practices and diasporas, conformities, and resistances. Notwithstanding the asymmetrical power relations and inequalities of social conditions between men and women that characterize many aspects of life in modern society, feminist senses remind us that we can individually and collectively take responsibility for empowering genders and creating cultural change. For example, gender semantics or phrases, such as *nwoke amu amu* (man of father's soil—literally, 'delivered to being son of the soil') as opposed to *nwanyi amumu* (born daughter, waiting to mature and move) and *di bi ulo* (husband, man who owns the house) as opposed to *nwanyi alualu* (a married woman), typically perpetuate the status quo. While this characterization of men and women through language may be relevant in that women are transitory and men are not, it is, nevertheless, pejorative to women and implies how identity and status are designed and accorded to men and women respectively. When such meanings have developed and become systematized, women speak with the nature, bodies, and social senses that men create for them. To 'escape' from being a woman is a wish consistently expressed among women, as was pointed out earlier. Feminist senses converge in social and cultural facts, and form grounds for the quest for release, for understanding, for gender safety and better status quo in all spheres, and for the sharing of gender flexibility and equality where it is merited and deserved in the changing traditional and modern fields of success and accomplishments.

Gender has, therefore, evolved from economic and sociopolitical processes of sociobiology and cultural conceptualization, and that concept now rests on what changing gender domains do with it, and make of it, in view of human relational and positional issues. It is hoped that this present work, along with further analysis, will fire up interest and make a contribution to bridging the gaps in our understanding of bridewealth power and gender practices—experientially, intellectually, and discursively.

As a whole, the search for opportunities that reach beyond tradition is an exploration of the new realities of gender. To effect change that would lead to more positive gender relations it is necessary that everyone be involved in achieving the vision of a new order. In the intuitive sense, the best gender practices must be able to see past the negatives or opposites so as to offer encouragement, challenge the process, and model the goal. Essentially, everyone should be enabled to act out of optimism and a hope for the better—and this applies even more so to women themselves.

Unfortunately, development at home and in diaspora apparently remains sluggish in that there is still a very real tendency to neglect feminist potential, especially with regard to the devaluation of women's participation in education, science, and technology. That we often take the human world as a homogenous whole, regardless of specific gender potentials and complementary forces, is a point that cannot be expressed strongly enough. It is crucial that we acknowledge that not only are human roles diverse, but the potential of individuals, as ascribed to them by their gender, is also a valid issue in the making and unmaking of identity and power relations. In this light, Ojukwu recently put forth a view critical to feminist potential in the political and development context when he asserted:

> "It is my opinion that ... women need to do more for themselves, however; because no matter how much I may claim to understand them, women understand themselves better. They, only, can make the propositions that will work for them,... Now, as a male, men are part of my political theorem. But both women and men must be included in any dialogue concerning our development. I say this very strongly; both genders must be accommodated, and no one dismissed. ... I hold against Nigerian women [*the fact that*],[3] they seem to take the easiest way out. As soon as they come together, they begin to look for male patrons to validate their female concerns! But this is not necessary; because they should fight their way out...not always rely on handouts by men" (Ojukwu in Conversation - *www.kwenu.com*, August 8, 2005).[98]

The message here is clear; women and men should become more upfront in the struggle to enhance their potentials and opportunities. The debate, therefore, must continue until the real level of accommodation is found and embraced by all in discourses of bridewealth dynamics, as well as in both the achieved and ascribed gender powers in the compelling cultural context of everyday lives. Whereas feminist sense must serve as a de factor force in development, understanding the culture of bridewealth necessitates understanding and appreciating the diverse issues around gender beliefs and practices—offered with a perspective on culture and life before, during, and after marriage. Gender-focused studies offer but a glimpse into the broad sweep of the cultural awareness that enriches theoretical discussions and formulations; and, hence, some obvious critical reformulations of gender and society. In this way, culture, contra Geertz's (1973:5) reference to it as the very foundation of human life, is, in this case, the very *foundation of gender* that works for the members of a group in their cosmoslogy of everyday reality. Gender, thus, weaves numerous webs of significations, and some of those webs are deep-seated in brdiewealth power and marriage.

Thus far, the analysis and interpretive senses of bridewealth can be congregated into the logic of one in search of meaning. By essentially bringing together a meaningful search of this reality, the Igbo signify themselves by rendering cultural and social expressions that enable them to understand and deal with their world within and outside of marriage. In that way, bridewealth powerfully constructs the fact that culture is not a power *sui generis*—that is, a thing that can, in itself, show purpose without firm connections to the other elements shaping life and society—rather, it is a context. Such a context is illustrated by bridewealth; bridewealth being something which can be concretely described and appreciated in its own right (cf. Geertz 1973). In addition, bridewealth is an effective ideology within which life is particularly defined after marriage. Not only does it map the problematic social reality of women and men in the quest for wealth or poverty, but it is also a creative matrix or prevailing condition of collective senses of social tradition and modernism. This is all, in turn, all too often is governed by the cultural forces of searching for wealth, and, if wealth cannot be found, settling for poverty. In the sense of articulating what constitutes right and wrong, power and authority, obligation and loyalty, bridewealth-demanded gifts and ceremonies elaborate upon all of those

---

3 For emphasis, the words in italics are mine.

concepts. In seeking to uncover the hermeneutic sphere of bridewealth, senses critical to both feminism and patriarchism intertwine and forge an understanding of the Igbo world in this regard.

Let me point out one last but important issue with regard to the concept of 'gender mainstreaming' in the modern world. By definition, gender mainstreaming refers to the process of assessing the implications for women and men of any planned action, including legislation, policies or programmes in all areas and at all levels for equal benefits insofar as inequality is not perpetuated. It means being assertive and deliberate in giving visibility and support to women's contributions rather than making the assumption that women will benefit equally from gender-blind development interventions. In other words, gender mainstreaming requires a focus on feminist senses such that improving the well-being of poor women ties in with the question of social justice in policy sectors. Repositioning bridewealth in this case through a gender mainstreaming approach will not look at women or men in isolation, but at both as sectors and beneficiaries in the development and reinforcement process. Feminist senses therefore are a major part of the issues served in different sectors – public and private.

More to the point, Otive Igbuzor, (*www.kwenu.com* 2006)[99] for example, has referred to and stressed the significance of gender mainstreaming as a planning tool. Gender inequality, he illustrates, is a constraint to growth and poverty reduction. A more equitable gender relation is an accelerator of poverty reduction, in particular when gender is mainstreamed into both state and national plans with emphasis on political, economic and socio-cultural equity. In this way, gender mainstreaming is to be considered a strategy critical for achieving social justice, economic equity and plan effectiveness. Underlining this is the fact that closing the gender gap created by bridewealth power in the light of feminist senses will help to stress that equity should not be seen as a favour to women. Neither is it to be viewed as just good politics

(Igbuzor 2006). Rather, it is good economics as well and will lead to poverty reduction and sustainable development.

# Chapter 13

# Summary and Conclusion

Marriage is, by tradition, an important value and institutional force to the Igbo, even to the degree that not marrying at the right moment carries with it significant implications. Indeed, marriage is a 'cultural will to life and personhood,' not only for the individuals involved but also for the families and larger kin groups within which the cultural realities and personal experiences that lie in the gender pattern itself are exposed. When, how, and who a person marries is vitally important to the larger kin groups such that their concern and involvement in ensuring the traditional status quo is valued, revealed, and reinforced throughout the marriage process. The society pays great attention, in respect to the social creation that marriage brings about, to marrying wealth or marrying poverty. Bridewealth, in effect, provides a holistic cultural prism for power within the genders. For the Igbo, bridewealth is a tool that functions to serve practical and symbolic gender purposes in many ways. As a tool for attaining status and power, it initiates and reinforces reciprocal effects on the creators—women and men, wife-givers and wife-takers, kin groups, and neighbouring communities. The tool of bridewealth is generated through these networks and, invariably, re-invents or reverberates—that is, changes and re-configures—the members' gender power and relations after marriage. Furthermore, bridewealth pulls out, injects, or breathes potential senses of difference and power on participants and, in so doing, entails them experiencing its implications in culturally relative dynamics. In other words, each person is unconditionally trapped within the forces of bridewealth, even while seeking greater meaning, inclusion, and equality.

Through structures that people in societies use to organize their lives—such as bridewealth—anthropologists explore the endogenous (*endo*—within, inside) processes that govern everyday lives in order to understand and describe them to others. Despite contributions this work may make to feminist discourse and anthropological knowledge, it should not be viewed with either a feminist or masculinist bias, but as a combination of the two in light of the roots of gender power. Neither should the views and analysis be exclusively arrogated to the likes of Margaret Mead, who preferred not to be called a feminist, but to that of femininity or feminine status in anthropological quests. My hope is that even if controversy of any sort should be found around this work, it will not be equal to when Margaret Mead, named 'Mother of the World' by *Time Magazine* in 1969, stated in her *Coming of Age in Samoa* that "…young women (her subjects) had casual sex before settling into satisfying marriages, which was contrary to Judeo-Christian cultural expectations." Admittedly, arguments raised concerning polygamy and cultural ways of managing excess women in society may be capable of capturing similar cultural, gender, religious, and ethical sentiments. In my analysis, however, bridewealth power initiates and shapes individuals through the expression of genuine beliefs and practices of kinship solidarity and alliance. In regard to expectations of respect and honour, the roots of gender relations are perceptibly social, cultural, familial, and individual—and this contribution has, through ideological arguments and case studies, provided instructive insights into this. For example, I showed with data how the Igbo view the marriage of their daughters as a validation of social benefits according to custom rather than as a loss. Unmarried daughters (and sons for the most part) are, on the contrary, considered a source of anxiety and a loss both in terms of the biological regeneration of life and in terms of material connections to the wider social and kinship circles. Even in terms of defining individuals as 'full people' who truly 'belong' to the society, marriage acts as an important measure. Given the fact that marriage secures and sustains idenity, and is regarded as a benefit both to self and others, Igbo data challenges the anthropological discourses that hold to the notion of "loss" in this matter. That said, the high cost of bridewealth is a central issue of concern that must be be reconsidered.[100]

This book has therefore attempted to demonstrate how bridewealth objectifies Igbo women in the patriarchal value system and exchange-of-power structure. It has revealed how Igbo women and men obey the rules of the kinship political economy of identity making and unmaking in terms of gender and power relations and meanings. It has equally shown how systems of meaning can, as such, be analyzed in terms of power relations between women and men. It further illustrates that gender and power are relational and positional concepts in themselves, and are not merely 'given' but 'constructed' in the axis of bridewealth, which provides position, meaning, and interpretation. Placing the Igbo bridewealth power of men and women in context thus becomes one way to analyze and understand a society's default power lines by identifying who does, or does not, have position and power, and the social expectations and implications of that. The reality of bridewealth permeates the politics of social payment among the Igbo, both at home and in diaspora, and emphasizes the fact that the struggle to gain position is strongly situated upon the males, thereby offering them the basis for gaining an unequal share of power, identity, status, and roles.

The gender divide is unique, and is distinguished by gender ideology, roles, and subjectivities that, taken together, allude to that to which bridewealth power is inherent. Bridewealth, when genderized, is a structure of dominance and submission that underlies the power of male-kinship interests, and this perspective is reflected in the ideas about male-female differences in bridewealth power in the Igbo culture. In examining Igbo gender relations and the power of bridewealth after marriage, this work has clarified the opportunities and implications of bridewealth negotiations, including both acknowledged and unacknowledged gender stereotypes.

On the playing fields of social equality and rapid social change, gender identities are revealed. While women and men negotiate marriage alliance through social payments, the implications of bridewealth become more noticeable after marriage. Bridewealth is an ideologically embedded trap for both women and men, and the definition and valuation of women's status through it is often a powerful tool. Both genders negotiate not only to find the 'best' mate, but also to mobilize kin networks in mediating roles, identities, and distances in order to connect to sources of wealth and opportunities for a better life in diaspora through migration. Difficulties posed by the intricacies of bridewealth and the social expectation to marry and be 'counted' in society result in women taking matters to new levels as they adopt innovative coping strategies—although they still seem to lose and suffer more than men in terms of flexible opportunities. In the changing gender relations in Igbo society, women can marry other women and thus become initiated into the strong-hold of power. The importance of this power is echoed in the specific and diverse ways that women take positions in society.

Despite expensive bridewealth, women and men continue to marry within the social idioms and ideological metaphors of bridewealth—but they yearn for a change for the better in order to liberate the power and bondage of bridewealth after marriage. In decades to come it is hoped the forces of bridewealth will loosen their hold and thereby lead to an increase in the female capacity to be heard, to negotiate, to take more inclusive roles, and to claim their rightful identity and equality.

The theories of gendered interculturalism suggest that women should act more pro-actively, carrying men along in the conjecture of alliance between the Igbo people at home and in diaspora. Feminism makes sense; in understanding the patriarchal structure through the study of bridewealth and power, men are encouraged to acknowledge the implications of unequal gender layering on their own lives in a changing Igbo society. It is hoped that this book has equally shown the benefits that feminist senses have to offer, and has emphasized that both men and women need to understand what feminism really entails in order to employ its dynamics in 'doing gender' in everyday life.

The logic of bridewealth power as a whole explains why popular media insights have often not found it easy to adequately define the root of male dominance in a more specific cultural and endogenous context. As this work demonstrates, this is partially because the 'bridewealth after marriage' theme has been so little discussed. In examining how men and women engage in the struggle of social payments, enact and/or redefine roles, and challenge and compete for the power underlying the beliefs and practices of bridewealth, it is crucial to consider both content and relevance. This, in turn, highlights those factors that actually promote differentiated rights and power, and how those rights and their related power idioms are assumed, assigned, and utilized in everyday life—even in the invention and re-invention of feminine and masculine discourses. Moreover, the work demonstrates that strong cultural and ideological forces have colluded with modernism, and, thus, both sexual inequality and increasing social opportunities are conjunctively stressed. It also boldly challenges some of the established ideas about sex, marriage, gender, and the male-power base given the ideological setting in which they are considered and rigorously analyzed. Not only does the ideological setting underpin feminist thought, it also yields viable insight into the treatment of bridewealth issues across the science of culture. Reproduced in this work, also, is the fact that related psychodramatic kinship social payments are constitutively a form of sociocultural history (of gender), identity, and power. Understanding bridewealth after marriage is invaluable in that it can largely construct not only the society's gender roots, but also how position and power, as they affect gender, are played out in a changing African society.

# References and Endnotes

Acholonu, C.O. 1995. *Motherism: The Afrocentric Alternative to Feminism.* LHHP: Women in environmental development series, Vol. 3, with Nigerian Institute of International Affairs (NIIA)

Afigbo, A. E. 1987. *The Igbo and their Neighbour: Inter-group Relations in South-eastern Nigeria.* Ibadan: University Press Ltd

Amadiume, I. 1997. *Reinventing Africa. Matriarchy, Religion and Culture.* London and New York: Zed Books Ltd

------------------ 1987. Male Daughters, Female Husbands: Gender and Sex in an African Society. London: Zed Books Ltd

Anderson, D.M. & V. Broch-Due (eds.). 1999. *The Poor are Not Us: Poverty and Pastoralism in Eastern Africa.* Oxford: James Currey.

Anderson, M. C. 2000. The Persistence of Polygyny as an Adaptive Response to Poverty and Oppression in Apartheid South Africa. *Cross-Cultural Research*, 34: 102-103.

Anyanwu, U.D. 1993. "Gender Question in Igbo Politics." In: U.D. Anyanwu and J.C.U. Aguwa (eds.) *The Igbo and the Tradition of Poltics.* Enugu: Fourth Dimension Publishers, pp. 113-119

Babangida, M. 1991. "An Address" on the Occasion of the Workshop on Strategies For Enhancing Women's Participation in Political Decision-making Process.

Abuja, May 7, p. 8

Bastian, M.L. 2001. "Dancing Women and Colonial Men: The Nwaobiala of 1925." In Brettell, C.B. & C.F. Sargent (eds.). 2001. *Gender in Cross-cultural Perspective (3rd edition).* Upper Saddle River, New Jersey: Prentice Hall.

Bell, D. 1981. "Women's Business Is Hard Work: Central Australian Aboriginal Women's Love Rituals." *Signs* 7:314-337.

Blackwood, E. Women's Intimate Friendships and Other Affairs: An Ethnographic Overview. In Brettell, B.C & C.F. Sargent (editors). *Gender in Cross-Cultural Perspective (4th Edition).* Upper Saddle River, New Jersey: Pearson-Prentice Hall.

Bolyanatz, A. 1996. "Musings on Matrilineality: Understandings and Social Relations among the Sursurungua of New Ireland." In Maynes, M.J. *et al* (eds.) *Gender, Kinship and Power: A Comparative and Interdisciplinary History.* New York: Routledge.

Bourdieu, P. 1980. *Le Sens Practique.* Paris: Minuit

Bourdieu, P. 1979. *La Distinction: Critique Social du Judgement,* Paris: Minuit

Brettell, C.B. & C.F. Sargent (eds.). 2001. *Gender in Cross-cultural Perspective (3rd edition).* Upper Saddle River, New Jersey: Prentice Hall.

Chuku, G. I. 1993. Economic Bases of Traditional Politic, in: U.D. Anyanwu and Aguwa, J. C.U (eds.) *The Igbo and Traditional of Politics.* Enugu: Fourth Dimension Publishers

Clarke, N.J. 1996. *Health, Illness, and Medicine in Canada (2nd edition).* Toronto: Oxford University Press.

Comaroff, J. L. 1980. Introduction. In: *The Meaning of Marriage Payments,* (ed.) J.L. Comaroff, New York Academic Press, pp. 1-47

Cronk, L. 1996. Reciprocity and the Power of Giving, in: J. Spradley, and D.W. McCurdly (eds.) *Conformity and Conflict. Readings in Cultural Anthropology, 9th edition,* pp. 157-163. New York: Longman.

Vansina, J. *et al.* 1982. *African History.* New York: Macmillan.

Davidson, B. A. 1965. *A History of West Africa.* Lagos: Pero Press

Devisch, R. 1993. *Weaving the Threads of Life: The Khita gyn-eco-logical Healing Cult Among the Yaka.* Chicago: University of Chicago Press

Dolphyne, A.F. 1991. *The Emancipation of Women: The African Perspective.* Accra: Ghana Universities Press

Douglas, M. 1966. *Purity and Danger. An analysis of the Concepts of Pollution and Taboo.* London: Ark Papers.

Dubisch, J. 1986. Culture Enters through the Kitchen: Women, Food, and Social Boundaries in Rural Greece. In *Gender and Power in Rural Greece.* New Jersey: Princeton University Press, pp. 195-214.

Ehrenreich. B. & D. English. 1973a. *Witches, Midwives and Nurses: A History of Women Healers.* Old Westbury, N.Y.: Feminist Press.

Ekejiuba, F. 1995. Currency Instability and Social Payments Among the Igbo of Eastern Nigeria, 1890-1990. In Guyer, J.I. (ed.) *Money Matters: instability, values and social payments in the modern history of West African Communities.* London: Heinemann, pp. 133-161

Ekejiuba, F. 1995a. Down to Fundamentals: Women-centred Hearth-holds in Rural West Africa. In: D.F. Bbryceson (ed.), *Women Wielding the Hoe: Lessons from Rural Africa for Feminist Theory and Development Practice.* Oxford: Berg Publishers, pp. 47-61

Ekejiuba, F. 1992. Omu Okwei, the Merchant Queen of Osomari. In B. Awe (ed.), *Nigerian Women in Historical Perspectives.* Lagos.

Ember, R. Ember, M, and P. Peregrine. 2005. *Anthroplogy (11th Edition).* Upper Saddle River, New Jersey: Pearson - Prentice Hall.

Emeka, L.N. 1991. Dead Folks Alive: "Igbo Funeral rites in the Broad Spectrum of Igbo Concept of Death." In: *Ahiajoku Lecture (Onugaotu) Colloquium.* Owerri: Directorate of Information and Culture, pp.10-33

Etienne, M. 2001. "The Case for Social Maternity: Adoption of Children by Urban Baule Women." In Brettell E. C. & C.F. Sargent (eds) *Gender in Cross-cultural Perspective (3rd ed)*. Upper Saddle River, New Jersey: Prentice Hall.

Ezeabasili, N. 1982. "Traditional Igbo Ideas about disease and its Treatment." In: O.A. Erinso (ed.) *Nigerian perspectives on Medical Sociology*. Virginia: Department of Anthropology, College of William and Mary. No. 19, pp. 17-28.

Feder, k. L. 2004. *Linking to the Past: A Brief Introduction to Archaeology*. Oxford: Oxford University Press.

Feldman-Savelsberg, P. 1996. Cooking Inside: Kinship and Gender in Bagangte Idioms of Marriage and Procreation. In Maynes, M.J. *et al* (eds.) *Gender, Kinship and Power: A Comparative and Interdisciplinary History*, pp.177-197. New York: Routledge.

Foucault, M. 1978. *The History of Sexuality Vol. 1: An Introduction*. New York: Random House.

Geertz, C. 1973. *The Interpretation of Cultures*. New York: Basic Books.

Gilmore, D.D. 1990. *Manhood in the Making: Cultural Concepts of Masculinity*. New Haven & London: Yale University Press.

Goody, J. and S. J. Tambiah. 1973. "Bridewealth and Dowry in Africa and Euroasia." In: J. Guyer and P. Peters (eds.) *Workshop on Conceptualising the Household*. Cambridge: Cambridge University Press.

Gordon, D. & P. Spicker. (eds.). 1999. *The International Glossary on Poverty*. London & New York: Zed Books.

Green, M.M. 1964. *Igbo Village Affairs*. New York: Praeger.

Growe, S.J. 1991. The Nature and Type of Doctor's Cultural Assumptions about Patients as Men. *Sociological Focus*, 24,3:211-23.

Guyer, J.I. 1995. The Value of Beti Bridewealth. In J.I. Guyer (ed.), Money Matters: instability, values and social payments in the modern history of West African Communities. London: Heineman.

Hagberg, S. 2001. *Poverty in Burkina Faso: Representations and Realities*. Sweden-ULRiCA

- Uppsala-Leuven Research in Cultural Anthropology: Uppsala University, Tryck & Medier.

Habu, M. B. 2004. "Nigerian Single Women in Diaspora: In the United States, for Instance" In *www.gamji.com*, April 4, 2004

Hall, C.M. 1992. *Women and Empowerment: Strategies for Increasing Autonomy.* Washington DC.: Hemisphere Publishing Corporation.

Hamilton, A. 1981. "A Complex Strategical Situation: Gender and Power in Aboriginal Australia." In Grieve, N. & P. Grimshaw (eds.). *Australian Women: Feminist Perspectives,* pp. 69-85. Melbourne: Oxford University Press.

Ibah, V.I. 1988. The role of women in the rural educational development in our society, in: *Report of the preliminary Seminar held by C.W.O Abuja Independent Mission,* 23rd January, pp. 1-7.

Igboanugo, S. 2004. USA Visa as Heart Breaker. In *nigeriaworld.com May 12, 2004.*

Iroegbu, P. & M. Izibili 2004. *Kpim of Democracy: Thematic Introduction to Socio-Political Philosophy.* Benin-City, Nigeria: Ever-Blessed Publishers.

Iroegbu, E. P. 2004. "The Meaning of Juju in Nigerian Political Culture (Parts:1, 11, 111)." In *www.gamji.com*, Feb.12, 2004; *www.lagosforum.com*, Feb. 6, 2004; and *www.lagosforum.com*, March 7, 2004 respectively.

---------------- 2002. "Marrying Wealth, Marrying Money: Repositioning Igbo Women and Men. In Saunders, B. and M.C. Foblets (eds.) *Changing Genders in Intercultural Perspectives.* Leuven: Leuven University Press.

---------------- 2004. "Re-Centering Bridewealth Power Between Igbo Women and Men at Home and in Diaspora." Paper submitted to *Department of African American Studies* on "Sisters Defining Sisters Conference: Redefining our Issues ~ Affecting Change." Feb. March. Temple University, Philadelphia – USA.

.............. 2004. Understanding HIV/AIDS and Combative Ways in Nigerian Society (Parts 1 & 11). In *www.gamji.com*, June, 2004). See also *www.lagosforum.com*, June, 2004.

Isichei, E. 1976. A History of the Igbo People. London: Macmillan.

Jenkins, M. & Miller, S.M. 1987. Upward Redistribution in the United Sates. In Ferge & Miller (eds.). *Dynamics of Deprivation*. England: Gower Publishing Company.

Jensen, R. 1997. Men's Lives and Feminist Theory. In Kendall, D. (ed) *Race, Class & Gender in a Diverse Society*, pp. 419-429. Toronto: Allyn & Bacon.

Kazemipur, A. & Halli, S.S. 1997. Plight of Immigrants: The Spatial Concentration of Poverty in Canada. *Canadian Journal of Regional Science* 20 (1,2): 11-28.

---------------- 2000. *The New Poverty in Canada: Ethnic Groups and Ghetto Neighbourhoods*. Toronto: Thompson Educational Publishing, INC.

Lancaster, R.N. & M. di Leonardo (eds.,). 1997. *The Gender Sexuality Reader: Culture, History, Political Economy*. New York & London: Routledge.

Lewis, O. 1966. The Culture of Poverty. In Harp & Hofley (eds.). *Poverty in Canada*. Scarborough: Prentice-Hall of Canada Ltd.

Lips, M.H. 1988. *Sex and Gender: An Introduction*. Mountain View, California: Mayfield Publishing Company.

MacKinnon, A. C. 1994. "Difference and Dominance: Sexuality." In Hermann A. C. & A.J. Stewart (eds.) *Theorizing Feminism: Trends in the Humanities and Social Sciences*, pp. 257-287. Oxford: Westview Press.

McClelland, D. C. 1972. *The Achieving Society*. New York: The Free Press.

Marx, K. 1973 [1939]. Grundrise. Britain: Penguin Books.

Mauss, M. 1950. *The Gift: Forms and Functions of Exchange in Archaic Societies*, London: Cohen & West

Menon, S. 1996. Male Authority and Female Autonomy: A Study of the Matrilineal Nayars of Kerala, South India. In Maynes, M.J. *et al* (eds.) *Gender, Kinship and Power: A Comparative and Interdisciplinary History*. New York: Routledge.

Melenyzer, B. 1991. Empowerment and Women in Education: A Critic of the Feminist Discourse. *Paper presented at the Eleventh Annual Conference of the Women's Consortium of the Pennsylvania State System of Higher Education. Shippenburg University of Pennsylvania.*

Middleton, R. DeWight. 2003. *The Challenge of Human Diverity: Mirrors, Bridges and Chasms (2nd edition)*. Waveland Press, Inc.

Miller, B. D. 1993. Surveying the Anthropology of Sex and Gender Hierarchies. In Miller, B. D. (ed). *Sex and Gender Hierarchies*, pp. 3-311. New York: Cambridge University Press.

Mitchell, C. 1957. Aspects of African Marriage on the Copperbelt of Northern Rhodesia, *Rhodes-Livingstone Journal*, vol. XXii, pp. 1-30

Modjeska, N. 1982. Production and Inequality: Perspectives from Central New Guinea. In A. Strathern (ed.) *Inequality in New Guinea Highlands Societies*, pp. 50-108. Cambridge: Cambridge University Press.

Mohammed, P. 1988. The Carribean Family Revisited. In Mohammed, P & C. Shephered (eds.). *Gender in Caribbean Development*. Pp. 170-182. Mona, Jamiaca: University of West Indies.

Nader, L. 1989. Orientalism, Occidentalism and the Control of Women, *Cultural Dynamics*, Vol. II, 3, pp. 323-355

Narotzky, S. 1997. *New Directions in Economic Anthropology*. London: Pluto Press

Narayan, D. et al. 2000. *Voices of the Poor: Can Anyone Hear Us?* Oxford: Oxford University Press (World Bank Document).

Nwankwo, A. 1993. The Igbo and the Tradition of Politics: An Overview, in: U.D. Anyanwu and J.C.U. Aguwa (eds.) *The Igbo and the Tradition of Politics*. Enugu: Fourth Dimension Publishers, pp. 3-8

Ohadike, D.C. 1994. *Anioma: A Social History of the Western Igbo People.* Ohio: Ohio University Press.

Oikelome, A. Wedding in Absentia: The new fad. In *Daily Independent Online, April 27, 2004.*

Okehie-Offoha, M.U. 1996. "The Igbo." In Okehie-Offoha, M.U. and M.N.O. Sadiku (eds.) *Ethnic and Cultural Diversity in Nigeria.* Trenton, New Jersey: African World Press Inc.

Okeke, E. P. 2001. "Negotiating Social Independence: The Challenges of Career Pursuits for Igbo Women in Postcolonial Nigeria." In Hodgson D.L. & S.A. McCurdy (eds.). *Wicked Women and the Reconfiguration of Gender in Africa.* Social History of Africa Series. Portsmouth, NH: Heinemann.

Omenuko, O. 1995. *Daily Sunray,* January 24

Onwuejeogwu, M.A. 1987. Evolutionary Trends in the History of the development of the Igbo Civilization, in the Culture Theatre of Igboland in Southern Nigeria. *Ahiajoku Lecture.* Owerri-Nigeria: Culture Division

Orji, J.N. 1990. *Tradition of Igbo Origins: A Study of Pre-Colonial Population Movements in Africa.* New York: Peter Lang.

Ortner, S.B. & H. Whitehead. 1981 (eds.) *Sexual Meanings: The Cultural Construction of Gender and Sexuality.* Cambridge University Press

Oyêwùmí, O. 1997. *The Invention of Women. Making an African Sense of Western Gender Discourses.* Minneapolis and London: University of Minnesota Press

Parkin, D. 1980. Kind Bridewealth and Hard Cash: Eventing a Structure, in J.L Comaroff, (ed.) *The Meaning of Marriage Payments,* London: Academic Press, pp. 197-220

Pinker, R. 1999. Do Poverty Definitions Matter? In Gordon, D. & Spicker (eds.) *The International Glossary on Poverty.* London & New York: Zed Books.

Randhawa, B.S. 1998. Is Empowerment or Autonomy Critical for Women? In Richardson, A. (editor) *International Multiculturalism: Preparing Together for the 21<sup>st</sup> Century*. Edmonton AB.: The Katana Learning Co. Ltd.

Ranger, T. 1983. The Invention of Tradition in Colonial Africa, in E. Hobsbawm and Ranger, T. (eds.) *The Invention of Tradition*, Cambridge: Cambridge University Press.

Rapp, R. 2005. "Thinking about Women and the Origin of the State." In Brettell, C.B. & C.F. Sargent (eds.). *Gender in Cross-cultural Perspective (4<sup>th</sup> edition)*. Upper Saddle River, New Jersey: Prentice Hall.

Rappaport, J. 1987. "Terms of Empowerment/Exemplars of Prevention: Toward a Theory for Community Psychology." *American Journal of Community Psychology* 15 (2): 121-177.

Reverby, S. M. 1987. *Ordered to Care: The Dilemma of American Nursing*. Cambridge: Cambridge University Press.

Rosaldo, R. 1989. *Culture and Truth: The Remaking of Social Analysis*. Boston: Beacon Press.

Salins. M. D. 1974. *Stone Age Economics*. London: Tavistock.

Schlegel, A. 1977 (ed.) *Sexual Stratification: A Cross-cultural View*, New York: Columbia University Press

Smith, R.T. 1956. *The Negro Family in British Guiana: Family Structure and Social Status in the Villages*. London: Routledge and Kegan Paul.

Stamp, P. 1990 *Technology, Gender, and Power in Africa*, Ottawa, Ont., Canada: International Development Research Centre (Technical Study/IDRC)

Stephens, W. N. *The Family in Cross-Cultural Perspective*. New York: Holt, Rinehart & Winston.

Stone, L. & James, C. 2001. "Dowry, Bride-Burning, and Female Power in India." In Brettell, C.B. & C.F. Sargent (eds.). *Gender in Cross-cultural Perspective (3<sup>rd</sup> edition)*. Upper Saddle River, New Jersey: Prentice Hall.

Strathern, M. 1982 (ed.) *Inequality in New Guinea Highlands Societies,* Cambridge: Cambridge University Press

Townsend, W. N. 2005. Fatherhood and the Mediating Role of Women. In Brettell & Sargent (eds.) *Gender in Cross-Cultural Perspective (4th edition).* Upper Saddle River, New Jersey: Pearson Prentice Hall.

The *Time Magazine,* 2004. "Special Issue on How Love Life Keeps You Healthy." Canadian edition, Feb. 9.

Uchendu, V.C. 1965. *The Igbo of Southeast Nigeria.* New York: Winston, Holt and Rhinehart

Uchendu, V.C. 1994. Igbo Marriage Systems: An Overview Lead Paper. *Ahiajoku Lecture Colloquium.* Owerri-Nigeria: Culture Division

Uchendu, V.C. 1995. Ezi na Ulo: The Extended Family in Igbo Civilization, *Ahiajoku Lecture.* Owerri: Culture Division

United Nations 1975. *World Plan of Action,* Mexico

United Nations 1980. *The United Nations Decade for Women,* Copenhagen

United Nations 1985. *Forward Looking Strategies for the Advancement of Women Beyond the UN Decade For Women to the Year 2000,* Nairobi

United Nations 1995. Action for Equality, Development and Peace, *Fourth World Conference on Women.* Peking.

Uwalaka, J. 2003. *The Struggle for Inclusive Nigeria… A Treatise on Igbo Political Personality and Survival in Nigeria.* Enugu: SNAAP Press.

Van Allen, J. 1976. "Aba Riots" or Igbo 'Women's War'? Ideology, Stratification, and the Invisibility of Women." In Brettell, C.B. & C.F. Sargent (eds.). 2001. *Gender in Cross-cultural Perspective (3rd edition).* Upper Saddle River, New Jersey: Prentice Hall.

Wolf. M. 1972. *Women and Family in Rural Taiwan.* Stanford: Stanford University Press.

# *Endnotes*

[1] Van Gennep, Arnold. 1966 (orig. publ. 1908). *The Rites of Passage*. Chicago: University of Chicago Press.

[2] For similar observations and claims on this, see for example, Butler, J. 1990. *Gender Trouble*. New York: Routledge Press.

[3] See Miller, B.D. 1993 in *Sex and Gender Hierarchies*, pp. 3-311. See also Hutter, M. 1988, *The Changing Family: Comparative Perspectives (2$^{nd}$ Edition)* p. 204. New York: MacMillan Publishing Company.

[4] See Judith Lorber's 1994 - *Paradoxes of Gender*. New Haven, CT: Yale University Press.

[5] For the 'field of power" and cultural adaptive response, see Bourdieu, *The Field of Cultural Production: Essays on Art and Literature,* edited and launched by Randal Johnson. New York: Columbia University Press, p.38ff. [See also David Palumbo-Liu & Hans Ulrich Gumbrecht's (eds.) *Streams of Cultural Capital* (1997). Stanford, California: Stanford University Press.

[6] Fieldwork was carried out for over twenty months and involved intensive participant observation and action research from 1996 through to 2001. Return trips (in 2002, 2003 and 2004) to the field provided additional insight.

[7] Tonye David-West, Jr. discussed some of these frustrations arising from trends in his article entitled "How about the Single Naija Ladies in the US? Who will Marry Them?" (see www.*nigeriaworld.com April 22, 2004)*. See also a critique of this pride on the side of females rendered by Murtala Bala Habu in *www.gamji.com*, April 4, 2004.

[8] While Marshall Salins's (1974) work focused on the subsistence economy of the hunter-gatherers of the Stone Age, the age was described as "original affluent society" (Salins 1974:1). Salins claims that the lives of the world's primitive people were happier as they had fewer possessions and exchanged and reciprocated their needs and wants. As such, there were no "poor people" in that poverty is neither counted by a certain amount of goods, nor is it just a relation between means and ends. Rather, it is a relation between people and, therefore, a social status. If so, Salins argued, poverty is an invention of cultural civilization by colonial monetization of goods and services – in this case bridewealth. We will not debate on this further here except to point out that the consequences of a colonial cash economy impacted bridewealth, and many Igbo women and men, we can assume, have become either poor or rich through current practices of bridewealth, marriage and kinship negotiations and alliance manoeuvring.

[9] For example: Ogbu 1978; Comaroff 1980; Parkin 1980; Guyer 1995; Ekejiuba 1995.

[10] See, for example, Al-Bishak, 1991.Misleading Polemics of Female Power. *Daily Times*, June 9, p. 22.

[11] Omenuko, O. 1995. *Daily Sunray*, January 24. Note it was not possible to speak of 'women' in general, let alone to describe them as 'weak' in pre-colonial times (Cf. Oyêwùmí 1997 on Yoruba).

[1] Iroegbu, P. & M. Izibili 2004. *Kpim of Democracy: Thematic Introduction to Socio-Political Philosophy*. Benin-City, Nigeria: Ever-Blessed Publishers.

[2] Wiredu, K. Philosophy and an African Culture. Cambridge: Cambridge University Press.

[3] *Bride burning* has been reported as a common and shocking event in India, specific to the culture and occurring in cases where men considered their wives to have brought in insufficient resources. This form of gender behaviour is foreign to Igboland, and we did not observe any cases as related to this experience in India

during our fieldwork.

4 *Aku nwanyi* guarantees the rights of the husband's patriline to the future children of this woman. It was not originally a 'payment'. Bride price is also spoken of, but it constitutes only a small fraction of the bridewealth signifying the bride's head (*ikwu ugwo isi nwanyi*). Bridewealth evokes the notion of collective wealth brought in by a suitor for the parents, kinsmen and women associated with the bride. *Aku nwanyi* is also *aku nwoke* (man's wealth). What a woman might 'own' *aku nwaniyi* though rarely spoken of, is represented as man's wealth; and it assumed and is treated as if, it entirely belongs to the husband without question.

5 I use the term 'gender' to mean: the relational structure between men and women, as well as the depiction socio-cultural forms of identity.

6 This bridewealth discourse can be taken up for further investigation to ground what we may here observe as two emergent conceptual theories of the quest for marrying. I am calling them "resources grab quest" for marriage and 'quest to be Mr. or Mrs. EX of this or that syndrome.' The latter, in turn, also refers to a 'single mother/father quest.' Each of these on its own pursues some underlying social and psychological undertones propelling women and men into marriage. I hope to focus on these further.

7 By the term 'call name' (*aha*) I mean a community, village or clan name with which each community is identified. Each community is associated with a name linked to apical ancestors as well as to connotations endowed by neighbours. This suggests that each identifies itself with how it is perceived by others. Further research is needed into how these names tie into colonial administration.

8 Military experiences in the development of the Nigerian political administration have also been called hopeless classism, juntarism, and stratocracy. The worst of Nigeria's despondency was experienced during the control of General Sanni Abacha, who subsequently died unceremoniously while in office. This was a time in history that social critics refer to as a maximum dictatorship characterized by self-

assertiveness and self-importance over the common people.

[9] Ottenberg, S. 1968. *Double Descent in an African Society: The Afikpo Village-Group*.Seatle & London: University of Washington Press.

[10] Nsugbe, P.O. 1974. *Ohafia: A Matrilineal Ibo People*. London: Oxford University Press.

[11] See Rose Uchem (2003) "Overcoming Women's Subordination in the Igbo African Culture and in The Catholic Church." In *CriticalHalf: Annual Journal of Women for Women International*, pp. 26-31.

[12] The scientific name of the kola-nut (*oji*) is *cola acuminata*. In Igboland, the kola-nut has strong cultural value and is used to welcome visitors. It is a seed that is usually presented to visitors and generally used in ceremonies and rituals of important dimensions. Life begins with a kola-nut presentation, blessing, sharing, and chatting. It opens the mouth and the heart of the people in a moment of discourse and deliberation. The kola-nut is a multireferential social symbol signifying life, peace, kindness, good-will, commensality, fraternity, and reconciliation.Women are forbidden from planting, climbing, plucking, or breaking kola-nut by men, who choose to perform those activities themselves because of the considered nature of the kola-nut as a symbol of sacredness and interchanging of hands. This also indicates how men regard women in the society in regard to the idioms of gender inclusion and exclusion in the rituals of everyday life. .

[13] A "myth" is an ageless story or event given a sacred meaning that people tell and refer to in order to shape social order and character. It helps in shaping people's consciousness and worldview and forges their collective sense of identity and value.

[14] See Abanuka, B. 1999. *Myth and the African Universe. Spiritan Publications*, Onitsha, Nigeria, pp. 77-79. See also Amadiume, I. (1987) – *Male Daughters, Female Husbands*, p. 28.

[15] 'Stem' and 'reach' are synonyms for 'extended' family.

[16] Delaney, C. 1991. *The Seed and the Soil: Gender and Cosmology in Turkish Village Society.*

Berkeley: University of California Press.

[17] The phrase "high school" is used here in preference to the senior secondary school (SSS) education level it is referred to in the areas we did research work.

[18] In the initial stages of inquiry about the compatibility of two lineages, a diviner—rather like a private detective—may be approached to investigate the lives and life-worlds of the respective lineages.

[19] In popular Igbo folklore-music such a woman is described as *oto n'aka nne* (a leftover in mother's hands).

[20] Generally, it is considered that women enjoy favourable positions in close kin marriages—a comparatively high status and degree of independence—because of the equal relationship between the bride and groom's families. Perhaps the social and emotional disembedding of women in exogamous marriages is the source of a woman's enduring powerlessness, a powerlessness that can be compensated for by the solidarity of polygynous marriages, pragmatic strategies, and free interpretations of a flexible system. Only when the system becomes rigid—as under Christian and colonial conditions—and conjoined to a cash economy is the situation likely to become one of deep oppression for women.

[21] Ukaegbu, A. O. 1970. "Fertility of Women in Polygamous Unions in Rural Eastern Nigeria." In *Journal of Marriage and Family 39, 1-4* (Feb. – Nov.: 397-404. When men engage in sexual relations with their wives, care is taken to ensure that only young wives will become pregnant, and elderly wives will support and nurture the young ones and their children accordingly. A man who has two or three young wives is not likely to impregnate them all at the same time, though this may occur, but not commonly. So, in each period of the year, farming and trading will continue as co-wives maintain the family.

[22] See John W. Whiting's (1964) contribution "Effects of Climate on Certain Cultural Practices" in Ward H. Goodnenough (ed.) *Explorations in Cultural Anthropology: Essays in Honor of George P. Murdock.* New York: McGraw-Hill, pp. 511-44. See also *Ember et*

*al* 2005.

²³ Quoted by Havelock Ellis, op. Cit, p. 502.

²⁴ Note that the Mormon Church, or Church of Jesus Christ of the Latter Day Saints, has allowed and practiced polygamy in the USA, although the USA government is opposed to this.

²⁵ Uchendu, V.C. 1994. Igbo Marriage Systems: An Overview Lead Paper. *Ahiajoku Lecture Colloquium.* Owerri-Nigeria: Culture Division.

²⁶ Green, .M. M. 1964. *Igbo Village Affairs.* London: Frank Cass and Co. Ltd.

²⁷ See also Amadiume, I. 1987. *Male Daughters, Female Husbands: Gender and Sex in An African Society.* London: Zed Books Ltd.

²⁸ Iroegbu, E.P. 2002. "Marrying Wealth, Marrying Money: Repositioning Igbo Women and Men. In Saunders, B. and M.C. Foblets (eds.) *Changing Genders in Intercultural Perspectives.* Leuven: Leuven University Press.

---------------- 2004. "Re-Centering Bridewealth Power Between Igbo Women and Men at Home and in Diaspora." Paper submitted to *Department of African American Studies* on "Sisters Defining Sisters Conference: Redefining our Issues ~ Affecting Change." Feb. March. 2004. Temple University, Philadelphia – USA.

²⁹ The bride price is a monetary gift given to the father or guardian of the bride. Bride price has been interpreted as compensation for the loss of a worker in a mercantile world, but it is also a way of maintaining prestige and covering wedding expenses (cf. C. Delaney 1991. *The Seed and the Soil: Gender and Cosmology in Turkish Village Society*, p. 119. Berkeley: California University Press).

³⁰ The 'vagina cock' (*okuko elu ikpu*) and the 'vagina yam' (*ji ikpu*) are prepared together in the house of the groom the same night or the following day, and eaten by the age grade members. The feasting offers them a moment to make sexual jokes among themselves, and to advise the new bride and groom about their sexual obligations and responsibilities to each other in the lineage setting.

³¹ Levi-Strauss, C. 1969b. *The Raw and the Cooked: Introduction to a Science of Mythology.* 3

(orig, publ. as *L'Cru et le Cuit*, Paris: Libraire Pol), New York: Harper & Row.

[32] Communities from near and far sneer at the Mbano people and call them '*ndi otuocha*'—that is, a group who calls or swears to the vagina. When this practice is challenged, the Mbano reply that the vagina is a source of life, a tunnel (*opi uwa*) through which one comes into the world, and calling to it is a sort of joking reverence to that source of emergence into the world. They do not seem to view the sexual jokes as being vulgar, but as a form of expressive metaphor and idiom in a situated form of gender relationship.

[33] Gioia et al 2005. *Literature: An Introduction to Fiction, Poetry and Drama (Glossary)*. New York: Pearson Longman.

[34] Turner, V. 1967. *The Forest of Symbols*. Ithaca: Cornell University Press.

[35] Morrison, R.B. & C.R. Wilson (eds.) 2002. *Ethnographic Essay in Cultural Anthropology: A Problem-Based Approach*. Itasca, Illinois: F.E. Peacock Publishers, Inc.

[36] White, A. L. 1949, 1976. "Symbol: The Basic Element of Culture," In Macionis J.J. et al (2004) *Seeing Ourselves*, (Canadian Edition), pp. 32-36. Toronto: Pearson Prentice Hall. See also "The Symbol: The Origin and the Basis of Human Behaviour," In *The Science of Culture: A Study of Man and Civilization (1976)*. Farrar, Straus & Giroux, LLC.

[37] Ingoldsby, B. B. 2004. "Mate Selection and Marriage Around the World," In Macionis, J.J. et al (eds.) *Seeing Ourselves* (Canadian Edition), pp. 357-363. Toronto: Pearson Prentice Hall.

[38] Informants noted how some men and women also resort to the use of medicine (*ija, ogwu, juju*) to achieve this. They also noted that women, especially those who are not lucky enough to secure an early marriage, now audaciously patronize Pentecostal Churches and Spiritual Houses for the purpose of performing prayers and rituals to marry and/or bear children.

[39] Stephens, W. 1963. *The Family in Cross-cultural Perspective*. New York: Holt, Rinehart & Harry N. Abrams.

40 For more details, see Iroegbu, P. 2004. "Perceiving Obasanjocracy in Nigerian Political Culture." at *www.gamji.com,Jan.2004*, *http://www.gamji.com/NEWS3226.htm*, and *www.lagosforum.com, Jan. 21, 2004*. This article argues that *Obasanjocracy* is what it takes to be good or bad, to lead or not lead, pollute or purify, alleviate poverty or enrich the rich, succeed or fail. It is a *mis-en-place*—a whirlwind blowing Nigeria no good and is perceived, and interpreted in Igbo language, as a spreader of evil and the ugly side of life as opposed to the good (*mma*), hence *obasanmma* versus *obasanjo* (the ugly, bad, suffering, difficulty).

41 Isichei, E. 1976. A History of the Igbo People. London: Macmillan.

42 Prof. Eyitato Lambo's "Breaking the vicious cycle of poverty, ill-health and underdevelopment in Nigeria (1)" was a paper delivered by the Minister of Health on the 5th College Guest lecturer, College of Medical Sciences, University of Benin, Dec. 18, 2003. In *The Guardian Online*, January 14, 2004)

43 See Laolu Akande in The Guardian, March 1, 2004.

44 In poverty literature, conceptual definitions of poverty abound—such as poverty being viewed as subsistence criteria versus relative deprivation (Whyte 1971), basic needs against relative perspective (Sarlo 1992, 1994), economic in opposition to socio-cultural condition (Oster *et al* 1978), physical versus social dimension (Ross *et al* 1994), and, more generally, absolute in contra position to relative definition. For more information on debates on this see Kazemipur and Halli (2000) and Hagberg (2001).

45 For more information on these poverty sectors, see Sten Hagberg's *Poverty in Burkina Faso: Representations and Realities* (2001, p. 67).

46 Hagberg, S. 2001. *Poverty in Burkina Faso: Representations and Realities.* Sweden-ULRiCA - Uppsala-Leuven Research in Cultural Anthropology: Uppsala University, Tryck & Medier.

⁴⁷ Kopker in Woodfin Camp – cited in Greeenwood D.J. and A. Stini 1977. *Nature, Culture, and Human History: A Bio-cultural Introduction to Anthropology.* New York: Harper and Row, Publishers.

⁴⁸ Greeenwood D.J. and A. Stini 1977. *Nature, Culture, and Human History: A Bio-cultural Introduction to Anthropology.* New York: Harper and Row, Publishers.

⁴⁹ Jenkins, M. & S.M. Miller 1987. Upward Redistribution in the United Sates. In Ferge & Miller (eds.). *Dynamics of Deprivation.* England: Gower Publishing Company.

⁵⁰ For more insight, see *Changing Childhood* (1979) edited by Martin Hoyles, pp.201-210. England: Writers and Readers Publishing Co-operative.

⁵¹ For details, see Bourdieu, P. & J.C. Passeron. 1977. *Reproduction in Education, Society, and Culture.* Beverly Hills, Calif: Sage.

⁵² Quadagno, J. and C. Fobes. 1997. The Welfare State and the Cultural Reproduction of Gender: Making Good Boys and Girls in the Job Corps. In Kendal D. (ed.) *Race, Class and Gender in a Diverse Society, pp.*253-273. Toronto: Allyn & Bacon. See also *Social Problems*, Vol. 42, No. 2, May 1995, pp.171-190.

⁵³ Nash, R. 1990 also discussed Pierre Bourdieu's insight on "education and social and cultural reproduction." See *British Journal of Sociology* 11:431-447.

⁵⁴ In their article, *Cultural Capital Educational Attainment and Marital Selection*, DiMaggio, P. & J. Mohr explored the ideological nexus and socio-educational implications of cultural assets. For more information see – *American Journal of Sociology* 90:1231-1261.

⁵⁵ As the writing of this book concluded, the news came from the NNPC (Nigerian National Petroleum Corporation) that 2,355 workers have been laid off. See *Guardian Newspapers Ltd.* December 21, 2004. The fate of these workers will be hanging in the balance, much like the fates of their counterparts in the Nigerian Ports Authority (NPA) and other Corporations and Ministries in Nigeria.

⁵⁶ In responding to poverty alleviation strategy to help the youth, Prof. Rev.

Pantaleon Iroegbu, in partnership with a German community, established a successful "Skills Acquisition College" in Umunumo in Ehime Mbano of the Imo State, Nigeria, where High School Graduates learn various sustainable occupational skills, including computer skills, soap and shoe making techniques, and a variety of fashion creation. Development here is perceived to fight poverty by empowering people to challenge it thanks to this proprietor's clear vision and model of development initiative.

[57] Lewis, O. 1966. *La Vida: A Puerto Rican Family in the Culture of Poverty – San Juan and New York*. New York: Random House.

[58] Mangin, W. (ed.). 1970. *Peasants in Cities: Readings in the Anthropology of Urbanization*. Boston: Houghton-Miffin.

[59] Cultural capital is an anthropological economic term used to mean social and cultural cues. The fundamentals of *cultural capital* include such elements as personal lifestyle, linguistic competence, familiarity with elements of high or educated culture that serve as a basis for inclusion or exclusion from levels of society, jobs, resources, and high status self-control, assertiveness, and poise.

[60] Maduagwu, A. 2000. Alleviating Poverty In Nigeria. In Africa Economic Analysis, www.afbis.com Retrieved August 6th, 2004.

[61] Arowolaju, S. B. 2004. "Obasanjo is Always Right – No Abject Poverty, No Evil in Nigeria." In www.nigeriaworld.com, Retrieved Wednesday, December 15.

[62] See Uk Guardian Unlimited, www.naijanet.com/news/source/2005/july/1/1002.html.

[63] See *The Punch*, July 13, 2005. In: http://odili.net/news/source/2005/jul/13/429.html

[64] According to the Finance Minister, Dr. Ngozi Okonjo-Iweala (see *Vanguard's Online News Analysis,* "Understanding Nigeria's Debt Situation", July 1, 2005, retrieved July 3) Nigeria's external debt stands presently at $34 billion. Dr. Okonjo-Iweala further states that Nigeria's debt problem is really "a Paris Club debt problem" at $28 billion, or 85%, of the sum total. The rest of the debt is owed to the multilateral institutions such as the African Development Bank and the World Bank

(8%), another 7% is owed to the London Club of commercial creditors and holders of Promissory Notes, and none is owed to IMF. This is a problematic situation, especially considering that the annual debt service amounts to US$3 billion plus domestic service debt of $1.4 billion. If these debts are serviced in order to avoid piling up more debt, nothing will be left in the Federal Capital budget to sort out Nigeria's investment needs and compelling social obligations on education and health. It has been argued that the search for debt relief is a vital financial economic issue for the country at the moment. Despite the fact that Nigeria does not belong to the Highly Indebted Poor Countries (HIPCs), its poor socio-econmic indices are similar to those of the HIPC countries. Even though the focus of UK's G-8 and EU's chairmanship this year (2005) will be Africa, seeking for debt relief is one of the options in which efforts have been concentrated in order to move the country forward in terms of its connection with the international community.

[65] See *The Guardian Online News*, Friday July 1, 2005, in: *www.nigeriaworld.com*.

[66] See KAIROS Africa – NEPAD – U.N. Statement – April 11, 2002, and also *www.web.net/~iccaf/debt/nepadun041102.htm*, retrieved June 20, 2005.

[67] Randriamaro Zo, The NEPAD, Gender and The Poverty Trap. in: KAIROS Africa, *www.web.net/~iccaf/debtsap/nepadgera.htm* retrieved June 28, 2005.

[68] See Aramide Oikelome's discussion "On marrying a poor man" in *Daily Independent Online*, Tuesday, February 24, 2004.

[69] Earlier scholars were less inclined to recognize this.

[70] See Bourdieu (1979:249-251).

[71] Mauss (1950: 174, 180, 192, 204, 233-4).

[72] N = *naira;* U$1 = +/- N135.

[73] See Laws of Eastern Nigeria, vol. 1V, 1963, Section 3.'

[74] Cf. Ekejiuba 1995. There is also a paper discussing 'Young Female School Leavers: Choices for becoming Important in Society,' which was delivered at *Mbano Joint Hospital Nursing School* (1996) during the course of one of my fieldworks.

75 This and the following two 'cases' are drawn from my field research in Igboland at various times—1996, 1998, 2000, and 2002. Other visits in 2003 and 2004 did not yield any significant changes in the process and stratification of gender involvement.

76 Babangida, M. 1991. "On strategies for enhancing Women's participation in political decision-making process," p. 8 (unpubl. workshop paper).

77 The numbers 419 come from a section in the Nigerian Criminal code, and refer to financial scams for obtaining by tricks (OBT), money from unsuspecting investors, individuals, and organizations. The scamming schemes often target their victims through unsolicited fax, email, or letter. Most write and plead themselves as victims in a letter, as reported most recently by a story by CTV about a Canadian 419 twist in which the scammer claims to be a member of a wealthy African family unable to get their fortune out of the country, or that they are in possession of a government contract that can be paid out to anyone listed on the document. Usually, the perpetrator claims to be a doctor, lawyer, top official with the Nigerian National Petroleum Corporation, or the child of an ex-general or other important person seeking a 'partner' who can assist them. These schemes always promise huge rewards—from the opportunity to double or triple your investment to a cut of millions of dollars worth of loot—in exchange for cash up front (CTV Staff writer – see *www.gamji.com* – retrieved Feb. 18, 2004).

78 For more information see Iroegbu. P (2001) *Healing Insanity: An Anthropological Study of Igbo Medicine in Southeast Nigeria*. Doctoral Dissertation. Anthropology - University of Leuven, Belgium.

79 Acholonu (1995:24) writes: "African cosmology identifies six different faces of the African Eve, each implying a different status and position for the woman within the family or community. They are, namely the woman - as wife, as daughter/sister, as mother, as queen, as priestess, as goddess, and as husband." The way in which these 'faces' are perceived centres around the varying degrees of power and autonomy woven into gender practices. Notable is the fact that the woman-husband, the sixth

'face of Eve,' was a phenomenon known throughout Africa, although such practices tend to be regarded by men as a transgression of male boundaries. For example, women involved in politics or trade are often stereotyped as a 'man-woman' *(oke nwanyi)*, the equivalent of a *'berdach'* in French. The North American Indians, where the practice of the 'man-like' woman is pronounced, have similarily related names for such women. In the case of the *'oke nwanyi,'* a woman is considerd to have become 'masculinized' and is taunted by male jokes (always pejorative—such a woman needs a strong stomach).

[80] Charlotte Spinks (2003) discusses the question of why African women join Pentecostal movements in her article entitled "Panacea or Painkiller? The Impact of Pentecostal Christianity on Women in Africa." In *CriticalHalf: Annual Journal of Women for Women International, Vol.1, No. 1, pp. 21-25.*

[81] In the context of gender, ritual, and religion, Diane Bell (1981) has discussed the experience of Australian aboriginals concerning the love rituals of women, particularly rituals that originally were viewed by ethnologists as magic and marginal to the central decision-making realm of men. In celebrating such rituals, Bell observed that aboriginal women negotiated, utilized, and maintained sexuality and marriages of their choosing through ritual tactics that fostered their power and social standing (cf. 1981:322).

[82] See Time Magazine, Canadian edition, Feb. 9, 2004.

[83] Gilmore, D. 1987. Introduction: The Shame of Dishonour. In Gilmore, D. (ed.) *Honour and Shame and the Unity of the Mediterranean.* Washington, DC: American Anthropological Association, pp.2-21.

[84] See Anne Phillips. 1998. "Introduction," *Feminism and Politics*, ed. Anne Phillips. Oxford: Oxford University Press, pp.12-15.

[85] See *Cultural Anthropology* (2nd Canadian Edition) 2004, by Miller *et al*, pp. 382-402. Toronto: Pearson.

[86] Meek, C.K. 1937. *Law and Authority in a Nigerian Tribe*, p. xi.

[87] For more information please see, for example, Chief Margaret Ekpo in Conversation with Onyeka Owenu, with The Chinua Achebe Foundation Interview Series in *www.kwenu.com*, retrieved July 23, 2005).

[88] See Boserup, E. 1970)'s *Women's role in economic development.* New York: St. Martin's Press.

[89] Jefremovas, V. 2000. Women are good with money: The impact of cash cropping on class relations and gender ideology in northern Luzon, the Philippines. In A. Spring (ed.), *Women farmers and commercial ventures: Increasing food security in developing countries.* Boulder, Co: Lynne Rienner Publishers.

[90] See: *The World Plan of Action* (Mexico 1975), *The Programme of Action for the Second Half of the United Nations Decade for Women* (Copenhagen 1980), *The Forward-Looking Strategies for the Advancement of Women Beyond the UN Decade for Women to the Year 2000* (Nairobi 1985), and *Action for Equality, Development and Peace of the Fourth World Conference* (Peking 1995).

[91] Florence Nightingale was born into a wealthy upper-class Victorian English family in 1820. Involved in the nursing of injured British soldiers in the Crimean War in Turkey, Nightingale championed gender-related rules that categorized nursing as a socially-related charitable activity that belonged to the caring world of women.

[92] See Iroegbu, P. Culture Conflicts in Genital Cleansing, Body and Sexuality in Africa. In *www.gamji.com*, Dec. 12, 2004. And also in *www.lagosforum.com* Dec.10, 2004.

[93] Notes and handouts taken at the "Train the Trainer Program for HIV/AIDS (for Africa, women and development) – May 22; 29, 2004.

[94] See Wolf Naomi's *Fire for Fire* cited in Haviland *et al* (2005) *Cultural Anthropology*, p.43. See also E. Esisenber & M. Ruthsdotter's *Living the Legacy: The omen's Rights Movement 1848-1998*. In National Women's History Project (1998a).

[95] See *Dose Daily Magazine*, August 24, 2005, p. 8. (*www.dose.ca*).

[96] Word in italics are mine.

[97] See Biddy Martin's *Femininity Played Straight: the Significance of Being Lesbian* argued

(1996). New York & London: Routledge, pp.78-80.

[98] See Ojukwu in Conversation with Prof. Nnaemeka Ikpeze & Nduka Otiono Part 2, in www.kwenu.com, August 8, 2005 of the Chinua Achebe Foundation Series, retrieved August 25, 2005.

[99] Igbuzor Otive has shown in his review of *Mainstreaming Gender* (www.kwenu.com 2006), retrieved May 16, 2006, how gender mainstreaming need be emphasized in planning political, economic, and socio-cultural equity. He argues that gender mainstreaming must be seen as a strategy for making women's as well as men's concerns and experiences an integral dimension of social policy.

[100] Reuben Abati has shown in his article entitled "Wives for Sale: N15, 000!" (*The Guardian Online*, January 27, 2006. See also *The Vangaurd Newspaper* of January 24, 2006, p. 8) how the Elders of Ekpeye Clan in Ahoada Local Government Area of Rivers State recently looked into the problematic of overripe spinsters and increasing population of university female graduates who cannot secure marriage due to high bride price. In this neighbouring region of the Igbo, marriage is viewed as a commercial transaction and families prepare their daughters to get the best out of the bridewealth as a compensation for their upbringing. As market forces are not working in the community's favour, the Elders pursued the road of pragmatism and common sense to re-peg the bridewealth transactions so that their daughters, as they mature to be acquired, will be able to win suitors and bring wealth and social connections.

# INDEX

419 scam, 115, 149, 170, 189-190

Abacha, Sanni, 114
Abortion, 49, 58
Acquired Immune Deficiency
    Syndrome (see *HIV/AIDS*)
Adoption, 51, 52
Agbiogwu, May Ezinne, 185
Age grade, 77, 78, 85;
    definition of, 77
AIDS (See *HIV/AIDS*)
Akande, Laolu, 99
*Akata* relationship phenomenon,
    149-150
Amadiume, 40, 43, 93, 134, 181

Babangida,
    General Ibrahim, 114, 147;
    Maryam, 114
Beijing Conference on Women, 186
Better Life for Rural Women,
    poverty program, 114
Bigamy, 149
Blair, Tony, 121
Boserup, 194
Bridewealth, 5-15, 48, 163, 221-26;
    and AIDS, 193-95, 198-204;
    ceremonies, 73; and feminism;
    206-220; and gender relations
    and perspectives, 24-26, 28, 33-
    34; ideology of, 31-35, 188-89;
    and marriage (*before, during,
    after*), 28, 33, 34, 190, 192, 226;
    and migration, 149-151, 142-44,
    184; modern, 34, 137-152, 156-
    57; negotiations/negotiating, 34-
    35, 74-77; paradox of, 165; in
    patriarchal structure, 33, 131,
    162; payments, 21-22, 142-43,
    144-45, 184; politics of, 187-
    88; and poverty, 117-18, 128;
    power, 6, 9, 142, 187, 213; pros
    and cons, 193; social code, 8;
    as social payment, 6, 7, 134,
    189; symbolism of, 9, 10, 22;
    theory of, 131-36; unfulfilled
    obligations of, 192
Bourdieu, Pierre, 10-12, 105, 131-35
Bride (*see also* wife),
    mail-order, 138-140;
    search for, 67-68
Buhari, General Mohammed, 114

Case Studies: 23-24, 25-26, 44-48, 66,
    145-46, 148, 151, 157, 159,
    170-71
Ceremony/ceremonies (see also *rituals*),
    bridewealth, 47, 73; marriage,
    21, 26, 38, 63-64, 83, 85, 94,
    159; kola-nut blessing, 44
Christian/Christianity/Christianization
    (*see also* missionization), 33-34,
    51-52, 77, 153-54, 157, 201;
    and bridewealth, 133; and
    monogamy, 60
Civil war, Nigerian-Biafran, 42, 137,
    184
Colonial(ism), 33-34, 44, 141-42, 153;
    invasion, 40, 180; penetration,
    182-84
Culture, *definitions of*, 11; Igbo,
    31-45
Cultural Capital, 110, theory of, 105

Daughters, 135, 223; lineage, 73, male,
    43, 135; value of, 33-34, 44
Destutt de Tracy, Claude, 31-32
*Di*, definition of, 64-65
Diaspora, 8, 209, 213-14, 217;
    marriage/seeking mates in, 25-
    26, 93, 137-150
Divorce, 60, 135, 163-64, 188
Directorate of Food, Roads, and
    Rural Infrastructure, 114

Ekpo, Margaret, 180-81, 185
Endogamy, 92
Exogamy, 92

Family/families (*see also* kinship/lineage);
    Advancement Program, 114-15; categories/traits of, 49; compatibility of, 68; Support Program, 114; unity between, 91-92, 132
Father/Fatherhood (*see* parent...)
Fieldwork *(see* Research Methods/Approaches*)*
Feminism/Feminist, 14-15, 29-30, 184-88, 193, 206-220, 222, 225; leftists, 211; male, 206-07, 213; movement, 6, 57; senses, 206-07, 214, 217, 225, definition of, 6; and poverty, 117-19
Fertility Cock, 77-83, 94
Foucault, 162

G-8, members of, 119; summit, 119-127
Gender, 5-8, 10-12, 56, 72, 82, 149, 151, 207-09; bridewealth and, 31, 33, 131; definition, 8-9; negotiate/ed/ing/ions, 8, 28, 120, 140, 162, 166, 171, 172-76, 190; positions/positioning, 5-9, 12; and poverty, 101-02, 112; equity/inequity, 179-181, 184-85, 206; ideology, 120, 159, 185; inequality (*see* Gender, equity); relations/relationships, 44-45, 165, 182; structuring of, 12
Geldof, Sir Bob, 121
Gettu, Tegegnwork, 99
Gilmore, David, 176
"Go Back to Land" poverty program, 114

Gowon, General Yakubu, 113
Green, 63,180
Green Revolution Program, 114-15
Gynaegamy (see *woman to woman marriage*)

Healers, 166-76
Habitus, (Bourdieu), 12
Hagberg, 100
HIV/AIDS, 193-204; statistics, 199, transmission/symptoms/treatments, 202-204
Human Immunodeficiency Virus (see *HIV/AIDS*)
Hopker, 103
Husband, 64-65, 82, 138, 144; female, 93, 153-56

Ideology, defined, 31-32
Igbo (*see also* Igboland), 36-45; celebrations, 20-21; and colonialism, 44-45; culture areas, 39; defined, 39; migration, 39, 40; origins, 39-40; and poverty, 105-06, 112, 113-19; pre/post colonial, 41-44; women's war, 181-82
Igboland (*see also* Igbo), 36-45; climate, 37; culture areas, 39; location, 37; map of, 36, 37; population, 37
Immigration (*see* migration)
Inheritance, 143, 162

Jensen, Robert, 206, 207

Kinship (*Kin, Kin membership, etc.*) (*See also* family and/or lineage), 9, 38, 43; alliance/allegiance, 29, 33, 46, 48, 76; in diaspora, 147; organizational styles, 161-65; participation in marriage, 6, 21, 63-64, 67, 161
Kleptocracy, 42, 115
Kola-nut, 64; blessing, 44, 68

Lambo, Prof. Eyitato, 98
Leith-Ross, 9, 180
Lewis, Oscar, 106, 109-112
Lineage, (*See also* family and/or kinship), 46, 49, 64, 69, 71-73, 85, 88, 135, 146, 161-63, 192
Live 8 Concerts, 121-22
Lorber, Judith, 9
Love potions, 168, 170-74, 175

MacFarlane, 56
Market days, 69-70
Marriage, arranged 90-92; child, 33; ceremonies, 63-64; in diaspora, 1137-52, exchange system, 7, 131-36, forms of, 51-61, 63, 89-92; foundation of, 63; ideologies, 6; in pre-colonial times, 46; modern, 51; negotiations, 74-77; traditions/traditional, 49, 63, 75; securing, 170-74; stages of, 69-74; woman to woman, 43, 93, 136, 153-56
Marx, Karl, 104
Match-making agencies, 139-40
Mate, selection/finding a, 89-83, 137-152, 153-58, 166-174
Matrifocal, households, 42
Matrilineal/Matrilneality, 161-65; households, 42
Mauss, Marcel, 10, 131-36, 142
Mead, Margaret, 193, 222
Migration/ Immigration, 25, 39, 40, 137-152, 184, 214
Missionization (*See* Christianity)
Monogamy, 57-61, 91; and Christianity, 60, 66
Mother/motherhood (See *Parent...*)
Murdock, 90 - 91

National Accelerated Food Production Program, 113
Neolocality, 209

New Partnership for Africa's Development (NEPAD), 122, 124-25
Nigerian Agricultural and Cooperative Bank, 113
Nnoromele, 43
Nwunye/nywanyi, definition, 64-65

Obasanjo, 97, 113, 116, 123
Oil, 113, 116, 118
Ojukwu, 217
Okonjo-Iweala, Dr. 124
Operation Feed the Nation, 113

Palm wine, 64, 68, 159
Paris Club of Creditors alliance, 120
Partner, selection (*See* Mate selection) Patriarchy/patriarchal, 45, 104, 131, 142, 153, 183, 189, 207, 210; and Bridewealth power, 6; ideology, 33; systems, 44
Patrilineage/Patrilineal, 43, 77, 93, 135, 161-65
Parents/Parenthoood/Parental, 7, 33, 47, 48, 49, 162, 169
Pre-/Post-Colonial, 42-44, 46, 132-36, 141-42
Polyandry, 43, 53, 54
Polygamy, 43, 53-54, 56-61, 66, 91, 149
Polygyny, 33, 51-56, 135
Poor, the (*see also* poverty), 96-97; critical groups of, 105-06
Postpartum sex taboo, 54-55
Poverty (*see also* Poor), 77, 96-130; alleviation programs, 111, 113-19, 123; causes of, 103-04, 109-112; culture of (Oscar Lewis), 109-112; defining, 96-99; etiology of, 103-09; G-8 summit and, 119-127; Hagberg's study of, 100; line, international and global, 100-01; marrying, 6, 127-130, 221; statistics, 98-99;

and women (*see also* women), 100, 127, 127-130; reform (see *alleviation programs*); reduction programs, (see *alleviation programs*)
Pregnancy, 55, 150, 169; premarital, 46-49
Premarital, pregnancy, 46-49; sex, 47

Research *(see also* Case Studies*)* methods/ approaches, 23-24
Ritual/Rituals *(see also* Ceremonies), 12, 37, 40, 42, 85-88, 116, 155, 183; healing, 41; women's role in, 43, 141-42, 77-83; fertility cock/vagina yam, 74-78; in finding a mate, 167-175
Robertson, Pat, 207

Said, Edward, 23
Salins, Marshall, 28
Shagari, Shehu, 114
Shaw, 40
Sex/sexual/sexuality, 172-73, 175-76; behaviour, 198-99; freedom, 212; postpartum, 54; premarital, 46, 48; ratio, 56; safe, 195-98
Social payments (*see* Bridewealth)
Stages of marriage, 63-88
"Staying on the road", 77
Strategies, bridewealth (*see* Bridewealth), for overcoming poverty (see also Poverty), 100, 106, 113, 116, 127; women's (*see also* Women), 127, 142, 170, 186, 187, 224
Structural Adjustment Program, 115

Symbols/Symbolic/Symbolism, of *akata*, 149-50; of bride-price negotiations, 76-77; of bridewealth, 9, 10, 22, 24; of fertility cock, 78-83, 94; fines, 47, of girl's names, 33-34; and human behaviour, 87-88; Igbo, 40; of marriage, 63, 65, 85-95; of money, 134; of a woman's worth; 75; of vagina yam, 78-83, 94; of washing of hands, 71; of shedding of tears, 83-85
Taboos, 40, 54, 202
Theory, of cultural capital, 105; of culture of poverty, 109-112; feminist, 211-13; of gift exchange, 131; of gift swap-over of bridewealth, 131-36; identity empowerment, 176-78
Traditionalism/Neo-traditionalism, 33, 142, 189, 209

United Nations, Conferences, 185; Human Development Report (UNDP), 101; Year of the Woman, 186-87
Uterine families (see *matrilineal*)

Vagina yam, 77-83, 94
Vansina, 40
Vidal, John, 115
Virginity, 46, 48, 202
von Ehrenfels, Prof. C., 57

Wealth, 190, celebrations of, 20-21; distribution of, 26; exchange, *(see also* Bridewealth*)* 7; marrying, 6, 22, 221
Western/ Westernization, 7, 28, 29, 59-58, 60-61, 92, 130-152, 209; aid, 115-16

Widow/Widowhood, 33, 65-67, 105, 132
Wife/Wives, (*see also* women and/or bride) 65-67, 71, 82, 160; co-wives, 52-53; giving/givers, 69, 75-76, 91; inheriting a, 65-67; searching for, 67-69; senior wife, roles of, 53; takers/taking, 69, 75-76, 91, 134
Wolf, Naomi, 206
Woman to woman marriage, 43, 93, 135, 153-156
Women (*see also* Daughters/Gender/Wives/Bride), as commodities, 1150-52; Beijing Conference on, 186; denigration/subjugation of, 6, 159, 193, 214; emancipation of, 190; empowerment of, 176-78, 214; exclusion of, 44; in health-care, 200-01; and HIV/AIDS, 202, 204; in politics, 185-87; and poverty, 28, 29, 100-02, 104, 110, 117-19, 127, 127-30; roles of, 43-50, 141-42, 149, 158-61, 182-84; sexuality of, 171-74; status/value of, 33-34, 51, 131, 138, 150-52, 169; unmarried, 50, 61, 91, 143, 156, 223; woman's war, 180-83; Year of, 186
World Development Report, 99

ISBN 1-4120-8100-9